NORTHERN IRELAND SINCE 1945

The Postwar World
General Editors: A.J. Nicholls and Martin S. Alexander

As distance puts events into perspective, and as evidence accumulates, it begins to be possible to form an objective historical view of our recent past. *The Postwar World* is an ambitious new series providing a scholarly but readable account of the way our world has been shaped in the crowded years since the Second World War. Some volumes will deal with regions, or even single nations, others with important themes; all will be written by expert historians drawing on the latest scholarship as well as their own research and judgements. The series should be particularly welcome to students, but it is designed also for the general reader with an interest in contemporary history.

Decolonization in Africa *J.D. Hargreaves*

The Community of Europe: A History of European Integration since 1945, Second Edition *Derek W. Urwin*

Northern Ireland since 1945, Second Edition *Sabine Wichert*

A History of Social Democracy in Postwar Europe *Stephen Padgett and William E. Paterson*

'The Special Relationship': A Political History of Anglo-American Relations since 1945 *C.J. Bartlett*

Rebuilding Europe: Western Europe, America and Postwar Reconstruction *D.W. Ellwood*

The Pacific Basin since 1945: A History of The Foreign Relations of the Asian, Australasian and American Rim States and the Pacific Islands *Roger C. Thompson*

Central Europe since 1945 *Paul G. Lewis*

International Relations since 1945. A History in Two Volumes *John Dunbabin*
The Cold War: The Great Powers and their Allies
The Post-Imperial Age: The Great Powers and the Wider World

Modern Indonesia: A history since 1945
Robert Cribb and Colin Brown

Peace Movements: International Protest and World Politics since 1945
April Carter

The Bonn Republic: West German Democracy, 1945–1990 *A.J. Nicholls*

Northern Ireland since 1945

Second Edition

Sabine Wichert

An imprint of Pearson Education

Harlow, England · London · New York · Reading, Massachusetts · San Francisco
Toronto · Don Mills, Ontario · Sydney · Tokyo · Singapore · Hong Kong · Seoul
Taipei · Cape Town · Madrid · Mexico City · Amsterdam · Munich · Paris · Milan

Pearson Education Limited
Edinburgh Gate
Harlow
Essex CM20 2JE
England
and Associated Companies throughout the world.

Visit us on the World Wide Web at:
http://www.pearsoneduc.com

First published 1991
Second Edition 1999

ISBN 0-582-32678-8 PPR

British Library Cataloguing in Publication Data
A catalogue record for this book is available from the British Library

Library of Congress Cataloging in Publication Data
A catalog record for this book is available from the Library of Congress

10 9 8 7 6 5 4 3 2
04 03 02 01 00

Set in Bembo

Printed in Malaysia

Contents

List of Tables

I. SOCIAL AND ECONOMIC

II. SECURITY

List of Maps

Abbreviations and Acknowledgements

AIA	Anglo-Irish Agreement
AP	Alliance Party
CAC	Continuity Army Council
CLML	Combined Loyalist Military Command
CSJ	Campaign for Social Justice
DCAC	Derry Citizens' Action Committee
DSD	Downing Street Declaration
DUP (PUP)	Democratic Unionist Party (before 1971, Protestant Unionist Party)
EEC, EC, EU	European (Economic) Community, Union
FEA, FEC	Fair Employment Agency, Commission
FF	Fianna Fail
FG	Fine Gael
GB	Great Britain
GDP	Gross Domestic Product
GOC	General Officer Commanding
IDB	Industrial Development Board
INLA	Irish National Liberation Army
IPLO	Irish People's Liberation Organisation
IRA	Irish Republican Army
IRSP	Irish Republican Socialist Party
LEDU	Local Enterprise Development Unit
NAC, NORAID	Irish Northern Aid Committee
NATO	North Atlantic Treaty Organisation
NDP	National Democratic Party
NI	Northern Ireland
NIAS	Northern Ireland Attitude Survey
NICRA	Northern Ireland Civil Rights Association
NIF	New Ireland Forum (1983/4)/Northern Ireland Forum (1997)
NILP	Northern Ireland Labour Party

NIO	Northern Ireland Office
NORAID, NAC	Irish Northern Aid Committee
OIRA	Official Irish Republican Army
OUP, UUP	Official Unionist Party, Ulster Unionist Party
PD	People's Democracy
PIRA	Provisional Irish Republican Army
PSF, SF	(Provisional) Sinn Fein
PUP	Progressive Unionist Party
RIC	Royal Irish Constabulary
RLP	Republican Labour Party
RSF	Republican Sinn Fein
RTE	Radio Telefis Eireann
RUC	Royal Ulster Constabulary
SACHR	Standing Advisory Committee on Human Rights
SAS	Special Air Service
SDLP	Social Democratic and Labour Party
UCDC	Ulster Constitution Defence Committee
UDA	Ulster Defence Association
UDI	Unilateral Declaration of Independence
UDP	Ulster Democratic Party
UDR	Ulster Defence Regiment
UFF	Ulster Freedom Fighters
UK	United Kingdom of Great Britain and Northern Ireland
UKUP	United Kingdom Unionist Party
ULDP	Ulster Loyalist Democratic Party
UP	Unionist Party
UPA	Ulster Protestant Action
UPNI	Unionist Party of Northern Ireland
UPV	Ulster Protestant Volunteers
UUC	Ulster Unionist Council
UUUC	United Ulster Unionist Council (or Coalition)
UUUM	United Ulster Unionist Movement
UUUP	United Ulster Unionist Party
UVF	Ulster Volunteer Force
UWC	Ulster Workers' Council

The publishers would like to thank the following for permission to reproduce copyright material: Basil Blackwell and the author for table I.1 from *Ulster: conflict and consent*, Tom Wilson (1989); Blackstaff Press for tables II.1, II.2, II.3 from *Northern Ireland, A Political Directory 1968–88*, W.D. Flackes and Sydney Elliot (1989).

Editorial Foreword

The aim of this series is to describe and analyse the history of the World since 1945. History, like time, does not stand still. What seemed to many of us only recently to be 'current affairs', or the stuff of political speculation, has now become material for historians. The editors feel that it is time for a series of books which will offer the public judicious and scholarly, but at the same time readable, accounts of the way in which our present-day world was shaped by the years after the end of the Second World War. The period since 1945 has seen political events and socio-economic developments of enormous significance for the human race, as important as anything which happened before Hitler's death or the bombing of Hiroshima. Ideologies have waxed and waned, the industrialised economies have boomed and bust, empires have collapsed, new nations have emerged and sometimes themselves fallen into decline. While we can be thankful that no major armed conflict has occurred between the so-called superpowers, there have been many other wars, and terrorism has become an international plague. Although the position of ethnic minorities has dramatically improved in some countries, it has worsened in others. Nearly everywhere the status of women has become an issue which politicians have been unable to avoid. These are only some of the developments we hope will be illuminated by this series as it unfolds.

The books in the series will not follow any set pattern; they will vary in length according to the needs of the subject. Some will deal with regions, or even single nations, and others with themes. Not all of them will begin in 1945, and the terminal date may similarly vary; once again, the time-span chosen will be appropriate to the question under discussion. All the books, however, will be written by expert historians drawing on the latest fruits of scholarship, as well as their own expertise and judgement. The series should be particularly welcome to students, but it is designed also for the general reader with an interest in contemporary history. We hope that the books will stimulate scholarly discussion and encourage specialists to look beyond their own particular interests to engage in wider controversies. History, and particularly the history of the recent past, is neither 'bunk' nor an intellectual form of stamp-collecting, but an indispensable part of an educated person's approach to life. If it is not written by historians it will be written by others of a less discriminating and more polemical disposition. The editors are confident that this series will help to ensure the victory of the historical approach, with consequential benefits for its readers.

A.J. Nicholls
Martin S. Alexander

Preface

Books like this which survey and interpret twentieth-century events necessarily rely on the publications of many scholars and investigative journalists. It is their work, at least in part acknowledged in the bibliography, to which I owe my greatest debt. Of equal importance, however, were my editors, in particular A.J. Nicholls, and my publishers, without whose suggestion to do so I should never have undertaken this study. Their encouragement and advice I appreciated greatly.

Special thanks are due to P.J. Jupp, A.T.Q. Stewart and Kevin Boyle who read all, most or part of the various drafts and provided invaluable criticism and constructive support. Any remaining errors and all views expressed are, of course, entirely my own responsibility. Thanks also to D.W. Harkness who let me use his library whenever books were not easily available elsewhere and, last but not least, thanks to Mary O'Dowd and Anthony Sheehan who introduced me to word processing and helped whenever my impatience and the computer's temperament were at odds.

Finally, I must acknowledge that having lived in Northern Ireland as an outsider for almost twenty years has given me a rare privilege for a contemporary historian: the opportunity to immerse myself in what I was studying without being totally part of it.

Belfast, April 1990

Preface to the Second Edition

With events in Northern Ireland having moved on since 1989, forward even, some might argue, however tentatively, and since the title of this book suggests an open ending, it is clearly time to provide the reader with an updated version.

While a good deal of substatial research has since been published on the period covered in the first edition, none essentially appears to contradict the interpretation offered here, and it was therefore felt that a major revision of the bulk of the text could wait for some possible future edition. The only exception to this is the period after the Anglo-Irish Agreement. The new chapter is thus intended to offer the reader a description and an explanation of the often confusing events since then. The almost completely revised tables and the updated bibliography will, it is hoped, give some help in understanding the most recent history of Northern Ireland.

Belfast, August 1998

To my Mother
Gertrud Wichert
1912–1998

Introduction

> The whole map of Europe has been changed. . . . The mode and thought of men, the whole outlook on affairs, the grouping of parties, all have encountered violent and tremendous changes in the deluge of the world, but as the deluge subsides and the waters fall we see the dreary steeples of Fermanagh and Tyrone emerging once again. The integrity of their quarrel is one of the few institutions that have been unaltered in the cataclysm which has swept the world.
>
> W.S. Churchill, 1929[1]

> To those who understand, no explanation is necessary. To those who will not understand, no explanation is possible.
>
> Graffiti on Falls Road, Belfast, 1980s[2]

These quotations encapsulate both the problems of Northern Ireland and the difficulties observers have faced in understanding them. Churchill's observation could have been made as easily after the Second as after the First World War, and the insistence that no outsider can understand those involved in the quarrel, which applies equally to both sides, highlights the irrational element in the problem. The quarrel is in the first instance about who should rule the province, less about how it should be ruled, although that, too, is an integral part of it. The history of the division of north-east Ireland's population into largely protestant unionists and loyalists (that is, loyal to the Union) on the one hand and largely catholic nationalists (that is, with the aspiration towards a united Irish nation state) on the other did certainly not begin in 1945, or even in 1922, although partition gave it a new focus.

1. Churchill, W.S., *The World Crisis. The Aftermath*, London 1929, p. 319.
2. Belfrage, Sally, *The Crack. A Belfast Year*, London 1988, p. 324.

The partition of the island into two separate political entities allowed reluctant unionists, who would have much preferred to remain an integrated part of the United Kingdom, to take over power in the region and nationalists to reject the arrangement, thus making sectarian rule inevitable. It was only after 1945, however, with the Ireland Act of 1949, that unionists could feel some confidence in their position, even though the province remained a constitutional anomaly within the UK. Yet nationalists, while willing to accept the economic benefits of belonging to the UK, were not able or willing to give their full allegiance to the state. The aspiration of the two communities thus remained irreconcilable: unionists wanted to remain members of the Union with Great Britain, while nationalists wanted the province to become part of the Republic of Ireland.

These mutually exclusive aspirations were underpinned by the cultural differences, expressed in religious and political terms, between the two sections of the population. It is argued here that it is to a large measure due to the 'backward' form of these cultures, and the 'backwardness' of the economy in which they were embedded, that the conflict in Northern Ireland has continued. This is a history of a peripheral region where the mainstream of European intellectual and political developments arrived late; and where many essentially nineteenth-century problems remained unresolved. Although unique in its particular history, it stands as an example of a region which, largely through its geographically remote position, remained 'underdeveloped' in an otherwise economically and culturally modernised and modernising postwar world. This was heightened by its economic disadvantages in a post-industrial world economy. While the war had forced Americanisation and modernisation on most of Western Europe, in Northern Ireland only the middle classes were gradually affected by this.

It was indeed the relative growth of the catholic middle classes after 1945 which began to challenge the status quo of sectarian rule in the 1960s, primarily in its civil effects. When this was carried further by revolutionary student demands to overthrow the existing political system, a protestant backlash became almost inevitable. The subsequent ossification of the vertical sectarian divide, however, was now combined with a horizontal social and economic division within each community, with the working classes of each side as the main carriers of the more conservative, irrational and extreme political philosophy, to be realised, if necessary, by violent means. The middle classes of each side would by and large have been willing to support a compromise. This new development meant that the traditional parties effectively lost control of working-class support and split. Out of this division new and more extreme parties, with predominantly working- and lower-middle-class support, emerged on both sides.

The lack of cultural modernisation made it comparatively easy to promote nineteenth-century versions of political nationalism, hand in hand with a very conservative catholicism on the one side, and a defensive and entrenched evangelism coupled with nineteenth-century notions of liberal democracy on the other. British governments' attempts at political modernisation from the 1970s onwards only increased the defensiveness on both sides. The impossibility of reviving the economy of the province kept unemployment high and the working classes conservative in their cultural and political perceptions. Both sides were defensive on two counts: firstly, the 'modernised' middle classes of each side appeared to be willing to cooperate with the 'enemy' on the other side, and secondly, the threat from the other side itself appeared to deny them their perceived basic rights. In moments of particular tension these amounted to existential fears and further promoted an antagonistic, confrontational political culture on both sides.

Thus in an age of superpowers and nation states willing to devolve greater powers to the European Community, the steeples of Fermanagh and Tyrone still stand for the integrity of an unresolvable quarrel. Part of that integrity is often a proud refusal to be understood by anyone who does not share the assumptions and general values of the protagonists of either side.

The ever-increasing number of publications on Northern Ireland, well over 5000 at the last count[3], seems to suggest that there are indeed some difficulties in understanding the 'Ulster problem'. Perhaps it is of significance that only a very small number of all these have been written by historians. Ever since the renewed eruption of communal violence in 1969 journalists and social scientists have understandably been in the forefront of interpreting Northern Ireland to the world. Comments and interpretations from outside the province have tended to assess Northern Ireland in terms of twentieth-century Western politics, that is, they have mostly judged events on the basis of rational principles and expectations, often taking their bearings from the civil rights campaigns of the 1960s. This, however, rarely captures the essence of the conflict which is historically determined and includes a great deal of 'irrational' behaviour and assumptions. 'Insider' interpre-

3. Teague, Paul, Introduction, in Teague, Paul (ed.), *Beyond the Rhetoric: Politics, the Economy and Social Policy in Northern Ireland*, London 1987, p. 1.

tations, on the other hand (however 'liberal' in meaning and approach), have almost invariably identified with their own side.[4]

Both inside and outside analyses have thus been sympathetic to one of the sides in the conflict in understanding (in the sense implied in the Falls graffiti), or at any rate, appearing to understand, its values. Most of this sympathy has been extended to the catholic population and its case, and unionists have found little support for their arguments. The reasons for this are in the origins of the recent conflict in the 1960s, and the 'reasonable' case for catholic civil and political emancipation in the province which has overshadowed subsequent events, as well as unionists' own failure to make their case in rational and unbiased terms. The fact that unionists have a perfectly rational, and in constitutional terms at least as convincing a case as nationalists has therefore largely been overlooked, or at any rate, rarely stressed.

The overwhelming majority of studies on Northern Ireland then are 'sympathetic' and almost invariably judgemental. They pre-judge events in the province's history and politics in the light of what ought to be or have been the case, or on the basis of their perceived stake in Northern Ireland. If the task of the historian, however, is to understand and explain, it is not sympathy but empathy that is required, and the suspension of judgement, at least until as comprehensive an understanding as possible has been reached. Only by assuming from the outset that every side is 'right' from their own perspective can the historian hope to understand and explain why things happened in the particular way they did.

While the author is aware of the ultimate futility of hoping to achieve impartiality, this study is an attempt to be as empathetic as possible and to find the causes that motivated people's action in the hope of arriving at perhaps some understanding. If the Falls graffiti were right, the writing of history would have to cease, and while one may be able to make a philosophical case for the impossibility to understand, it would also mean the end of the historian's craft.

Disregarding that philosophical possibility then, the short introductory part of this book tries to show how the partition of the island confirmed in the north-east of Ireland a politically divided society and how that division had far-reaching economic and social consequences. The expansionist aims of the Southern state together with the uncertain commitment of London to Northern Ireland drove unionists on

4. Various interpretations of the Northern Ireland problem are examined in Whyte, John, *Interpreting Northern Ireland*, Oxford 1990.

to the defensive, while catholics withdrew into non-cooperation with the state.

The second part traces developments from the outbreak of the Second World War to the eve of the new 'troubles' in 1969. It argues that the province's governments after 1945 could feel reassured on several grounds. The explicit confirmation of Westminster's support for the region in conjunction with the application of British welfare legislation to Northern Ireland slowed its economic decline and helped to create a North which grew increasingly different from the Southern state whose economy as well as its social legislation fell well behind. Cautious optimism about the future prosperity of the province grew in the fifties and into the sixties. As catholics began to profit at first from educational reforms, but then also from the improving economic conditions, the catholic middle classes grew larger in size and soon also more articulate in their demands for equal civil rights. This implied their acceptance of the Union with Great Britain and suggested their willingness to cooperate with the state. While most unionists cautiously welcomed this, it also generated a vociferous protestant minority opposition to any such catholic rights. It was the clash between the anti-liberal elements in unionism with the ever more outspoken supporters of civil rights that precipitated the crisis of 1969–72 and threw Northern Ireland back into nineteenth-century modes of politics. This interrupted the process of modernisation that had begun in the sixties, even though it had not yet reached the working classes. Politics and population, and in particular the working classes, thus reverted to the ancient sectarian power politics of fear and violence. The slide into civil war could be halted only by London's intervention.

In the third and largest part particular emphasis is placed on the years 1969 to 1972 in which the ground was laid for the political events of the following two decades. It shows the increasing gap between moderate politicians in Belfast and London who were trying to implement reforms which would meet the civil rights demands and the politics of the streets in the province which drew on ancient fears and hardened into total rejection of any compromise. Before the former were completely defeated the British government took over and began to rule Northern Ireland directly. Direct rule was and remained an attempt to find a compromise and establish consensus politics. It is argued here that the failure to achieve this can only be understood in terms of the mutually contradictory aspirations of the two communities. The number of people willing to support these aspirations violently was normally quite small, but their very existence could, in times of tension, generate enough traditional fears on either side to make any compromise impossible. Since the extremists had succeeded in establishing themselves firmly in the economic, social and political life of the province, this study concludes that a solution to the problems of Northern Ireland, short of an economic miracle which might have helped to modernise the working classes and thus obliterate their need to cling to their fundamentalist political and cultural values, was not available.

The last two decades of the century, however, saw developments which for the first time offered the promise of a successful compromise which might end direct rule. It was the militants of both sides who were willing to try a political solution, realising that political cooperation with each other rather than violence was more likely to further their own political aims, even if in the process they had to concede some of these. Whether or not this would lead to an accommodation of the two political sections of the community remained to be seen.

Perhaps it needs finally to be stressed that this is a history of Northern Ireland, and not of the 'Ulster Problem'. In so far as Northern Ireland has an international dimension[5] this has only been touched upon in the relevant context, but not explored to any extent. The focus of this study is therefore predominantly on Belfast and the province and only occasionally shifts to London or Dublin.

5. See Guelke, Adrian, *Northern Ireland: The International Perspective*, Dublin 1988.

PART I

1921–1939: The Roots of the Problem

Introductory

The division of the population of Ireland into 'Unionists' and 'Irishmen'[1] has deep historical roots and draws its sustenance from the centuries-old separation by religious as much as economic and social developments. This gained sharper political focus during the Home Rule debates of the later nineteenth century. Ulster Unionism began to supersede Irish Unionism: where the latter was generally associated with landlords, the former had a much wider social base in the industrialising area of the north-east, comprising not only the gentry but businessmen, the professions and the clergy, farmers as well as agricultural and industrial workers. The threat of Home Rule becoming a political reality endangered the religious, economic and social interests of these groups. Their growing fear of extinction led to tighter organisation and increasing intransigence and to further polarisation. They tended to equate Home Rule with Rome Rule which would not only threaten their religion but also their markets and their social position in society; and, since fear did not lend itself to subtle differentiation between shades of nationalism, this led to the conviction that revolutionary extremism threatened their political way of life. The need to be loyal to King and Empire, and violently so if necessary, became uppermost: Home Rule was to be defeated at all costs.[2]

Because of its numerical and geographical limitations the strength of Ulster Unionism was underestimated by both London and Dublin politicians, each absorbed in their own problems. Southern Ireland was at war with Britain from 1919 and assumed, as nationalists had before,

1. Lyons, F.S.L., *Ireland Since the Famine*, London 1982 (revised edn.), 287ff; Beckett, J.C., 'Northern Ireland', in *Journal of Contemporary History*, Vol. 6, No. 1, 1971, 121ff; Stewart, A.T.Q., *The Narrow Ground*, London 1977, *passim*; Wilson, Tom, *Ulster. Conflict and Consent,* Oxford 1989, pp. 1-50.

2. Lyons, *Ireland*, p. 186 and *passim*.

that unionism could be coerced and that there was no need for conciliation, while Westminster assumed that the provision of a Council of Ireland would eventually persuade the North to throw in its lot with Dublin. A closer look at even the more recent history of nationalism and unionism in Ireland could have convinced both parties that theirs was a misjudgement. The roots of the division pre-dated partition; the constitutional, political and economic separation of Ireland ossified this division.

CHAPTER ONE

The Constitutional Compromise

When the six counties in the north-east of Ireland accepted the Government of Ireland Act (1920) 'as a final settlement and supreme sacrifice in the interests of peace . . . although not asked for by her representatives'[1] their politicians thereby admitted defeat, and settled for a compromise that allowed different and mutually exclusive interpretations of its meaning to grow which would lead to the political difficulties and ultimate stalemate of the 1970s and 1980s.

The Home Rule debates of the later nineteenth century had raised the expectations of the catholic minority population in the north-east for greater political participation and social and economic equality (by 1911 the population of what became the six counties of Northern Ireland comprised around 39 per cent catholics and 61 per cent other denominations, while the population of Ulster as a whole was about equally divided), while protestant fears of being swamped by a catholic government from Dublin, which would have no experience of an industrially expanding economy, grew culminating in the 'Ulster Crisis' of the two years prior to the war when Ulster unionists showed themselves ready to stage a rebellion should the Home Rule Bill become an Act of Parliament.[2] The war offered a respite for the British government, but with the events of 1916 a fourth and final Home Rule Bill became necessary, and with it the need for partition in order to accommodate the dissenting minority in the North. Following the logic of the Ulster plantations and the industrialisation of the Belfast area not all Ulster was separated from the rest of the island, but only six coun-

1. Sir James Craig in a letter to Lloyd George, 1921; quoted in Lyons, *Ireland*, p. 696.

2. Stewart, A.T.Q., *The Ulster Crisis*, London 1967.

ties – Antrim, Armagh, Down, Fermanagh, Londonderry and Tyrone – leaving Cavan, Donegal and Monaghan within the borders of the Free State (see map, p. 260).

The Government of Ireland Act, which entered the statutes on 23 December 1920 and began to operate from June 1921, was meant for all Ireland and envisaged an ultimate reconciliation between North and South; the end of partition and full integration, it was hoped, could be achieved through the operation of a Council of Ireland. For Westminster this settlement seemed to offer a solution to the Irish problem: the majority of the North had been appeased, they would have a Unionist majority in their parliament, while the South was fighting over the terms of the agreement with Britain. The signing of the Anglo-Irish Treaty in December 1921 made the Irish Free State a self-governing dominion but did not touch the status of Northern Ireland under the 1920 Act. If Northern Ireland wanted to opt out, a Boundary Commission was to come into operation. Disagreement over the Treaty led to civil war in the South and confirmed the fears of the protestants in the North. The North meanwhile was left with an Act which was meant to provide a constitutional framework for the whole of the island, but had not envisaged a six-county unit to cater on its own in political and economic terms.

The birth of Northern Ireland was thus accompanied by external threats and constitutional, political and economic insecurities and uncertainties. Its parliamentary system was closely modelled on Westminster with an upper house, the Senate, a House of Commons which elected most of the Senate by proportional representation and was itself elected by universal suffrage and the single transferable vote (this reverted to the British practice of the simple majority system in 1929). The Crown was represented in the person of the Governor.

The powers of government and parliament in Northern Ireland remained limited, subordinated to Westminster and, because of the provision for a Council of Ireland, not fully independent of Dublin. Responsibility was given only for certain internal affairs that did not fall directly under overall United Kingdom legislation (for example taxation, communication and coinage). Financial affairs remained a major problem throughout the existence of the Northern government. Because Northern Ireland opted out of the Free State, it was never a fully integrated part of the United Kingdom, nor did it achieve the degree of independence granted to British dominions, which gives some justification to the occasional reference to its status as semi-colonial.

British hopes that the Council of Ireland envisaged in the Act would materialise and would eventually lead to reunification soon proved to be mistaken. Craig and Collins agreed in 1922 that little could be achieved by its institution and suggested regular meetings at governmental level instead. But relations deteriorated fast and contact ceased altogether.

The first Northern Irish parliament consisted of forty Unionists, six Nationalists and six Sinn Fein representatives and met in Belfast City Hall on 21 June 1921 without the Nationalist and Sinn Fein delegates. The cabinet consisted of seven members under the leadership of Sir James Craig, and a Senate of twenty-six was elected which contained no Catholics as a result of their non-attendance. Later meetings were held in the Presbyterian College until Stormont, the parliamentary building, was opened in 1932.

Of the new ministers only Craig had held government office before, although most of the others had some experience in political affairs. The civil service was initially manned from the old Irish administration, largely protestants who wanted to transfer to Belfast from the South, but soon extended with local recruits, at first mostly ex-servicemen. Its first head was an Englishman, Ernest Clark.

The administration began its work under perilous conditions: with Dublin hostile, documents had often to be smuggled to the North; political developments in the South threatened the territorial integrity of the North and doubts remained about not only the financial basis for the area, but also its responsibility for public order as it did not at first have a reliable security force at its command. The religious dimension of the social division in Northern Irish society was evident in every area of social and economic life. As neither side was content with the form political events had taken (protestants wanting more independence, catholics not seeing their nationalist aspirations fulfilled), values, traditions and local customs clashed frequently, leading to a boycott of the new government by large sections of the population. This was not helped by the economic decline that set in, once the immediate postwar boom was over, and led to growing unemployment in both industry and agriculture. The resulting unrest and social conflict tested the new administration whose survival remained in doubt, and forced it into policies of resilience and toughness rather faster than it could have anticipated.

The work and ultimate failure of the Boundary Commission, promised by Lloyd George to realise the principle of self-determination, and which reported in 1925, highlights the continuation of the distrust within the divided community, felt between its constituent parts and towards their respective centres of allegiance, Dublin and

London. The nationalists' hopes for the transfer of part of the border counties were not fulfilled, while the unionists experienced four years of fear about further curtailment of their political unit which was of limited economic validity as it stood.

The Unionist government therefore felt that it could trust only itself and the part of the community it represented, however limited its power. It had to develop pride in its own ability to rule well and democratically so that it could not be swept aside by Westminster. Given its geographical separation from Britain, full integration into the UK might well have opened the door for London to come to some arrangement with Dublin about the six counties. All unionist power and future prospects thus rested on the maintenance of the constitutional status quo, and their insistence and proof that they could govern as well as Westminster. These circumstances not only supported the growth of a distinct unionist nationalism, but they also helped to form the pattern of expectation in the population, the protestant part of which quickly showed its disapproval whenever the government could not deliver, as well as initially very strong, but always festering, disapproval and distrust from its catholic section.

The Westminster model of democracy, with its basic two-party system and firm government based on clear majorities and general consensus of the population on how it wanted to be governed, was, of course, superimposed upon political conditions which not only were not suited to it, but which contradicted it. There was no consensus about the quality of the system, reinforced by the fact that the unionists' 'natural majority' would mean their domination of government in perpetuity. This is not to suggest that unionist government would by definition be bad, i.e. inept or corrupt, but that given the constitutional versus the political circumstances, it would require an extraordinary amount of economic and political good luck for it ever to become democratic government. On a very few occasions in its history it looked as if it might have had that luck, but more often than not the reverse was the case, and each crisis revived and continued the traditions of mistrust, fear and defensiveness of a community that remained uncertain and split about its allegiances.

With a population of about 1.5 million of whom roughly one third were catholics, and the presbyterians the largest protestant group (e.g. about one third of all protestants in the Greater Belfast area), Northern Ireland was more industrialised than the South but had no raw materials of its own; moreover its most prominent industries, shipbuilding and linen manufacture, had begun to decline; its agriculture was backward; and the general health of the population was one of the poorest in the British Isles. Culturally, too, the North had been deprived, since the centre of artistic activity had been Dublin, where most talented people moved if they wanted to stay on the island. With a relatively small professional class, Northern Ireland was disadvantaged, compared with the South, in all but industry, and even that had begun to decline. The new government, if it wanted to prove its worth, had thus to attend to general prosperity, agriculture, education, culture and public health in order to compete successfully with the South and overcome the neglect of the past (Westminster and Dublin Castle had naturally concentrated on amending grievances in the South).

The greatest problem, however, underlying all the above and never fully solved, was that of the legitimacy and survival of the Northern government. Since the constitutional compromise was accepted by only two-thirds of the population, but rejected and partly violently opposed by the rest, the government had to use force itself in order to stay in power. The resulting unrest amounted to something close to civil war: between 1920 and 1922 almost 300 people were killed, three times that many wounded, hundreds interned and £3 million worth of property destroyed. The curfew in Belfast was not lifted until 1924. Since the first target of extreme republicanism was the police force, it is perhaps not surprising that the Royal Ulster Constabulary (established by the Constabulary Act NI of June 1922 to succeed the RIC) evolved not only as a law enforcement service but also had to fulfil military functions.

Violent republicanism aimed to destroy whatever and whomever could be said to represent the British administration, claimed to speak for the whole minority population and frequently used that civilian population as a shield. This reinforced the divide between the denominational communities and was thus socially much more destructive than the civil war in the South: catholics who did not support violence but stood for the tradition of constitutional nationalism were suspected of membership of, and identified with, the IRA. The denominational geography of Belfast became ever more important (as it never had in Dublin) to the location and understanding of violent incidents, shootings, evictions or house-burnings. Religious identities more than ever before became national identities, often promoting reprisals, but always fear, and soon spread to the workplace where holding on to a job had become more difficult, and keeping your own side's workplaces for your own side thus became paramount.

When the RUC was established to curb the violence, after it had become apparent that the old RIC could not cope with the particular problems of law enforcement in Northern Ireland, it already had a forerunner in the Ulster Special Constabulary (based on the Special Constabulary [Ireland] Act 1832) which had been recruited from 1920. There were three categories of these: 'A' Specials, full-time members who were to operate throughout the province; 'B' Specials, part-time members to serve only in their own districts; and 'C' Specials, the reserve. In 1921 a new branch was added, the 'C1' Specials who were to have a semi-military training. By the end of that year there were 8000 A Specials, 25,000 B Specials and 11,000 C1 Specials who were part-timers but could be called up for full-time duty. A great number of ex-servicemen entered the Specials which were effectively organised by Captain Basil Brooke (later Prime Minister and Lord Brookeborough) and were helped with arms and equipment from the army. The Specials continued after the disbandment of the RIC and operated, particularly in rural areas, more as a security than a police force, where their special local knowledge was an extra asset. A and C Specials were eventually abolished and only the B Specials remained.

The RUC was established in June 1922 under the Northern Ireland Parliament Act and was limited to a number of 3000, a third of which was expected to be filled by catholics but not surprisingly never was; often well-founded fear of intimidation and persecution by the IRA and/or specific catholic–nationalist communities saw to that. The nucleus of the new force, about half its membership, was taken over from the abandoned RIC. By 1922 there were about 50,000 part- or full-time policemen (including the Specials) working in Northern Ireland, helped by thirteen battalions of British troops. They tried to operate a strategy of containment and prevention, particularly in the border areas which were much affected by events in the South and where the worst incidents occurred. Given the size of the community, the activities of the police and the violence affected virtually everyone, reinforcing social and religious divisions, fear and apprehension about the 'other side', and made resort to violence at moments of political difficulties and uncertainties endemic, a feature that has remained a socio-political part of the province's landscape.

The legal authorities and methods used by the Northern government, once it had taken over the police from the British government, were much the same as those used by the UK in Ireland in the past under the terms of the Civil Authorities (Special Powers) Act (Northern Ireland) 1922. Under the Act the Minister of Home Affairs for Northern Ireland had considerable powers which he could delegate to 'any officer of the police'; these included search and arrest without warrant, appropriation of documents and other property, destruction of buildings, questioning of witnesses, banning of meetings and publications, and the prohibition of approach to specific places. Later these were extended, originally as temporary measures, to internment and exclusion orders. The latter became controversial only when they were later turned into permanent measures. The original Special Powers Act was thus much changed and extended through the years of its existence. The Act allowed the government powers which amounted to martial law in peacetime. The Act was renewed annually until 1933 and then made permanent.[3]

The need for security and the suspension of normal law thus became a feature of Northern Irish life, making government possible but also guaranteeing a relatively (set against the record of previous centuries[4]) peaceful evolution of the province. It eventually gave protestants a feeling of security, if it also reinforced their belief in their natural right to rule. But its very existence confirmed the fears of the nationalists and republicans, as it failed to persuade most of the minority population that they were living in a liberal–democratic state and society from which they could expect equal political and social rights. The misgivings of the latter were emphasised by the British legal system which made no provision to grant or rectify civil rights in the courts.

The only area in which one can talk of Northern Ireland as being an integrated part of the United Kingdom is that of finance, even though the principle of parity in standards and social services with the rest of the country was not fully established until 1938. Financially Belfast could never be independent from London. The financial provisions of the 1920 Act had envisaged separate budgets and an 'Imperial Contribution' for the whole of the island. After partition this, while not repealed, became a fiction: not enough revenue could be raised in the province to pay for the transferred services (in particular housing, education and health), or even to attempt to catch up with the mainland. A Joint Exchequer Board was set up, representing the UK Treasury and the NI Minister of Finance, to allocate funds, while the 'Imperial Contribution' was made flexible from 1925 onwards and was charged on Northern Ireland's revenue only after other allocations had been made; so it became an indicator of Northern Ireland's prosperity, showing clearly, for instance, the depression of the 1930s and the boom during the later war years.

3. Palley, Claire, 'The Evolution, Disintegration and Possible Reconstruction of the Northern Ireland Constitution,' in *Anglo-American Law Review*, Vol. I, 1972, pp. 368–476; for a brief assessment see Arthur, Paul, *Government and Politics of Northern Ireland*, London and New York 1984 (2nd edn), 17ff.

4. Beckett, 'Northern Ireland', p. 124.

The financial dependence of Stormont on Westminster curtailed any real independence of the Northern Irish administration, but it also helped, once full parity was established and Britain could afford the social legislation of the 'Welfare State', to push Northern Ireland's fortunes after 1945 ahead of the South, loosening the ties of allegiance by which the minority felt bound to Dublin.

The major reasons for the continuing volatility of the constitutional and therefore political structure in Northern Ireland have thus to be looked for in the constitutional compromise and its political consequences. The political and constitutional aspirations of the two communities were mutually exclusive. While the minority could imagine the realisation of their aims in the South, the majority gratefully grasped at the possibility to employ the British system which would guarantee their rule, and which could be defended as being democratic by virtue of copying the British model. Out of this grew a siege mentality and an Ulster nationalism for the protestant/unionist community which never dared to open up the system fully, and an attitude of at least caution but mostly resistance and rebellion among the frustrated catholic/nationalist groups. If national self-determination was to be a basic human right, then both sides from their respective points of view were right, and the constitutional compromise turned out to be the root for the ultimate impossibility to reach a political compromise. Only an abundance of economic good fortune and continued great prosperity might have made a liberalisation possible. But that was not to be.[5]

5. Background information for this section can be found in Lawrence, R.J., *The Government of Northern Ireland*, Oxford 1965; Buckland, Patrick, *Ulster Unionism and the Origins of Northern Ireland 1886–1922*, 2 vols, Dublin and New York 1973; and Shearman, Hugh, *Northern Ireland 1921–1971*, HMSO, Belfast, n.d. [1971].

CHAPTER TWO

Economy and Society

THE ECONOMY

Throughout most of its existence Northern Ireland has had to put up with a substantially lower level of prosperity than the rest of the UK. As already indicated, some of the reasons for this derive from its lack of resources and the failure of the 1920 Act which left a geographically small area dependent on the good will of the Westminster government. Unemployment averaged between 20 and 35 per cent as the staple industries of shipbuilding and linen were contracting. Manufacture had a considerable way to travel in order to reach a wider domestic market. While the population increased, the province was starved of capital, private firms rather than limited companies dominated, and savings were drawn into the national economy. There was little industrial diversification as the internal competition increased. Improvements in the productivity of agriculture only raised the unemployment figures further, while government intervention was patchy and of very limited success.

By 1921 every single public service in Northern Ireland was backward compared with its British counterpart: health, transport and communications, housing and education. Its agriculture was fragmented and backward. Its regional economy had specialised in shipbuilding and textiles since industrialisation, and this made its economy vulnerable in the chaotic international atmosphere of the 1920s and 1930s. Yet, as in Britain, government responsibility and intervention to the necessary degree were not considered desirable, although given the particular social and political pressures facing Stormont governments, there were attempts at government assistance which preceded those of British governments, none of which could overcome the peripheral and disadvantaged position of the economy.

The war of 1914–18 had particularly benefited the economy of the north-east of Ireland. It had brought increased demands for its traditional produce: linen, agricultural products (in particular butter, pork, eggs, beef and flax) and shipbuilding, because of both the specific requirements of the war economy and the interruption of traditional trade patterns which decreased imports and thus boosted the home market which continued to fuel the economy for up to eighteen months after its end. This prosperity was reflected in low unemployment, a great deal of overtime work and eventually in higher wages and an improved living standard which was sustained by the consumer boom immediately following the war.

As elsewhere in Europe the postwar boom was succeeded by a depression which did not allow the industries of Northern Ireland to operate at full capacity ever again during the inter-war years, while unemployment remained at around 20 per cent. The effect of partition on the economy is disputed, but on balance the benefits to Northern prosperity seem to have been greater than the damage caused by an (economically) arbitrary border, or the setting up of a fiscal boundary between Britain and Northern Ireland could have done. The only Ulster counties which truly suffered from partition were those included in the Free State, Monaghan, Donegal and Cavan. Traditionally poor, they remained so in this period with a possible improvement through the prevalence of cross-border smuggling after 1932 in the period of 'economic war'.[1]

Industry and agriculture, despite the debilitating circumstances of the period, however, performed well. Forty to fifty per cent of the working population were employed in the staples of shipbuilding, linen and agriculture. Their decline, and the inability to attract many new and faster growing industries to the province, account for the level of unemployment, averaging 20 per cent in the 1920s and 27 per cent in the 1930s, the largest figures in any region of the UK, and possibly aggravated by insurance benefits which may have reduced emigration.

The decline of the staples has to be seen primarily in terms of international developments. The interruption of the war had forced

1. Johnson, D.S., 'The Northern Irish Economy 1914-1939', in Kennedy, Liam and Ollerenshaw, Philip (eds), *An Economic History of Ulster, 1820-1939*, Manchester 1985, p. 190; this section is greatly indebted to Johnson's article.

British shipbuilding into a much more competitive position as other countries were compelled to develop their own industries. This together with the boom of 1919–20 meant that there was an overcapacity worldwide and orders for the Belfast shipyards declined rapidly, although they still maintained their percentage of ships launched within the UK as well as their worldwide reputation. This was made possible by their involvement in diesel-powered shipping which increased in importance throughout the period, and specialisation in liners and large merchant ships. Finally the industry benefited from feeling able to import cheaper foreign metals (which British shipyards embargoed) and from Stormont's guarantee against default on loans from banks or insurance companies. The good overall record of the industry was maintained despite the slump of the early 1930s after which Belfast actually increased its share in the British market and also began to diversify into railways, oilpipes, engines, trains, etc. Only in the late 1930s, with new naval contracts helping the British yards, did Belfast begin to fall behind the rest of the UK.[2]

As in the case of shipbuilding, the linen industry performed well and held its own under adverse circumstances. Here the warboom was untypical in that linen had begun to decline prior to the war, which only heightened the effect of the postwar slump. Output declined drastically; UK exports of linen (most of which came from the province) fell by almost three-quarters while the number of people employed in the industry fell by about one third between the boom of the early 1920s and 1930. From then onwards, however, matters improved: the devaluation of the pound and protection from dumping stabilised and improved the internal as well as the external markets. Given the shrinking market for linen (which was worldwide and permanent) the industry as a whole held its own in the inter-war period, even though it suffered its due proportion of depression and unemployment.

The difficulties agriculture encountered in this period have also to be seen in an international context, as there was an oversupply of agricultural products worldwide as a result of the war, i.e. non-belligerent countries had expanded their production because of the increased demand during the war. Hence prices fell, and drastically so in the run-up to the Wall Street Crash. The effect of this on Northern Ireland's farming was aggravated by the traditionally small size of farms which reduced output even further (only 46 per cent of Britain's level

2. *Ibid.*, p. 193; Parkinson, J.R., 'Shipbuilding', in Buxton, Neil K. and Aldcroft, Derek H. (eds), *British Industry between the Wars*, London 1982, p. 96.

in 1924). Even if a short-term structural change had been possible, the strength of the agricultural lobby at Stormont could easily have prevented it, as agriculture by the mid 1920s still employed one third of the male and one quarter of the total labour force. On the other hand, the fact that the agricultural strength of the province lay in livestock rather than in cereals provided a safety net and made the industry less vulnerable to the slump in the world market which was much more favourable to the former sector of the industry. Relative to Britain, Northern Ireland could thus even improve its position in agriculture in this period, although it remained far behind in absolute terms: its output never got above 52 per cent of that of Britain. Similarly the income in agriculture rose in Northern Ireland in absolute terms, due to emigration and the consequent slight increase in the size of holdings, but also to the growth in livestock numbers. Yet living standards in the industry remained very low if compared with the industrial sector or with Britain; this was highlighted when agriculture was brought under the cover of the Insurance Acts in 1936 with the result that farm labourers were often better off out of work than in employment.

However reasonably the three major industries performed in the inter-war period, the fact remained that they could not escape the depression. Like most UK regions, Northern Ireland did not attract any of the new growth industries like motor vehicles, electrical engineering and chemicals which tended to concentrate nearer the capital with easier access to transport and markets. Looked at in the UK context, the province was by no means the area with the steepest decline; Wales and the north of England suffered worse. Given the financial restraints on Stormont and the unwillingness of Westminster to take full responsibility for economic developments in the regions (despite the commissioning of reports on some of the problems), new industry found little inducement to come to Northern Ireland (the Special Areas legislation in Britain itself was not a great success either, in terms of the number of new jobs it created in depressed regions). The only major and, in the context, belated exception to this was the setting up of the Short and Harland aircraft factory in 1937 which benefited from the increase in armaments as part of the beginning defence and war preparations.

The building and service industries were the only sectors which increased employment in the inter-war period, particularly in education, government administration, professional services and distribution businesses. Because the economy as a whole did not grow sufficiently to absorb the labour made redundant by the declining industries, unemployment and emigration to the more prosperous parts of the UK increased. Real incomes thus rose by only 10 to 15 per cent as opposed to about one quarter in the UK as a whole. A greater involvement by the province's government may have been desirable, but was not a realistic option.

When the financial provisions of the Government of Ireland Act, 1920, passed into law amidst an economic boom, the Northern economy was in as promising a state as it had ever been before, giving the misleading impression that the Belfast government would easily be able to meet not only expenditure within the province but also contribute substantially to the 'imperial' fund of the UK Treasury. The onset of the depression from 1921 increased necessary expenditure, but also considerably reduced revenue. Belfast, following Westminster's example, responded to the economic setback with increased spending on social services: old age pensions, unemployment and sickness benefits, and support grants towards the derating of agriculturally worked land. Unionist governments, despite the hardly affordable costs of this exercise, felt in no position to deny their supporters the benefits that other British citizens enjoyed. Earnings per capita and government revenue were, however, considerably lower than in Britain, which not only made it difficult to sustain the social services embarked upon, but led furthermore to disgruntled employers' complaints that unemployment benefit was so close to the wage level that it resulted in a great deal of voluntary unemployment.[3]

Westminster did not help, as it would after 1945, by transferring funds to ease the Northern government's burden, since its own expenditure, heavily depressed by the need to service the huge National Debt that the Great War had produced, was difficult enough to control. The only contribution it felt it could, and did, make was, as already mentioned, to turn the Imperial Contribution into a residual one. By the beginning of the 1930s the Northern Irish Imperial Contribution had thus become a token payment. Overall, however, the province was treated with more parsimony than other regions of the UK.

This resulted in severe financial restrictions for the unionist governments: however much they may have wanted to, and there were a number of schemes to help the various particularly badly affected sectors of the economy, there was little or no money for new initiatives, rationalisation of industry, or subsidies to attract new industries to the

3. Johnson, 'The Northern Irish Economy 1914–1939', 203f; on the whole question of finance see Buckland, Patrick, *The Factory of Grievances*, Dublin and New York 1979, pp. 81–104.

province. The financial impotence of the Stormont governments does not appear, however, to have added to the difficulties of the Northern Irish economy,[4] as these were, as suggested above, due mostly to historical conditions and contemporary international economic circumstances. The area in which there was improvement, some of which at least was due to government intervention, namely in agriculture, came through regulations from Westminster in the 1930s rather than from the regional government.

There was then in Northern Ireland a disadvantaged economy, not helped by political developments of the time but not particularly hindered by it either. While the standard of living was improving in absolute terms, there were none the less high levels of unemployment and the size of farm holdings in the province was small.

Housing can serve as a good example for this relative improvement: conditions in the late 1920s and 1930s were clearly improving. About one sixth of the population moved into new houses between 1926 and 1937; 50,000 new dwellings were built in the twenty years before the war, which compares poorly with England and Wales but has to be seen against the background of a virtually stable population (17 per cent increase in England and Wales), very little internal migration and a much lower marriage rate. On the other hand, families in Northern Ireland tended to be larger which meant that greater numbers of people occupied newer houses (newer than in Britain because of the later start of industrialisation). The population census also shows that – a reversal of British conditions – housing was worse in the countryside than in urban areas, indicating greater marital fertility in rural areas as opposed to towns. The relative improvement in housing came to an abrupt stop with the beginning of the war: while the blitz destroyed in excess of 3000 houses, no new houses were built for the duration of the war despite the greatest increase in the population since the Famine.

In the health sector a similar picture emerges: a general improvement, while Northern Ireland maintained its bottom of the league position when compared with other regions in the UK and the Irish Free State. In two areas, however, the province's record was particularly poor, namely in infant and maternal mortality and in deaths from tuberculosis. This is no doubt a reflection of the generally lower living standards and inferior nutritional, housing and medical services; higher mortality from tuberculosis was primarily due to inferior nutrition,

4. Isles, K.S. and Cuthbert, N., 'Economic policy', in Wilson, T. (ed.), *Ulster under Home Rule*, Oxford 1955, pp. 137–82.

while maternal and infant deaths, as reported at the time, highlighted the lack of medical services which 'might reasonably be expected in a city [Belfast] of its size and importance'.[5] During the period life expectancy did improve, however, and so did general health.

Education, too, improved gradually while remaining considerably behind Britain, particularly for children from poorer families. The sectarian division of education made a rational application of available resources more difficult and helped to maintain 'inefficient' small schools, especially in the countryside. But primary schooling improved markedly. A great number of new schools were built, teacher training improved and school attendance rose substantially. But the number of children receiving secondary education remained low in comparison with Britain.

The responsibility for social conditions in Northern Ireland lay with the local authorities. Municipal and county councils often did little or nothing to improve facilities, even when urged by Stormont to do so. Financial restrictions may have been part of the problem, but the conservative attitudes which prevailed among the representatives on the councils, and which did not consider change desirable, offer a more convincing explanation. The most significant point, however, is that Northern Ireland, while remaining relatively deprived throughout the period, in absolute terms experienced considerable improvements for the vast majority of its population. Housing, health and education improved, and employment increased, as did the number of private cars. With the foundation of the Electricity Board of Northern Ireland in 1932 electrification proceeded most rapidly and consumption rose almost threefold in the following six years. Drinking and drunkenness declined, replaced by other leisure activities such as cinema-going, radio-listening, and increased active and passive participation in various sports, much as in Britain.

Social conditions, while clearly influenced by sectarianism, were accompanied by much less violence than hindsight might suggest. The average number of incidences of violent deaths was lower than in Britain and largely clustered in the early 1920s and mid 1930s. Improving living standards appeared to contain sectarian violence.

Most historians have suggested that the economic difficulties Northern Ireland encountered in the inter-war period contributed substantially to its political problems. Seen in perspective, however, this was not necessarily the case: compared with other regions in the UK the province appeared to be doing badly, if by no means worse than some

5. Quoted in Johnson, 'The Northern Irish Economy 1914–1939', p. 212.

other areas, but by its own standards it did quite well. The misleading picture that often arises has its origins, at least in part, in the availability of statistical information. While quite detailed figures are available for the province, this is rarely the case for other regions with the result that Northern Ireland more often than not is compared with the whole of the UK rather than with other regions, a comparison in which it is bound to be disadvantaged.

The rather traumatic origins of Northern Ireland have to be remembered when one considers the question of who benefited most from the economic improvements that did take place. It is perhaps not surprising that a good deal of discrimination against catholics did occur in many areas, considering the embitterment, frustration and fear on both sides, as referred to on previous pages. As catholics were often reluctant to cooperate with unionist governments, or prevented through intimidation from doing so, so unionist governments equally were wary of trusting catholics and admitting them to local or central government posts. This raises the question of how society evolved under the new constitutional arrangements after 1921.

SOCIETY

As has already been pointed out, the six counties that make up Northern Ireland comprise a small territory with a population of about 1.5 million. Economically the east of the province, counties Antrim and Down and including the city of Belfast, are industrialised, comparatively prosperous areas, while counties Londonderry, Tyrone and Fermanagh belong to the agricultural and less developed west, county Armagh in the south falling between the two categories. With the growth of the staple industries there had been migration to the east of the province (e.g. 63 per cent of the population lived in the Greater Belfast area by 1937). This encouraged accusations of discrimination against the less developed areas not only from catholics, but equally from protestants in the affected areas. After 1921 and partition, through which Londonderry, the second city of the province, lost its hinterland, Belfast naturally dominated Northern Ireland, and any new industries, if only for convenience, settled as near to it as possible.

This economic–geographical division may have been no different from other regions in the UK, or indeed anywhere else in Europe, but it mirrored the religious divide: the east of the province was dominated by protestants, where they made up 71 per cent of the population, whereas three-fifths of the population in the western regions were catholics. Given the perpetual fear and tension, accusations against loyalists that they pursued only their own interests were common, even if they did not reflect the full historical reality.

The census of 1926 broke down the religious affiliations as follows: 33.5 per cent Catholics, 31.3 per cent Presbyterians, 27 per cent Church of Ireland, 3.9 per cent Methodists, 4.3 per cent others. This remained roughly the same until at least the 1960s, the higher birthrate among catholics being largely absorbed by emigration. Sectarian divisions intertwined with socio-economic issues have always been an integral part of Irish and Northern Irish history. It is the field which in common with history has provided the most consistent myths and thus perpetuated conservative, or more often reactionary identities and policies.

While Ulster protestantism and Irish catholicism shared a conservative attitude towards theology which tried to resist any cultural and social modernisation and secularisation, there was a fundamental difference in the political dimension of their respective religious theories and practices. The monolithic strength of catholic faith and organisation appeared not only to threaten the protestant, but it also suggested to him an enslavement of the individual to his priest and his Church, while the protestant felt free to be in direct communication with his God without the interference of an intermediary. The unity of catholicism made for the confidence and security that allowed its members to ignore protestantism; the divisions and disputes about doctrine within protestantism could be overcome temporarily, and in non-theological terms, only through unity against catholicism which offered a sinister fascination to protestants. The tyranny of Roman Catholicism thus became a religio-political myth irrespective of the historical and political reality which proposes a much more complex relationship between catholic faith and catholic politics. In turn, and almost as a defensive counter-myth, there was a close identification between the 'reality' of the Bible and politics in the protestant mind.[6]

While protestants were neither denominationally nor politically ever quite as monolithic as might appear from the outside,[7] they did gain the upper hand in Northern Ireland after 1921 by sheer force of num-

6. O'Brien, Conor Cruise, *States of Ireland*, London 1974, 284ff; Buckland, Patrick, *A History of Northern Ireland*, Dublin 1981, 3ff; see further: Beckett, J.C., 'Ulster Protestantism', pp. 159–69, and Kennedy, David, 'The Catholic Church', pp. 170–81, both in Moody, T.W. and Beckett, J.C. (eds), *Ulster Since 1800*, second series, *A Social Survey*, London 1958 (2nd edn).

7. Arthur, *op. cit.*, 37ff; Buckland, *History*, p. 4 and *passim*.

bers, reinforced by the Westminster model of democracy which does not safeguard minority political interests. If protestants could therefore overcome their internal divisions and maintain a common front, they could rule in perpetuity. This was perceived as true by both sides, but naturally interpreted in different, equally defensive ways. The result was that the overriding focus of identity remained 'religious', while social and economic divisions played a secondary, though often integrated role. Trade union and labour organisations which tried to persuade workers otherwise had only limited success: non-'religious' parties lost importance at times of political crisis, and trade unions found that workers managed to divide their loyalties as long as they were not asked to declare their priorities, when the vast majority invariably put their immediate economic interest second, because only by declaring their membership to their 'caste' could they hope to maintain their social, and therefore also economic standing in the community.

The protestants

Where protestants found it easiest to unite and maintain a common front was in their common unionism, that is the maintenance of the border, and their opposition to 'Rome rule', that is the encroachment of Dublin or their northern supporters of the Free State or Eire on their right to rule. But since their governments had real responsibility accompanied by very little real power, they had to convince their supporters again and again that only unity could keep them in power, since economic circumstances did not permit a successful wooing of the nationalist section of the population. One way of appeasing unionist supporters was by discriminating in their favour in representation and education, and to a lesser degree in governmental appointments and law and order.

Given that the province had effectively a one-party system in the inter-war period, parliament played no real role, and any real power lay with the regional government itself and its administration. Judging by the number of ministries – the Prime Minister's, Finance, Home Affairs, Education, Labour, Agriculture and Commerce – Northern Ireland certainly was meant to be governed a great deal for the size of its population.[8] This structure was, however, run by a very small num-

8. For a detailed account of government in this period, see Buckland, *Factory*.

ber of individuals: only twelve people served in the cabinet between 1921 and 1939, some of them continuously. This made for growing expertise, if also for an increase in the average age of the cabinet. The majority of these men came from a landed background with business interests and/or experience, representing the upper social and economic strata of unionism but at the same time identifying with and being perceived as representing the true interest of the protestant community as a whole. Their defensive political attitude would not easily be shaken by catholic/nationalist disapproval from within the province or by criticism from south of the border.

It has often been suggested that for these reasons unionist ministers lacked vision, were narrow-minded and unable to adapt to changing circumstances. But considering their limited power, the economic and political circumstances of the time, the conservative nature of the region they were ruling, and the amount of good luck required to turn Northern Ireland into a prosperous and democratic society based on consensus government, perhaps on balance the critics have been too harsh. To expect Northern governments to have done substantially more for the minority population is perhaps to underestimate the various pressures they had to operate under, including those coming from their own supporters with whose perceived problems they identified, and to overestimate the financial and political flexibility open to them. It is quite clear that there were attempts, if perhaps not always as wholehearted as one might have hoped for with hindsight, to extend the social services and even to look at the interests of the minority, but these were mostly stalled by the Ministry of Finance and its need to balance the budget.

The general attitude of unionist cabinets towards government was largely a reflection of the British example: a reluctance to intervene substantially, to allow the economy to find its own way and innovate and interfere only when absolutely necessary. Part of this was also a reflection of their insecurity which was based on their limited experience in government, further exaggerated by the need to follow the opinions and views of their supporters rather than lead them – a necessity which became a tradition still prevalent today; this very defensiveness, with regard to both Westminster to whom they wanted to prove that they could govern well, and Dublin to whom they wanted to show their true independence and difference, made them vulnerable, as their government was not supported by an overwhelming consensus among those they governed.

It has further been argued that Sir James Craig, later 1st Viscount of Craigavon, with his experience in British politics and his contacts in

Westminster and Dublin, was the only politician in Northern Ireland able to give 'unity and direction to the region',[9] but failed to do so by lacking the imagination necessary for new departures and by refusing to assert himself when it came to developing long-term plans and initiatives for the province. His style of leadership may not have been brilliant but it was certainly popular, making government appear accessible and open, as well as meeting the expectations of the unionists. His emphasis on local issues may have restrained even further the possibility for long-term change, but if once again the pressures of the time are taken into account, the need to appease the protestant community in the first place, and the ethos of government, it is difficult to see how different leadership could have produced substantially different results.

The bulk of the new civil service which was to serve the government was recruited locally (making it one of the growth sectors of the economy): a few appointments were political, but most were made by Selection Boards following the British practice which was based on merit. As with ministers there was a slow turnover of senior civil servants, and standards of competence were generally high. The different images that the civil service had in the two communities highlights once again the divergent expectations and prejudices existing in the population: while unionists complained that there were too many 'disloyal elements' in the services, nationalists tended to identify it exclusively with the protestant sector of society. These attitudes affected applications as well as recruitment: catholics never came remotely near being proportionately represented in the civil service; as in the police, catholics in the lower ranks of the service made up about 10 per cent, and not much more than 5 per cent in the administrative grades.

While civil service recruitment did not discriminate on religious grounds, recruitment into the police was meant to produce a force which was deliberately and explicitly representative of the population, and one third of places was reserved for catholics. The government, however, did little especially to attract catholics to join, and furthermore found it difficult to trust them with senior positions. While the power of the civil service was limited by the government, it none the less could run the regions and gain influence in many areas of detail, if not on sensitive issues like security or the border. The civil service, then, was not a protestant administration in either intention or policy, but was expected to be just that by both communities.

9. Buckland, Patrick, *James Craig Lord Craigavon*, Dublin 1980, p. 124; Harkness, David, *Northern Ireland since 1920*, Dublin 1983, p. 91.

The single most important force of social integration for protestants was the Orange Order. Born out of the rural tensions in Armagh in the late eighteenth century, it became and remained in the nineteenth century a semi-secret socio-political society to which by the twentieth century about two-thirds of adult male protestants belonged. It was the Orange Order which more or less openly made certain its members joined the police and helped to cement the identification of protestantism with unionism and Orangeism as a defence against any possible aspirations to power from the catholic community. The strength and social power of the Order also helped to undermine any original intention by Northern Irish governments to apply the law fairly and justly, and irrespective of the political persuasion of the perpetrators of crimes. In practice discrimination against catholics/nationalists was most marked in law and order, representation and education, where political loyalty was often given the overriding emphasis. This was done only partly to prevent a loss of support from the protestant community, but at least as much in the conviction that nationalists by definition threatened the constitutional status quo and thus the rationale of the existing social and political order.

The ground for this (almost) irreconcilable division of society was laid in the early unstable years of the province, and there was little prospect in the 1920s and 1930s that change might be possible. While unionist governments tried to govern as well as circumstances permitted, the dominant issue remained the constitutional one, and every attempt to cut across this issue, be it on political or social lines, failed.

Unionism thus dominated on every political level: Westminster, Stormont, and in a disproportionate number of local authorities. Social and economic life was similarly dominated, supported by the geographical location of industry and agriculture, the Ulster Unionist Council (the major political organisation dating from the beginning of the century) and the Orange Order. In view of the political and constitutional origins of Northern Ireland, it is not surprising that unionists should have tried to consolidate their power in the face of what they could only perceive as a threat to their very existence and to the political system that guaranteed their survival. The perception by unionists/protestants of nationalists/catholics as not trustworthy – and there are a great number of quite extraordinary examples of this bias asserting itself in individual cases within the administration[10] – predated the partition of Ireland but became the staple myth of protestant politics, continually being fed and refuelled by the particular interpre-

10. Buckland, *Factory, passim*, and Buckland, *History, passim.*

tation of events it suggested. The mirror image of this myth can be found in catholics' perception of protestants.

The catholics

Irish nationalism in the late nineteenth and early twentieth centuries had found its fiercest opponents on the island in Ulster Unionism and had made little effort to conciliate the north-east or appease its fears. The idealism as well as the ideology of nationalism focused on national integration and Home Rule and paid little attention to its denigrators or the protestants of eastern Ulster who felt genuinely threatened by it.[11] The 1920 Act took no account of these historical hostilities and identities, offering only limited safeguards for the protestant minority in a Home Rule Ireland and, by the same token, for a catholic minority in Northern Ireland governed by majority rule. Furthermore, Westminster made no use of its sovereignty in operating them, when Ulster Unionists felt they had to opt out of a United Ireland a year later. Catholics in turn now felt as threatened in the province as unionist protestants had before partition: they generally refused to accept the Unionist government or to cooperate with it, since their wish to be ruled from Dublin had not been fulfilled. They felt their nationalist aspirations frustrated, and their attitude towards the government therefore remained one of passive or active resistance.

Despite the Unionist government's reluctance to use coercion, as provided for in the Special Powers Act, and Craig's early attempts to come to terms with J. Devlin, the leader of the Northern Nationalists, and Michael Collins, the Southern leader, the general perception of unionism by catholics did not change. The discrimination they encountered was thus not only the result of pressures from the Unionist rank and file (as in local government, for instance) or the government's attempts to appease their supporters, but was also due in no small measure to the Nationalists' refusal to cooperate.

The best and clearest example of this can be found in their unwillingness to join the Lynn Committee of 1921 which was set up to consider and examine the education system. The catholic hierarchy refused to appoint representatives, and protestants were left to guess at and make arrangements for the education of catholic children as best they could. Whatever they did under these circumstances would lay

11. Buckland, *History*, 1ff; Lyons, *Ireland, passim.*

them open to accusations of prejudice, manipulation and discrimination.

The Local Government (NI) Act which abolished proportional representation was a very clear attempt to reduce nationalist successes in traditionally marginal areas such as Fermanagh and Tyrone County Councils and Londonderry Corporation. The fact that this provision became law, despite Dublin's intervention in Westminster, showed once more, on the one hand, that Northern nationalists felt Dublin had to speak for them as they had not been given a political voice of their own, and on the other hand it confirmed yet again unionist suspicions that catholic loyalties were not invested in Stormont or Westminster.

The vicious circle of Ulster politics had thus started from the very beginning: nationalists felt they had little choice but to opt out of the state they had never chosen to live in, while unionists' worries about nationalists' hostilities were confirmed and they in turn felt reluctant to serve in the police, civil service, or other public bodies of the 'foreign country' they found themselves living in.

Catholic/nationalist loyalties and allegiances could therefore become clearly defined as lying outside the existing system, as, so it was claimed, were their religious allegiances. Each side could easily see their views confirmed by events. Not only did law-makers and law-enforcers discriminate against, and have a suspicious attitude towards the minority community, but justice itself (despite the fact that the first Lord Chief Justice in Northern Ireland was a catholic) – professionalised in 1932 – was dominated by protestants most of whom had unionist connections.

The socially most unifying force for catholics was in the first instance their Church which made secular organisations like the Ancient Order of Hibernians less necessary or attractive than their protestant equivalent. The conservativism of the Irish Catholic Church and its long-standing political involvement on the side of nationalism reinforced its function as a focus of identification of nationalism with catholicism by protestants/unionists. As unionist cultural and political identity incorporated a British-protestant tradition, so Irish catholicism served the same end for nationalists.

Economically catholics tended to be over-represented among the unemployed and the economically and socially lower rated occupations, and under-represented in the upper occupational classes and the higher status industries like engineering. Feeling exploited and suppressed as a group, this further fuelled their perception of discrimination in their everyday work experience. It is therefore not surprising that catholics felt little inclination to join the police or government services generally, not only because there were repeated incidents of discrimination within these services, but because their community identity forbade participation and required a defensive attitude, which might even extend to sheltering and protecting the recurring activities of the IRA.

While the official nationalist policy of all-out boycott of public bodies began to change in the mid 1920s, the spirit of non-cooperation had become as much part of its ideology as the 'natural right to rule' had become imbedded in unionist consciousness. Even if it had been possible to reverse some of the voluntary ghettoisation that nationalists had inflicted upon themselves, it would probably have implied giving up the notion of a united Ireland which in the inter-war period was not really a viable option for them: the Free State was not a brilliant success story, but Northern Ireland did not appear to do much better for its catholic inhabitants, and at least, they felt, a united Ireland would give them greater freedom than they possessed.

One of the most unfortunate effects of non-cooperation was the lack of proper political organisation. Even when abstentionism was abolished, nationalists refused to function as an official opposition. Part of the problem was divisions within the nationalist camp itself which split into constitutionalists and republicans. Because their focus was a united Ireland and not the improvement of Northern Ireland, they missed the opportunity of properly representing and defending the catholic interest. For the same reason there were barely any political organisations in existence outside parliament. Whatever claims there were for non-sectarian aims by the leader of the Nationalist Party, it remained a catholic party and showed little tendency to act in any but the general interest of the catholic community.

The organisation which benefited most from this political withdrawal was the Catholic Church which flourished in the province in the inter-war period. As already pointed out, it provided a social, intellectual and political all-Ireland focus in which the reality of Northern Ireland seemed to be no more than a passing misfortune, and all would be well once Ireland was united. It justified and encouraged non-cooperation and helped to increase the alienation between the two traditions, fuelling unionists' fears as well as offering them a justification for discrimination. As Patrick Buckland has put it: 'Catholics helped Unionists to put them into the position of second-class citizens by refusing to participate and challenge for positions in official life'.[12]

12. Buckland, *History*, p. 67.

As among the protestant working classes, political and religious sectarianism prevented the formation of an effective working-class party, which may have cut across the denominational divide on economic and social issues. The general apathy towards Northern Irish politics (interrupted by occasional excitement about events south of the border) only emphasised this. The unique exception was the non-sectarian unemployment riot of 1932 which lasted several days and erupted in protest against the non-application of British relief to the unemployed of the province.

The society which emerged in Northern Ireland in the inter-war period thus continued to be divided into two sections whose group solidarity existed in a general cultural framework, based on opposing and partly mutually exclusive religious and political assumptions and expectations. Any perception of social and political realities drew its framework from the specific historical references of its group and assumed the other side to be different and by definition hostile. Both the identity of one's own group and the view one held about the other, were based largely on myth, but the myth of one's own seemed to reflect a positive, experienced reality, while that of the other was negative, an 'enemy image'. There was little attempt to bridge that gap, and ignorance about the other side, its religious and social beliefs and practices, became a hallmark of the province's social and political reality.

Taking political and economic developments of the period into account, it can be seen how Northern Ireland evolved into two mutually hostile camps who grudgingly accepted each other's existence, but were willing to expect the worst of each other and would certainly never surrender to each other.

PART II

1940–1968: The Limits of Modernisation

Introductory

When the British government declared war on Germany in September 1939, Lord Craigavon immediately offered to 'place the whole of our resources at the command of the Government in Britain',[1] as well he might have done, since with the emergency of war the scope of the Imperial Parliament widened and Defence Regulation 55, for instance, allowed governmental control over production, distribution and prices of goods throughout the UK.[2] The Air-Raid Precaution Bill of 1937 had already contained provisions to apply it to Northern Ireland, and the Bill for the Civil Defence Act of 1939, too, gave powers to the province's parliament to adopt it. Only the Military Training Act, 1939, the Reserve and Auxiliary Forces Act, 1939, and the National Service (Armed Forces) Act, 1939, excluded Northern Ireland. This became a much debated issue and Northern Irish governments frequently, but without success, requested that it be changed.

The London government did use its powers of delegation frequently, however (there were over 100 delegations by 1944), so that in effect it can be argued that the government of the province grew stronger rather than weaker as a result of the war. The creation of a Ministry of Public Security, under a minister of cabinet rank, and the conferment of special powers to it by the Ministries Act (NI), 1940, 'to take such steps and precautions, and to issue such orders, as the said Minister may consider necessary for public security, civil defence, the co-ordination of civil defence services and the protection of persons and property from injury or damage in the present emergency'[3] effectively meant that powers and functions could be transferred from other ministries under order from the Governor.

1. Lawrence, *Government*, p. 63.

2. Quekett, Arthur S., *The Constitution of Northern Ireland. Part III: A Review of Operations under the Government of Ireland Act, 1920,* HMSO, Belfast 1946, p.1.

3. *Ibid.*, p. 10.

With Eire remaining neutral, Northern Ireland's geographical position gained in importance, particularly after the fall of France, making her, through the advantage of her ports to the empire, for the first time an essential part of the UK. This was reflected in the London government's changed attitude towards Belfast and not least by Churchill's much quoted assurance to Prime Minister Andrews in 1943 that 'the bonds of affection between Great Britain and the people of Northern Ireland have been tempered by fire and are now, I firmly believe, unbreakable'.[4]

Given Northern Ireland's peculiar position at the north-eastern corner of an otherwise neutral island, there were naturally great worries about possible sabotage of war-vital installations, such as docks, shipyards and aircraft factories.[5] The frontier to the South was 'open', there was a functioning German embassy in Dublin, and the IRA would certainly not let the opportunity pass to undermine the authority and stability of the North. Ironically there were restrictions on movement to Britain, but none on traffic to Eire. Internal security was thus a crucial matter, with the IRA an ever-present potential fifth column. When invasion was feared in 1940, a number of IRA members were interned during May, along with enemy aliens.

Under the pressure of war Stormont curtailed non-essential expenditure, especially public works and local authority spending. This affected the planned improvement of transport and housing particularly badly. Emergency legislation was introduced to prepare for civil defence and control civil life; the most important of these measures was the issuing of identity cards, food rationing, and compulsory tillage to 'plough for victory' in Britain's war effort. Even in the short term the latter resulted in a revolution in agriculture: marketing methods as well as the grading and slaughtering of livestock were drastically rationalised and improved. The importance of the province's food-producing industry increased as the war went on and great efforts were made by the Ministry of Agriculture to improve output. The power of the Ministry grew. The Minister, Sir Basil Brooke, wrote a letter to every single farmer urging him to increase tillage, and this personal effort showed remarkable results: the acreage ploughed in 1943 was almost double that of 1939. The Ministry also encouraged and helped with agricultural training and the mechanisation of farming with substantial success.

The result was not only that Northern agriculture by 1945 was so modernised that it differed very substantially from the now 'backward' South, but also that the efforts made to help feed Britain during the

4. For example Harkness, *Northern Ireland,* p. 102; Lawrence, *Government*, p. 64.

5. Blake, John W., *Northern Ireland in the Second World War,* HMSO, Belfast 1956, p. 80.

war had immediate consequences for the agricultural infra-structure of the province, i.e. the industry moved away from Belfast as its main market and could thus widen its base throughout the region. This strengthened the economy to such an extent that the yield in revenue during the war increased more than it did in Great Britain, even though the yield of revenue per head of population remained lower than in Britain.

With the booming economy, unemployment decreased; industrial employment increased by 20 per cent, as war-related industries worked at full capacity and soon expanded, especially shipbuilding, engineering and aircraft manufacture.[6] General prosperity thus improved: in 1939 income per head of population had been three-fifths of that in Britain, while by 1945 it stood at three-quarters. When Brooke was appointed to head the Ministry of Commerce in the 1941 cabinet of J.M. Andrews, he made great efforts to reorganise and coordinate the local machinery of war production, to utilise its capacity and the Northern labour force more efficiently. When he became Prime Minister in 1943, he continued these policies alongside the initial preparations for postwar policies.[7]

The war brought not only changes in the power of the regional government, but also a revolution in finance. With the province's economy flourishing, Britain promised parity of social services as a reward for Northern Ireland's contribution to the war effort. The new generation of ministers, brought into the government by Brooke, realised the widened scope for commerce and education that postwar reconstruction would offer. The war highlighted, as it did in Britain, the many social grievances and neglects that the province had suffered in the past: in the wake of the blitz on Belfast, for instance, it was estimated that about 5000 houses had been uninhabitable before the war. This resulted in a review of housing needs which concluded with the urgent requirement for slum clearance, closely followed by proposals for improvements in health and educational services, urban reconstruction and planning, and suggestions for improvements in urban and rural service facilities and planning regulations. By June 1944 a Ministry for Health and Local Government was established.

While Brooke and his government pursued energetic planning policies which not only included the working classes but brought their representatives into government for the first time, he and his colleagues paid as little attention as previous unionist governments had to any special needs of the minority community. It was out of fear of,

6. Probert, Belinda, *Beyond Orange and Green. The Political Economy of the Northern Ireland Crisis*, London 1978, 66f.

7. Harkness, *Northern Ireland*, p. 99.

and in deference to, nationalist opinions and attitudes towards the war that conscription had not been introduced in Northern Ireland, despite the marked enthusiasm for the war among the protestant community. The British government even considered trading Irish neutrality for partition in 1940, but, probably wisely and largely for lack of response from the South, eventually dropped the idea.[8] The neutrality of Eire confirmed unionists in their hostility to and suspicion of the Southern state, despite de Valera's clear anti-IRA attitude and notwithstanding that this included capital punishment. Many catholics joined the war effort, both in the British army and in voluntary services at home. The IRA campaigns of 1940 and 1942–44 had little support or success in either North or South. Yet only two of the eight Nationalist MPs attended parliament during the war, and because of the fear and uncertainty about extremists' activities and Southern neutrality, the Ulster Special Constabulary and the Special Powers Act remained active and in force.

The possibility for a new, less divided identity for the population of the North which the shared experience of the war, both in suffering and in prosperity, might have offered, was thus not realised. While the war helped to differentiate the North from the South in a historically new way and turned citizenship in each of the parts of Ireland into different experiences, it had not enough force to overcome the ancient divisions. Established hostilities had been confirmed as early as the spring of 1939, when the Northern bishops of the Catholic Church issued a statement of opposition against conscription, even though unionists were themselves worried about the prospect of having the 'subversive' part of the population being trained in arms. In many ways the war strengthened and fulfilled unionist identification with Britain and by the same token hardened their attitude to their catholic fellow citizens who had not, and could not have in their view, shared the experience of drawing together in defence of the fatherland, since they did not accept it as their country in the first place. Not surprisingly, catholics did have reservations in taking the oath of allegiance or participating fully in the war effort, and while support for the IRA did not increase, neither did the interest in parliamentary procedure. Supervision of and discrimination against catholics continued, as Brooke saw no need to appeal to the minority community.

At the end of the war, then, the Union with Britain was greatly strengthened, the economy booming, and there was great promise for future prosperity and parity with Britain, but the essential sectarian–political division within the province's society and body politic was much as it had been before.

8. *Ibid.*, p. 90.

CHAPTER THREE

The Welfare State

Rather than a smooth transition from war to peace and a more prosperous Northern Ireland in which the unionist 'ascendancy' would be unshakably certain, the Belfast government found itself faced with a majority Labour government in London which was by no means convinced that partition was the only available option for Ireland. Furthermore, the prospect of a 'socialist' central government which threatened to continue state control into peacetime was bound to clash with conservative unionism at Stormont. A constitutional debate ensued in which real self-government was set against full integration into the UK.[1] Either solution promised to overcome the dichotomy of power versus responsibility, but unionists were divided on which was the more viable. While the 'Irish Question' was no longer an issue at Westminster – Northern Ireland remained with the General Department of the Home Office until 1969[2] – the newly founded 'Friends of Ireland', a group of Labour MPs, were committed to look after the interest of the Northern Irish minority and the ultimate unification of Ireland.[3]

These developments seemed to open up the whole constitutional question all over again. The vast majority of Ulster unionists wanted to maintain partition, yet a substantial number began to think of dominion status and real independence from Westminster as an alternative to Britain's 'socialism' and a guarantee against the ending of partition. But the arguments against independence, largely economic, carried the day. While 1945 resembled 1920 in the exuberance of the

1. Lawrence, *Government*, 74ff; Harkness, *Northern Ireland*, 106f.
2. Arthur, *Government*, p. 72.
3. Buckland, *History*, p. 83.

immediate postwar economy, the economic lessons of the inter-war period had not been forgotten: the province's economy, and in particular its industrial sector, was not sufficiently diversified to survive another world recession without outside help. Furthermore, if Northern Ireland wanted to adopt any of the expanded social services that were envisaged for postwar Britain, she would certainly not be able to finance them herself, and thus the advantage won over Eire during the war would be lost, and Labour would be offered further ammunition to end partition.[4]

The Ireland Act (1949) affirmed the province's territorial integrity and constitutional position within the United Kingdom, while declaring the Republic of Ireland no longer part of the British Commonwealth.[5] This offered the minimal assurances unionists required despite the existence of a less friendly government in Westminster, as it gave the Northern Irish parliament veto power against any attempted ejection of the province from the UK and Commonwealth; in other words, devolution remained constitutionally the safest form for the maintenance of the status quo, even if it implied the adoption of some of Britain's more 'socialist' measures.

Financial dependence of Stormont governments remained what it had been before the war, with one significant change: the Imperial Contribution could in effect now be negative. Britain was going to help pay for the welfare legislation it suggested. By necessity this would imply greater involvement of Westminster in Northern Irish finance and thus effectively diminish Stormont's power. Parity of services and taxation between Great Britain and Northern Ireland was guaranteed, but it was once again the Joint Exchequer Board which made the ultimate financial decisions. What Stormont governments lost in power they gained in the satisfaction of their electorate, however, since Britain helped to finance the social legislation that could never have been sustained out of the province's revenue.[6]

This did not affect the population until the second half of the 1950s; as in Britain, the late 1940s were years of austerity for Northern Ireland. But the revolution of an expenditure-based system transformed the province over the next decade, and it is necessary to look at the changes in the most important areas, most of which had sectarian implications and were therefore not as easy to implement as in Britain.[7]

4. Harkness, *Northern Ireland*, p. 107.
5. Lawrence, *Government*, p. 75.
6. *Ibid.*, 77ff.
7. Buckland, *History*, p. 83.

Arguably the most far-reaching changes took place in the field of education.[8] The Education Act (NI), 1947, revolutionised access to secondary and further education and made a norm what the Lynn Committee had only proposed with its scholarship schemes which had only reluctantly and minimally been adopted by the province's local authorities. It became now their duty 'to contribute to the spiritual, moral, mental and physical development of the community by making available efficient education at each stage'[9] of primary, secondary and further education. The Eleven Plus examination was introduced, which enabled brighter children to receive grammar-school education irrespective of their economic and social background.

The White Paper of December 1944 prepared the ground for this and immediately and predictably opened a fierce debate about the traditionally controversial issues of appointment of teachers, religious instructions and grants to voluntary schools. Since 1930 schools in Northern Ireland had had their teachers appointed through the schools' management committees in which in particular the Churches' interests had become firmly entrenched. This proved impossible to change, thus continuing to force teachers to canvass and to allow religious institutions considerable influence over the appointment of teachers.

Religious education, similar to the English Act of 1944, provided for non-denominational (except in voluntary schools) worship and instruction, with ministers of religion being permitted to supervise religious instruction and to offer additional denominational teaching where and when required. Catholics objected to the implied denominational bias of collective worship in state schools. Protestants, on the other hand, were incensed by another change of the Education Act (NI), 1930: since then it had been possible to compel teachers to give Bible instruction. As the Attorney-General now ruled this illiberal and unconstitutional, the province's protestant churches organised campaigns to ensure Bible teaching in all state schools, and a number of conferences between the government and religious representatives were necessary to make them reluctantly accept the point.

The main controversy, however, arose over the grants to voluntary schools, most of which were under catholic managements. These schools had received the cost of their teachers' salaries and half the cost of running expenses, new buildings and reconstruction from public funds. To raise the other half had been difficult before the war, but

8. Lawrence, *Government*, p. 3.
9. *Ibid.*, 117f.

would be all but impossible after it. The White Paper proposed to increase the grant provided school managements would accept one third local authority representation on the committees. This the voluntary managers would not accept, and the government had to give in if it did not want to end up with a totally unequal education system. The Minister of Education, Lt-Col Hall-Thompson, settled for a compromise: 65 per cent grants for the running costs, new buildings and reconstruction for all voluntary schools, and a full grant for all managers who would accept a statutory committee.[10] Furthermore, educational authorities were now also obliged to provide free medical inspection and treatment, transport, milk, meals, books and other requisites.

The Bill was fiercely attacked from both sides, nationalists demanding 100 per cent grants for all schools, unionists warning against the continuing appeasement of the Catholic Church. Once again the by now traditional pattern of prejudice, mistrust and entrenched power positions of the two communities asserted itself. The result was an Act that dramatically changed educational provisions for Northern Ireland without touching upon (or being able to touch upon) the social divisions which, while rooted in the community, were continued and perpetuated in the schools. Significantly, under pressure from the Grand Orange Lodge which discussed education in December 1949, Hall-Thompson had to resign his post, even though his successor, H.C. Midgley, found that nothing fundamental could be changed.

In 1948 the formidable task to put the Act into practice commenced; the most pressing and important aspects were teacher training and new schools. In almost every respect this was a success. Teacher training improved remarkably, new county and voluntary schools were eventually built and many old ones extended and modernised, although many obstacles had to be overcome in consultation with the different interests involved to diminish the duplication of county and voluntary schools. The grammar-school system was reformed by a compromise, as most of them (sixty-seven out of seventy-seven by 1947) were voluntary and had long traditions of independence which they were not willing to give up. Henceforth 80 per cent of places were reserved for qualified pupils and paid for by local authority scholarships, while the remaining places could be filled with fee-paying pupils.[11]

10. *Ibid.*, p. 121.

11. This was somewhat modified in 1950; see Lawrence, *Government*, p. 123, note 2.

Thus education was modernised in Northern Ireland, even beyond the English system in some respects, but this was done at the expense of continued, and arguably increased, socio-religious segregation.[12] The intransigence of both sides forbade a compromise in this most vital field, which in turn once more increased the grievances of the poorer section of the population (though their schools were academically as successful as state education), and confirmed protestant suspicion about the existence and continuation of a catholic cultural state within the state. This latter point had, of course, a basis in reality: the catholic hierarchy was clearly more concerned about the impact of state education – and state schools were open to all pupils – on their flock than their protestant counterparts. This attitude is again not very surprising, however, given that they dealt with what they perceived to be a protestant state.

As indicated on previous pages, the war had highlighted the poor health of the province's population. A Select Committee on Health Services came to the conclusion that immediate action was required and proposed the establishment of a Ministry of Health to overcome the inefficient and uncoordinated existing administration of health. A new Ministry of Health and Local Government was created in 1944 under William Grant which, with the help of the Public Health and Local Government (Administrative Provisions) Act (NI), 1946, the Public Health (Tuberculosis) Act (NI), 1946, and the Health Service Act (NI), 1948, restructured health care in the province, succeeded in overcoming many decades of neglect and paid extra attention to areas of special need.

The new structure largely followed the implementation of the Health Service in Britain. General medical, dental, pharmaceutical and eye services were administered by the Northern Ireland General Health Service Board, which was, as was the new Northern Ireland Hospital Authority, appointed by the Minister. Thus the remnants of the Poor Law disappeared with the responsibilities of the local authorities for hospitals and tuberculosis. District and borough councils were left to administer matters of hygiene, such as water supply, housing, refuse collection and sewage. As Northern Ireland's local government structure was founded on the English example, the adaptation of these measures caused few administrative problems. Following the principle of parity and the province's government's signing of the Social Services Agreement in 1949, the scale and standard of the health

12. Buckland, *History*, p. 90.

services in the region operated in parallel with Britain and long-needed reforms could be undertaken.

But even in this area sectarianism intruded: a large catholic teaching hospital in Belfast refused to be taken over by the state and was as a result deprived of any funds while still treating patients of all creeds most of whom were insured, thus indirectly subsidising the Health Authority. This provoked the expected passionate debate in which sectarian arguments were rehearsed by both sides. While attempts were made in the 1950s to solve the matter, a solution was not yet forthcoming.

Housing was another area which the war had shown to be insufficient and backward. Hostilities had also interrupted the building of new dwellings and the repair of old ones. The housing survey commissioned by the Ministry of Home Affairs in 1943 showed that about 70 per cent of all existing houses needed repairs and the minimum number of new houses required was 100,000, twice that if slums were to be cleared and overcrowding eliminated.[13] The new Ministry of Health and Local Government undertook this formidable task with the Housing Act (NI), 1945. The existing distinction between rural and urban housing was abolished, the administration rationalised, and councils became housing authorities. A new housing agency, the Northern Ireland Housing Trust, was established which was to build dwellings at the Exchequer's expense and manage them thereafter.

In housing Northern Ireland benefited more from state aid than in any other of the social services, and quite disproportionately so if compared with other regions of England and Wales. This was partly a reflection of the province's special needs and its backwardness in this field, but also a confirmation of the principle of parity in all social services with the rest of the UK. The annual rate of construction more than doubled in the twenty years after the Act, although the 100,000 new dwellings mark was not passed until the early 1960s. Improved housing may appear to be a straightforward economic issue, but the allocation of housing by the authority lent itself to sectarian discrimination, and was indeed frequently used by politicians within the election borders of their constituencies to maintain their majority (see pp. 104 and 108 below).

Regional planning, which emerged very strongly in Britain after the war, met with little success in the province. The Ministry did not develop an overall central plan for Northern Ireland and local authorities were often too small to employ planning officers. Despite a

13. Lawrence, *Government*, p. 152.

great number of suggestions and plans that had been put forward during the war, none was implemented after it. It was only in the 1960s that the province began to grow aware of the advantages of regional planning and started gradually to consider limiting the ever-growing city of Belfast and the building of a new town.

It was also only after 1945 that the Poor Law and boards of guardians finally disappeared in Northern Ireland. The new social security was modelled closely on the British example, although the province followed slightly different practices in the administration of local welfare services. But in this field, too, Northern Ireland was brought into line with a modernised welfare safety net.

The initial reluctance of conservative unionist cabinets to implement the 'socialist' legislation from Westminster, in case this threatened their right to rule, soon evaporated as the province grew more prosperous and left the Republic of Ireland economically well behind.[14] They found, to the contrary, that social legislation not only posed no threat but helped them to maintain their political dominance. The adoption of British social policies, however, implied a financial dependence on Westminster which went well beyond that of the inter-war period. The raised expectations of the protestant population could and would act against any thought by unionist politicians of independence or dominion status for the province; it tied the fate of the 'protestant ascendancy' even more firmly to the good will of British governments.

Protestant political dominance thus became even more entrenched, while the minority population did not take advantage of the inherent weakness of this situation and continued to combine any justified complaint about social, economic or political grievances with demands for the reunification of the island. Despite the fact that Northern Ireland was now very firmly separated from the South in very real social and economic terms, there was no indication that either the impact of the war or the emergence of the welfare state had dented the old issues and identities on which sectarianism thrived. On the fringes of Europe and only indirectly in touch with the rest of the 'modern world', Northern as well as Southern Ireland remained parochial and derived their respective identities from earlier centuries, unimpressed by war or modernisation.

In the economic field concerted efforts were made, as in Britain, to avoid the recurrence of a postwar slump like that experienced after the

14. Bew, Paul, Gibbon, Peter and Patterson, Henry, *The State in Northern Ireland 1921–72. Political Forces and Social Classes*, Manchester 1979, p. 125.

First World War. Government, through the Industries Development Acts (NI), 1945–1953, provided inducement for the expansion of industrial firms and businesses, and the infrastructure was greatly improved. But, as indicated, there was still no overall regional planning, and the underlying deterioration of the old, essentially nineteenth-century economy continued. Not enough new firms could be attracted and not enough new jobs created to make up for the decline and closures of the older industries. Unemployment could never be reduced below 6 per cent. The only sector of the economy which carried its war successes into the postwar period was agriculture: it continued to increase the volume and value of its output and boosted the export figures.

The Agriculture Act of 1947 assured a regular review of farm prices, and guaranteed markets for all major products. This led to the better use of surplus production, particularly through milk and potato processing, and the canning industry increased considerably. The Ministry of Agriculture also oversaw the implementation of the Drainage Act (NI), 1947, which made drainage a national charge financed through central and local funds.

The changes brought about by economic diversification and the continuing decline in the staple industries were reflected in changes in society. But this had as yet no distinct effect on the sectarian divide: changes occurred within the two communities rather than between them.[15] Urbanisation, and with it migration to the east of the province, continued. Agricultural employment contracted and well over 50 per cent of the population now lived in urban areas.[16] Towns grew larger: there were ten with populations over 10,000 by 1951. While the denominational distribution remained roughly the same, catholics increased their share in the overall population from 33.5 per cent in 1937 to 34.4 per cent in 1951. The balance within towns changed with migration, and the marginal increase in catholics was more apparent in some places, particularly so in Belfast and Londonderry.[17] The birthrate among catholics had begun to fall but remained higher than the protestant one, while emigration, which had previously maintained the balance, had declined considerably.

Continuing attempts to bridge the sectarian divide, at least among the working classes, were made by British and Irish trade unions, but while the unionisation of the labour force increased speedily, neither

15. Buckland, *History*, 94ff.
16. *The Ulster Year Book 1953*, HMSO, Belfast 1953, p. 36.
17. *Ibid.*, p. 39.

these nor specifically created cross-border all-Ireland trade organisations showed any success in reconciling the divided parts of the community.

Changes in the economic structure of the province and the introduction of the welfare state did, however, affect the social structure of the catholic section of the population. Before the Second World War catholics had been under-represented in the urban and rural middle and upper classes.[18] The improvement and extension of secondary and higher education, as well as the increased demands of the new industries for better trained and professionally educated managers, after 1945 encouraged the catholic middle class to expand and diversify. The proportion of catholics in professional and managerial occupations thus began to rise.

While the catholic middle classes grew in numbers and confidence, the catholic working classes were adversely affected by the economic changes. Contracting agricultural employment and the growth of non-manual but low-grade occupations forced them down the social scale within the working classes. An increased number of catholics became unskilled manual workers, while protestant workers succeeded in replacing skilled manual work with semi-skilled and lower-grade non-manual work, thus shifting the socio-economic balance at the bottom even further in their favour. As there was little economic contact between protestants and catholics at this level, the sectarian divide was not affected by this.

Segregation between the communities remained strongest in the most important social areas: residence, education and marriage. While in urban areas residence appears to have been the essential means of maintaining the divide, in rural life mixed marriages, i.e. between protestants and catholics, were very rare indeed, thus limiting any social contact to one's own group. Residential separation was particularly evident in large towns and cities, and especially in Belfast where it had increased and solidified since partition, encouraged by intimidation and local politics in times of crisis.

This seems to have been reinforced by the prevalence of almost total segregation in education on the primary and secondary level which showed clearly marked differences in the emphases placed on particular aspects of the curriculum studied by catholic and protestant children.[19] Their cultural bias was augmented, for instance, by distinctly unionist and nationalist perspectives in the teaching of history, or

18. Buckland, *History*, p. 96.

19. Insufficient research has as yet been done in this field. But see Magee, Jack, 'The Teaching of Irish History in Irish Schools', in *The Northern Teacher*, Winter 1970.

the continued separation of games: catholic schools played Gaelic games, while protestant ones pursued rugby, cricket and hockey, though they would occasionally play each other at soccer. The school system not only reflected and strengthened the cultural divide, but was expected to do so by the communities. Mutual ignorance about each other and stereotyping therefore continued, and on whatever level social intercourse might occasionally take place between members of the two groups, it was always marked by the strict avoidance of controversial and political topics.

Catholics began to participate more actively in politics after 1945.[20] They contested the June election of that year and returned ten Nationalist members and one Socialist Republican. They took their seats at both Stormont and Westminster, where the return of a Labour majority promised better things to come. This was backed up by extra-parliamentary organisations: an Anti-Partition League, predominantly of middle-class members, organised rallies and focused its activities and propaganda on the removal of the border. Soon politics south of the border also looked more promising for nationalists, when de Valera's Fianna Fail lost the election of 1948 and the new coalition government contained both Labour and extremist republican elements.[21]

This hopeful outlook did not last, however; the Election and Franchise Act (NI), 1946, maintained the prewar system and did not democratise it further as Britain would in 1948,[22] i.e. the Queen's University constituency was maintained, allowing plural voting and preventing the redrawing of electoral boundaries. Gerrymandering could thus be maintained and 'the delicate balance of Unionist control would not be disturbed'.[23] Most legislation following this was equally disputed and equally divisive. Protestant churches and the Orange Order fought, as indicated, over the 1930 conscience clause in the Education Bill, while the Catholic Church worried about the extension of state control and demanded different but equal treatment. Although voluntary schools got only 65 per cent capital expenditure grants, the Minister for Education had to resign over attempts to make further financial provisions for catholic schools in 1949, showing the strength of feeling among unionists and the Orange Order and, furthermore, the tight control protestants could maintain on governments. Tensions in constitutional relations were also obvious in the

20. Harkness, *Northern Ireland*, 113ff.

21. Lyons, *Ireland*, 590f, points out the irony in the Republic's renewed drive for reunification while all of Europe was redivided in the aftermath of the war.

22. *The Ulster Year Book 1947*, HMSO, Belfast 1947, 15f.

23. Harkness, *Northern Ireland*, p. 115.

debates and fights over Belfast's catholic Mater Hospital (see above, p.48), which suggested once again that catholics were required to pay extra for the maintenance of their religious beliefs and practices.

Unionists, and in particular their business interests, were more concerned with the implied 'socialism' of the new legislation. They objected to, and successfully limited, government intrusion through the Statistics of Trade Act (NI), 1949, and pushed through against much opposition the Safeguarding of Employment Act (NI), 1947, which imposed a strict residence qualification upon people wanting employment in Northern Ireland.[24] These, and the exclusion from peacetime national service, continued to separate the province from the rest of the United Kingdom.

The greatest impact on unionist sensitivities and fears, however, was made by the anti-partition drive in Eire after 1948. This had begun with the debates over the Northern Ireland Act, 1947, which enlarged the powers devolved in 1920 to enable 'the Parliament of Northern Ireland to exercise more freely and fully its general legislative powers', mainly in the areas of health, transport and electricity.[25] The anti-partitionist lobbies in the South attacked this legislation vigorously. While Attlee assured Brooke that there would be no constitutional change for the North, the Dublin parliament began to debate the Republic of Ireland Bill and the Anti-Partition League launched one of its major campaigns, both at home and internationally. This enabled unionists to focus on a single issue in the February 1949 general election and so increase their dominance by an additional 12 per cent of votes, even though it also helped to concentrate the anti-unionist vote.

The exclusive concentration by Prime Minister Costello of Eire on sympathies for the minority only helped to keep the constitutional issue in the forefront and cemented the division in the North.[26] After Irish withdrawal from the Commonwealth, the Labour government gave assurances and guaranteed that Northern Ireland would remain within the UK as long as its parliament wished. The Irish Republic was enraged and the Unionist government reassured. But the pressure from the Dublin government on Westminster and Stormont about partition continued, domestically and worldwide, for a number of years.

Had, then, the effect of the war and the implementation of the wide-ranging welfare legislation succeeded in creating a new identity

24. *The Ulster Year Book 1950*, HMSO, Belfast 1950, p. 198.
25. *Ibid.*, p. 16.
26. Harkness, *Northern Ireland*, 120f.

for Northern Ireland? In some respects it had: the constitutional compromise, by now the best available option for the protestant ruling groups, had been confirmed and underwritten quite explicitly by Westminster. This removed uncertainties and reassured the initially shaken unionists, but it also implied that they need not search for changes in the policies they pursued, or in their attitudes towards the minority community. Greater government involvement slowed down the decline of the economy, but the accompanying changes in the economy also led to the beginning of structural changes in society. These, in conjunction with the welfare legislation, would gather momentum over the next two decades and would ultimately create pressure for political changes. By the 1950s it was not only the unionists who had gained in confidence, but also the catholic middle classes. The relative social and economic prosperity of the North increasingly separated it from the South, and Northern catholics, without perhaps noticing or admitting it, began to differ from their Southern counterparts. The long-term consequences of this were not apparent until the later 1960s. Meanwhile sectarian divisions remained as deep as ever, arguably even furthered by the social and economic developments of the late 1940s and 1950s.

CHAPTER FOUR

The Fifties: Social Change and Political Stagnation

The 1950s can perhaps be seen as the most successful period in the experiment of devolution. Once the principle of parity with Britain was established and could be implemented, unionist governments ruled the region with little or no interference, or interest for that matter, from Westminster. An extension of Stormont's powers was never seriously considered and London paid little attention to how the devolved powers were used by the regional government. The constitutional situation was generally accepted as 'the only feasible compromise between the conflicting sentiments of loyalists and republicans'.[1] As the Cold War established itself, it could even be argued that partition was not only in the province's best interest, but equally beneficial to the USA and NATO.[2] Occasionally concern was expressed about the Civil Authorities (Special Powers) Act which remained in force and could potentially be used to establish a unionist dictatorship. But the IRA campaign of the mid 1950s justified its continued existence while doing little for the bad reputation of Northern Ireland in Great Britain and the United States as a region in which civil rights were treated too lightly. As Britain reconstructed its foreign and domestic policies and politics to suit the postwar conditions in Europe and worldwide, the 'Irish problem' which had become the 'Ulster problem' since 1912–14 remained on the shelf – 'benign neglect was the British policy towards

1. Wilson, T.(ed.), *Ulster*, p. 202.
2. Falls, Cyril, 'Northern Ireland and the Defence of the British Isles', in *ibid.*, 79ff.

Ulster',[3] and Stormont governments were left to cope on their own. This they continued to do, taking full advantage of the financial assistance now available from London.

THE ECONOMY

To build on the successful war economy into the 1950s had, as indicated on previous pages, proved to be less difficult than after the First World War, but was by no means an easy task. At the beginning of the decade, the Annual Register reported that '1950 was on the whole a year of uneventful austerity, with prices steadily rising and money growing more scarce'.[4] While central government aid was now more readily forthcoming, this could not halt the decline of the staple industries nor do very much to change the structure of the economy. Both the government-commissioned 'Economic Survey of Northern Ireland' by Isles and Cuthbert and the Hall Report of 1962 were critical of the economic policies pursued in the province: the old industries were still heavily relied on at the expense of a reform of the infrastructure which might have stimulated new economic growth.[5]

The postwar boom had lasted longer than the previous one, but by the late fifties and early sixties it had faded and Northern Ireland experienced a radical fall in economic activities and drastic changes in her manufacturing industries. It was now that the province became the most disadvantaged area in the UK, while those regions which had shared her fate in the 1930s (e.g. parts of Scotland, Wales and Merseyside) were participating in almost full employment. The changes her economy encountered were unparalleled anywhere else in the UK, despite the fact that she was struggling quite successfully against substantial odds arising out of her natural disadvantages. As the Wilson Report concluded for the decade, 'While precise accuracy is not to be expected in a statistical comparison of this kind, it would be hard to

3. Rose, Richard, *Northern Ireland. A Time of Choice*, Washington DC, 1976, p. 20.

4. Macadam, Ivison (ed.), *The Annual Register of World Events. A Review of the Year 1950*, London 1951, p. 75.

5. Isles, K. S. and Cuthbert, N., *An Economic Survey of Northern Ireland*, HMSO, Belfast 1957; *Report of the Joint Working Party on the Economy in Northern Ireland* (Hall Report), HMSO, London 1962, Cmnd 1835.

dismiss the broad conclusion that the rate of growth of production in Northern Ireland has been above the national average.'[6]

An indication of the changing structure of the economy can be found by comparing the percentage share of employment and GDP in 1951 and 1961.[7] In 1951 agriculture held 18 per cent of the labour force and contributed 17 per cent to GDP, industry employed 44 per cent and contributed 41 per cent to GDP, services employed 38 per cent and contributed 42 per cent. By 1961 there was a marked increase in services and a parallel decline in industry and agriculture, particularly obvious in the case of agriculture (agriculture employed 13% = 12% of GDP, industry 42% = 40%, services 45% = 49%). These figures also indicate a fairly good level of productivity; but again the most successful one is the service sector. The province's economy had a relatively narrow and fairly specialised industrial base, not only covering the home market but exporting worldwide, in particular textiles, shipbuilding and engineering. In a small regional economy in which large firms dominated, the encouragement of outside investment in order to overcome existing disadvantages also resulted in high levels of imports and exports in relation to GDP. The consequence of this had traditionally been great vulnerability to changing trends in international trade and fluctuations abroad. This in turn put restraints on the kind of fiscal policies that could be employed to achieve an expansion of domestic economic activities.

The specialised industrial structure of the economy and the well above national average unemployment influenced economic developments in this period as much as the particular constitution of the province which allowed the regional government considerable powers of control over industrial growth. Isles and Cuthbert have suggested that the effects of the monetary and fiscal policies of governments, during at any rate the early fifties, were not altogether positive.[8] The benefits of special investments were largely absorbed by other regions through the expenditure of increased income on goods imported. This not only did little to raise the level of employment, but also, they argued, aggravated the inflationary tendencies in the economy as a whole, while any steps to curb inflation would increase unemployment. They

6. *Economic Development in Northern Ireland* (Wilson Report), HMSO, Belfast 1965, Cmd 479.

7. Kennedy, Liam, *Post-War Ireland* (work in progress), to which this section is particularly indebted; forthcoming as D.S. Johnson and Liam Kennedy, 'The Two Irish Economies since 1920', in Moody, T.W., Martin, F.X., Byrne, F.J. and Vaughan, W.E. (eds), *A New History of Ireland*, VII, Oxford.

8. Isles and Cuthbert, in Wilson, T. (ed.), *Ulster*, 92ff.

concluded that on the whole the limited provincial self-government produced only marginal benefits for the Northern Irish economy.

The population of Northern Ireland continued to increase during the decade, from 1,370,921 in the 1951 census to 1,425,042 in 1961, raising the average population density from 262 to 272 per square mile (compared with England and Wales – 790, Scotland – 174, and the Irish Republic – 106), and with this came further urbanisation, from 53.1 per cent in 1951 to 54 per cent in 1961; two-fifths of the whole population now lived in Belfast and the surrounding area.[9] The outstanding features of the industrial structure remained the predominance of agriculture as the single largest industry, the absence of other extractive industries, and the concentration of industrial workers in very few industries. Farms remained small, largely family-worked with seasonal employment of outside labour, although the number of persons employed in agriculture continued to decline from 148,370 in 1952 to 112,000 in 1962. While farming had been modernised as a result of the war and was in considerable advance of the Irish Republic, Northern Irish farms still suffered from a deficiency in agricultural mechanisation in comparison with Britain. The importance of agriculture in the economy and its still large share in the total income was reflected in the governments' attempts to improve standards of husbandry (the province maintained its preference for livestock) and marketing procedures.

The lack of domestic sources of principal minerals continued to hinder the development and expansion of industry. It raised the cost of power and reduced profitability.[10] Furthermore, it largely determined the structure of the industrial sector with its large proportion of workers in few industries. The small size of the domestic market dictated an export-orientated production which in turn tended to result in light industries with relatively low transport costs. There was a fall of over 28 per cent in those employed in textile manufacture between 1950 and 1961, while the numbers employed in shipbuilding, ship-repairing and marine engineering fell by over 16 per cent.[11]

By 1950 the future for agriculture began to look promising again: postwar scarcity had given way to agricultural surpluses in some commodities.[12] European agriculture reached its prewar level of output by 1950. Britain did even better: by 1952 it had raised its prewar agricul-

9. *The Ulster Year Book. The Official Yearbook of Northern Ireland, 1963–1965*, HMSO, Belfast 1965.

10. Isles and Cuthbert, in Wilson, T. (ed.), *Ulster*, p. 101.

11. Hall Report, p. 68.

12. Kennedy, Liam, *Post-War.*

tural output by 50 per cent. Most European countries, however, resorted to protectionist policies in order to support their home producers. Thus access to the international market became more difficult and price trends grew more unfavourable. Under these circumstances Northern Ireland's agriculture benefited in particular from its secure access to the British market with the implied price guarantees and subsidies. The net agricultural output increased by 2 per cent per annum between 1950 and 1959, though this was accompanied by a 12 per cent fall in farm sector income. The changes in output included a restructuring of output. There was continual growth in pig, poultry and egg production, encouraged by the availability of imported cheap foodstuffs. By 1950 farmyard products accounted for about half of the value of total agricultural output, declining slowly to 44 per cent in 1959. The acreage tilled contracted, partly due to the cheap grain policy of the UK. By 1950 about three acres of pasture existed for every one of tillage; by 1959 the ratio was five acres to one. Cattle and sheep production, however, increased, from 28 per cent of total output in 1950 to 32 per cent in 1959, while dairying's share of output declined from 23 per cent in 1940 to 16 per cent in 1959.

These structural and volume changes were a reflection of changes in the input: tractor power had replaced horses, and great improvements had been made in the quality of animal breeding, fertilisers and seeds. The number of tractors – 16,000 in 1950 – doubled over the decade, while the number of males employed fell by 27 per cent. This growth in efficiency did not, however, have serious social consequences as the agricultural sector in the province's economy was balanced by industrial developments.

In the industrialised world the 1950s were characterised by rapid technical change, productivity gains, fewer tariff restrictions than in the agricultural markets, and a buoyant trade, but Northern Ireland did not fully benefit from this in either industry or employment. The difficulties of the restricted structure of her industry, as indicated above, did reappear after the new prosperity of the war years and in the immediate postwar period. Both the composition of her industries and the openness of her regional economy made her vulnerable to cyclical fluctuations, and the capital goods produced by her shipbuilding and engineering industries were particularly affected, while the linen industry increasingly produced luxury goods which were no longer in steady demand. The result was that the region felt every decline in the UK's economic cycle more strongly than other areas. The narrowness of the economic base – shipbuilding and engineering on the one hand, and textile and clothing on the other (in 1952 44 per cent of insured males and 82 per cent of insured females of the total industrial sector were employed in these industries) – only increased this vulnerability.

The extended commitment to, and dependence on, old industries, however, began to change: clothing, light engineering and shipbuilding started to adjust to modern market demands. There was a marginal increase in employment during the 1950s in the clothing and engineering industries. World demand in shipbuilding remained buoyant beyond the initial postwar boom and almost doubled over the decade as a whole. The level of employment at Harland and Wolff's Belfast ship-yards, the province's largest single industrial enterprise, was maintained at about 20,000 throughout the decade. Other engineering employment increased, and the construction sector benefited greatly from the effects of public investment, be it roads, hospitals, factories, health and welfare services or housing. Only the linen industry began a steady decline, once the 1940s boom was over. Not only was it affected by a serious international recession in textiles during 1951–52, but the competition from mostly cheaper synthetic and other natural fibres made trading increasingly difficult. The number employed in textiles fell by a third from the early to the late fifties, but this masks the even steeper decline of linen as new textile firms developed beside the old declining industry.

The engineering sector, too, experienced some diversification: new, mainly British firms or their subsidiaries introduced changes from heavy mechanical to lighter and electrical engineering. If the Northern Irish economy was to have a future, as the old industries were declining, the industrial base had to be restructured in order to create new jobs for those lost in the old industries. Government policy tried to attract outside investment to the province as well as aid existing industries directly through financial grants which would help to modernise and expand them, as expressed in the Re-equipment of Industry Act (NI), 1951 and the Capital Grants to Industry Act (NI), 1954.[13] The significant result was that, while virtually no new jobs were created through financial aid to existing indigenous enterprises, outside firms, newly established in the province, promoted new jobs at the rate of 3000 per year. This was insufficient, however, to absorb either the displaced workers from the declining industries or the labour flow out of agriculture. This explains the overall decline in employment with the sole exception of the service sector, which expanded in the wake of the social reforms implemented in the late 1940s and early 1950s.

13. *The Ulster Year Book 1953*, p. 114, and *The Ulster Year Book 1956*, HMSO, Belfast 1956, p. 119.

The 1950s can thus be seen as a period of transition in which industry was restructured and employment patterns changed. The growth rate of industrial output increased by an average of only just over 2 per cent over the decade, reflecting the adjustment problems industry had to overcome. The growth of manufacturing output was even lower at below 2 per cent per year.[14] Contributory reasons for this slow growth may be found in the lack of dynamism in the traditional industries; in the case of linen, export demands were falling, while shipbuilding encountered serious problems of supply. The UK economy as a whole, furthermore, grew very slowly, thus not providing the stimulus of an expanding market; and private investment in manufacture was low: less than 4 per cent of GDP per year during the decade. Local enterprise had to cope with the structural changes needed and the low profitability connected with these adjustments, while outside investors and new firms may have suffered from the province's peripheral location and the higher cost of transport, thus not contributing as much to the overall growth as might have been expected.

Unemployment remained at an average of over 7 per cent per year throughout the 1950s, much lower than in the inter-war period but still four or five times as high as in Britain, although the social effects were reduced by the welfare system. Emigration, too, continued, averaging 7 per 1000 of the population throughout the decade. While no longer very high, it none the less helped to keep unemployment down. All this made for a slowly rising living standard, an expanding consumer market, and particularly improved the life of the working classes.

Given the important long-term effects of economic changes in the 1950s on social and political developments, it is desirable to attempt a more detailed assessment of the underlying reasons for the persistent unemployment and governments' attempts to ease it on the basis of the Hall Report. Sir Robert Hall's Joint Working Party on the Economy of Northern Ireland, which had been appointed 'to examine and report on the economic situation of Northern Ireland, the factors causing the persistent problem of high unemployment, and the measures that could be taken to bring about a lasting improvement',[15] reported in 1962. Its proposals were based on a thorough analysis of the province's economy and, while concentrating on the causes of unemployment, it not only provides a summary of the success and failure of the economy, but also continuously compares it with economic performance in Great Britain.

14. Kennedy, *Post-War*.
15. Hall Report, p. II.

While the powers of Stormont were restricted – nine-tenths of revenue was imposed and collected by Westminster – the very fact that it supervised a separate administration meant that it was in a position to develop and practise wider employment promotion policies than the UK government. The parity between Great Britain and Northern Ireland in services and expenditure also extended to basic wage rates in manufacture, since 80 per cent of organised labour in the province belonged to UK-based unions. It should be stressed, however, that this did not lead to equal levels of earnings: more often than not Northern Irish wages remained at the basic level. The prospect of the Northern economy being able to export to the Irish Republic was considered remote, unless both the South and the UK joined the European Economic Community.

Hall stressed the disadvantaged nature of the Northern economy which meant that jobs had to be found both for those dismissed from the contracting old industries and because of the natural expansion of the population. This could be achieved only by making its industry competitive with the rest of the UK fast enough to decrease unemployment, which would necessitate that transport and material costs had to be lower than in Britain. Because of government assistance to industry, capital costs were already lower and so were labour costs: the average earnings of male workers in manufacture were lower than in Britain (the average income per head of the population was even lower than that, about 74 per cent of Britain's in 1959–60). But while the zeal and discipline of the workforce were considered to be good, there was notably less of a tradition of diversified industrial skills than in Britain and the average net output per operative was well below the UK as a whole: about 68 per cent by 1957. (Perhaps it is worth while to remember that Hall compared a region to the whole of the British economy; if regional comparisons had been made, a different picture might have emerged.) Lower productivity and lower labour costs could, however, not be set off against each other; the disparity in productivity was greater than that of earnings.

The Report pointed out that while linen, shipbuilding and the aircraft industry were all in difficulties for reasons not related to the special difficulties of Northern Ireland, these problems might restrict their ability to diversify. It was recognised that linen had diversified as far as it could and had developed new fibres and fabrics, and that it could now be expected only to hold its ground, while other textiles had widened their scope, in particular into hosiery, carpets and carpet yarns, and artifical fibres like rayon, acrilan, nylon and tylane. Shipbuilding, consisting largely of Harland and Wolff and ancillary works and sub-contractors, had only recently encountered severe problems, but had kept its workforce of about 23,000 stable until 1961. The future of the aircraft industry, consisting mostly of Short Brothers and Harland, 70 per cent of whose shares were owned by the UK government, would depend on their ability to attract new contracts and perhaps join the recently rationalised organisation of British firms. Employment in this industry had fluctuated greatly over the decade.

A few large and a number of small firms in engineering and metals, diverse in origin and character but historically related to the supply needs of the textile industries, had begun to widen the range of their products and increased their activities under the impact of the industrial development programme. A trend towards lighter engineering products had begun: oil-well equipment, computers and tabulators, radio and electrical equipment, wires and cables, cameras and gramophone equipment were now produced in the province. Employment in these sectors had increased from 14,700 in 1954 to 20,900 in 1962, which was due not only to the complementarity of these businesses but also to the fact that an increasing number of diverse firms were attracted to the province. 'The introduction into the Northern Irish industrial community of the energetic executives and technicians of new industry help to establish an attractive atmosphere for the newcomer', noted the Report.[16]

Agriculture, while declining in numbers, remained the largest employer. Individual holdings were down to 72,000 from 87,500 in 1949, and the number of people employed in the industry was down from 101,000 to 73,000, which included a fall in paid employees from 29,000 to 16,000.[17] As already pointed out, this was due largely to mechanisation: where there had been about 850 tractors in 1939, there were now about 30,000. The Small Farm Scheme and the Farm Improvement Scheme encouraged amalgamation of holdings and the elimination of uneconomic units.[18] This had resulted in further rationalisation and an increase in efficiency and output which had increased by over 80 per cent since 1938. Most of this happened in livestock and related products, more than 60 per cent of which was exported to Britain.

The Hall Report, as was its brief, paid special attention to the trends in employment. It concluded that the fall in the number of persons in agricultural employment roughly mirrored the rise in the building and construction sector, that employment in the textile and clothing sector fluctuated but changed little overall between 1950 and

16. *Ibid.*, p. 7.
17. *The Ulster Year Book 1950*, p. 64.
18. *The Ulster Year Book 1963–65*, 74f.

1960, and that the decline in the staples was made good by the growth of the new industries. The large increase in employment in the services – 18,500 more in 1961 than 1950 – was due largely to public investment in education and health. The number of insured employees rose from 438,000 in 1950 to 449,500 in 1960.

These trends were largely similar to those in Great Britain, but with significant qualifications: the increase of potential employees was greater in the province than that of potential employment. The natural increase of the population was about 15,000 per year, the net migration about 9000 of whom more than half of the insured workers went to Great Britain. As a result unemployment in the province throughout the 1950s remained at over 30,000. There were seasonal fluctuations for male and cyclical changes for female employees, mostly in the textile and clothing sectors. Furthermore, the new firms decreased the number of the unemployed by less than the number of jobs they created. The reasons for this may be found in men returning from Britain once jobs became available in Northern Ireland, and women, particularly in country areas, may have taken up new employment without previously having been registered as unemployed.

Unemployment was particularly concentrated in the Greater Belfast area and especially so for craftsmen and skilled workers. Outside a radius of twenty miles from Belfast there was no concentration of unemployed craftsmen to be found. Shipbuilding and general engineering accounted for 68 per cent of unemployment in the Belfast area and made up 57 per cent of the province's total. The remainder was largely to be found in the building trade: three out of seven builders in Belfast were unemployed, but only one in nine outside it. The unemployed were also relatively young, i.e. the majority under forty-five, and nearly half of them were general labourers with little or no training. Some 40 per cent of all women registered as unemployed had no training or experience, and four-fifths of those belonged to the textile and clothing trades.

Yet the economy was growing faster than in the United Kingdom as a whole. The index of industrial production rose from 89 in 1950 to 125 in 1960, an increase of 40 per cent, while the UK index rose by only 35 per cent. Personal income per head had been £168 in 1950–51 and had risen to £284 by 1959–60. The corresponding figures for Britain were £221 and £378 respectively. While the jobs created through new industries and employment in the services kept pace with the rise in the working population and the fall in employment in the old industries, unemployment remained high since surplus employment could not be created.

Before suggesting remedies, the Hall Report analysed the measures that had been taken to create employment and how effective they had been. In contrast to Britain, governmental measures covered the whole of Northern Ireland and not just development districts, and the inducements offered to outside investors and native firms were greater. The assistance given to agriculture – and the province received a relatively larger share of this than other regions in the UK as well as additional small subsidies for geographical remoteness – also eased unemployment, even though it was not intended for that purpose. Industry was helped mainly through the Capital Grants to Industry Act (NI) (see above, pp. 50, 60) and the Industries Development Acts (NI). Most aid to new firms came under the Industries Development Acts; this could comprise aid of almost any kind, but was in fact mostly capital assistance. The grants of up to one third of capital costs went mostly into factory building, indicating a clear preference for new industrial developments. In other words, the Capital Grants Act provided incentives to re-equip or provide for minor extensions of existing industries, while the Industrial Development Acts offered special incentives for new industries or substantial extensions of existing ones. The maximum grant under the former was fixed, while under the latter account could be taken of all manner of aspects, e.g. the amount and type of employees relative to expenditure or the potential growth of the enterprise, in order to determine the amount of inducement required.

Other subsidies came in the form of reduced prices for coal and forms of power derived from coal, or the derating of industrial premises by 75 per cent (this compared with only 50 per cent in Great Britain), although rates constituted only about 1 per cent of net output and derating therefore did not constitute a large inducement. A total £750,000 of subsidy was distributed between 1953 and 1962 to industrial users of coal who used more than fifty tons per year, since coal was more expensive in Northern Ireland than in Great Britain because of the additional transport and delivery costs. The benefits of this appear to have been uneven: large firms with large usage benefited disproportionately, and since the subsidy did not apply to oil users, it may also have operated as a disincentive to switch over to oil.

The success of re-equipment aid to firms to improve productivity is also difficult to assess; it seems to have stopped the further contraction of existing enterprises and thereby preserved jobs. The linen industry, for example, was given about £4 million in aid between 1956 and 1961; jobs in the industry declined over that period from 52,000 to 42,000. It is impossible to estimate how many more jobs might have been lost without subsidy and the only conclusion that can be drawn is that aid must have had some effect.

One may thus conclude that the Northern Irish economy in the 1950s was probably more successful than ever before in its history while still causing concern for governments; the heritage of outdated staple industries and the geographical periphery of the province made it virtually impossible to reduce unemployment any further and thus allow the region to catch up with the rest of the UK. The ironic result was that, while Northern Ireland did unprecedentedly well by its own standards, it became in the 1950s economically the most backward region in the country in almost all respects.

THE RULING CLASSES: GOVERNMENT, PARTIES AND POPULATION

While by 1961 unemployment in Northern Ireland was still five times higher than in Britain, the more important fact was that more people than ever were employed. This remained not without effect on the political scene. There can be little question that the 1950s were a politically and socially more tolerant and less violent period than the prewar years, and it is of some significance that the four university seats at Stormont were held by Liberals and that the non-sectarian NILP (Northern Ireland Labour Party) captured four Belfast seats in the 1958 general elections.[19] The Annual Register for these years reported repeatedly that apart from occasional IRA violence which never amounted to very much, 'the political life of the province was unexciting',[20] a clear indication that the old controversies were taking a rest, or even became traditions, less and less relevant in the increasing relative prosperity of the later 1950s.

Sir Basil Brooke, created Viscount Brookeborough in 1952, who had replaced John Andrews as Prime Minister on 1 May 1943, remained in this position until 1963. Brooke, born in 1880 and educated at Winchester and the Royal Military Academy, Sandhurst, was a County Fermanagh landowner, a member of the Church of Ireland

19. Lawrence, *Government*, p. 100.

20. *The Annual Register of World Events. A Review of the Year 1957*, London 1958, p. 72.

and the Orange Order, who had been involved in unionist politics since 1921. He presided over a party, the Ulster Unionist Council, which, under his leadership and with the help of the 'benign neglect' of the London Home Office, no longer attempted in any sense to provide the policies of a 'national' party, as it arguably had under Craig's guidance in the inter-war period. The 'protestant ascendancy' seemed to be secure, and a certain amount of triumphalism crept into unionism; more often than not Brookeborough played the Orange card and relied on anti-catholic speeches. He rejected any attempts by Unionists to adopt catholic candidates for parliament.[21]

Brooke's standing in the Unionist Party and the protestant community was not least based on his achievement of securing Northern Ireland's constitutional position in 1949, thus putting him in a historical line with Carson and Craig.[22] But he was equally concerned about the improvement of the province, as seen in his personal interest in farming, his concern for social welfare and the attention he paid to the alleviation of unemployment. However bigoted he might have been as an individual, he certainly presided over one of Northern Ireland's most successful periods in history.

A new constitution had changed the leadership structure of the Ulster Unionist Council in 1946, enlarging the Standing Committee of the party and making it more representative of its membership: the dominance of the landowners, which had been in evidence since 1905, began to decline. The real link between the party and its leader became the Executive Committee which was made up of local and institutional representatives and the party leadership. This body was potentially the most powerful in the party: it could possibly influence the leader and certainly had the right to challenge, if not depose him. It was also the body in which principles of policy could be debated. It was the chairman of the Standing Committee and ex officio member of the EC, Sir Clarence Graham, who suggested in 1959 that catholics should be able to join the Unionist Party and be selected for parliament, and another member of the Standing Committee, Sir George Clark, Grand Master of the Grand Orange Lodge of Ireland which was also represented on the EC, who rejected this suggestion: 'It is difficult to see how a Catholic, with the vast differences in our religious outlook, could be either acceptable within the Unionist Party as a member or, for that matter, bring himself unconditionally to support

21. Buckland, *History*, p. 102.

22. Harbinson, John F., *The Ulster Unionist Party, 1882–1973. Its Development and Organisation*, Belfast 1975, p. 145.

its ideals.' The Prime Minister topped this soon afterwards with 'There is no change in the fundamental character of the Unionist Party or in the loyalties it observes and preserves. If that is called intolerance I say at once it is not the fault of the Unionist Party. If it is called inflexible then it shows that our principles are not elastic.'[23] The Executive Committee felt obliged to issue a statement to confirm what the leaders of the party and the Orange Order agreed on, and Sir Clarence Graham duly signed the statement. Tolerance was barred to the fringes of the party. Unity was still essential to maintain protestant rule, and in order to keep unity the divisions in society had to be stressed.

The UUC had employed full-time professional staff from 1905 and was particularly well served by William Douglas as Secretary to the Council from 1941 to 1963, during which time he also served as Superintendent to the Whip's Office. Douglas's political views were totally confined by the constitutional issue, but his talent lay in judging and organising the Unionist vote.[24] He combined an awareness of politically exploitable issues with an ability to get all available Unionist votes into the ballot boxes that mattered. The realisation of Unionist political majorities was in no small measure due to his election organisation, no mean feat in a province where a great number of legal and semi-legal tricks were generally employed to win elections. His party management ensured the unity of the party and provided the link of a strong personality, himself, between party headquarters, the parliamentary party and the Prime Minister.

Harbison has shown that the political attitudes that evolved and became the party's political identity between 1905 and 1944 were centred on the constitution, anti-socialism and anti-catholicism.[25] Little had been allowed to change by the 1950s, even though some practical 'socialism' had crept into the overall conservative and paternalistic policy of the party. The main advantage of the UUC was that it did represent all protestant social classes and different shades of unionist opinions which helped to reinforce its essential identity which combined the constitutional issue with anti-catholicism.

The network of local Unionist constituency organisations was the oldest in Ireland, dating back to the last years of the nineteenth century. Its association with the UUC provided the basis for successful electioneering in both regional and general elections. There is no collected evidence of the socio-economic composition of the local associ-

23. Quoted in *ibid.*, p. 44.
24. *Ibid.*, 50ff.
25. *Ibid.*, 54ff.

ations, but they appear to have been fairly representative of the protestant population in their respective areas. The constituency associations selected candidates for elections, following a loosely similar pattern. Since there was no limit to the financial contribution a candidate could make to the funds of the local organisation, and selection often meant a guarantee of election if the seat was well chosen, technically the link between property and power had not been broken.[26] The other important feature was that there appears to have been considerable pressure from the constituency organisations for the candidate to be a member of the Orange Order.

The relationship between MPs and their constituencies is by no means clear; while the general pattern appears to suggest that local elected representatives could generally pursue the policies they liked provided they maintained a fairly clear line on the constitutional issue, there were a number of examples where sitting candidates were defeated at selection conferences because they supported causes in parliament of which their constituency organisation disapproved.[27] In the UUC the local associations constituted about a quarter of all delegates and there is little evidence to suggest that they ever successfully influenced Unionist policy. Their main function seems to have been to provide the voluntary labour which kept the organisation together and by implication reinforced the commonly held beliefs about the Union and the policies necessary to preserve it.

The link between religion and politics within the Unionist Party continued to be provided and maintained by the Orange Order. It was the entrenched power position of the Order which made it ultimately impossible to open the party to catholics, however liberal some of the party members might have grown. The very great majority of Unionist MPs were members of the Orange Order, including one woman.[28] The local Orange Hall served as a social as well as a political focus where much of the groundwork for Unionist electioneering was done, such as knowing the exact size of the Unionist vote at any given moment. More often than not candidates were selected in the Orange Hall, and frequently delegates from the Orange Lodges outnumbered those of the constituency organisation at these conferences. During elections the local Orange Hall became the centre of all Unionist activity, the headquarters for canvassing and 'the engine-room of the Unionist Party machine in any given locality'.[29] The Order has to be

26. *Ibid.*, p. 79.
27. *Ibid.*, 82f.
28. *Ibid.*, 90f.
29. *Ibid.*, 92ff.

seen as predominantly an integral part of the party despite its religious origins,[30] as J.M. Andrews, who was then its Grand Master, put it in a speech in 1950: 'While I agree that we are mainly a religious body, the Order has been in the front rank for generations in preserving our constitutional position. The Orange ritual lays it down that it is the duty of the Orangeman to support and maintain the laws and constitution.'[31] This support for the constitution was its only political point; it did not have anything resembling a political programme beyond it, and in practice Orangemen were free to join other parties provided they supported the constitutional status quo. Yet every prime minister of Northern Ireland has been an Orangeman and so have 95 per cent of all elected Unionist representatives in parliament. The protestant middle classes often distanced themselves from the institution as being beneath their social and intellectual dignity, and their attitudes pointed to a marginal liberalisation of unionism, at least in the larger towns and in Belfast, while tolerance and liberalism were not seen as virtues in the countryside.[32]

An indication of the self-confidence that unionists felt in the 1950s is the fact that their two parliamentary parties, at Westminster and Stormont, functioned quite independently of each other. It was only towards the end of the decade that it was felt some liaison ought to be established to enable the Unionist parliamentary parties to speak with one voice. The Westminster MPs, for historical reasons as a rule, took the Conservative whip, which did not mean that Unionists at Stormont voted exclusively for conservative legislation; sometimes quite the reverse, as the case of the National Health Services Bill of 1948 showed, a dilemma which perhaps was helping to prolong a decision on how better to coordinate Unionist parliamentary policies at Stormont and Westminster.

It is interesting to note to what extent the Unionist parliamentary candidates were representative of their electorate. Westminster MPs had always been, and still were, quite unrepresentative of the party or the unionist community, while representation at Stormont, although also dominated by the business and professional classes, had at least some members from the intermediate and lower classes.[33] There was, however, a steady decline in business representation (42.5 per cent of

30. For a history of the institution see: Gray, Tony, *The Orange Order*, London 1972.

31. Quoted in Harbinson, *Unionist Party*, p. 94.

32. Barritt, Denis P. and Carter, Charles F., *The Northern Ireland Problem. A Study in Group Relations*, London 1962, 62f.

33. Harbinson, *Unionist Party*, 107ff.

all MPs in 1921, 40.6 per cent in 1949, and 22.2 per cent in 1969) and a corresponding rise in the intermediate (22.5 per cent in 1921, 27 per cent in 1949, and 19.4 per cent in 1969) and professional groups (22.5 per cent in 1921, 33.3 per cent in 1949), although the 1969 figures are slightly misleading as that election was fought on quite exceptional issues (see p. 110 below). Agrarian representation at Stormont was always comparatively low, which is not to suggest that the influence of the landed classes was insignificant but that the seats they held in parliament were only one indication of their potential and real power. In terms of social class the 1950s saw a gradual decline of the over-representation of social class A (at an all-time high in 1949 with 89.2 per cent) and a widening representation of classes B and C1. Overall, however, the Unionist parliamentary parties at Stormont and Westminster remained upper middle class.

The legislation supported by the Unionist parliamentary parties was conservative, but included a very strong desire to improve conditions and life in the province. As they understood democracy to mean majority rule, so they believed that it was their responsibility to look after those they ruled, and of course, in particular those who supported them and agreed with their interpretation of the constitutional issue. The 1950s was an easy decade in this respect, since Northern Ireland had indeed never had it so good.

The anti-socialist attitude which was part of unionism did not prevent the parliamentary parties from supporting state intervention in the economy. Pragmatically they realised that the province could overcome its geographical and economic disadvantages only with the help of the state, and legislated accordingly. The acceptance of this bore fruit in the early and later 1960s, with the Matthew Report of 1963, a Regional Survey Plan for Belfast, and the Wilson Plan of 1965 which looked into the economic development of Northern Ireland. The finance for this had, of course, to be negotiated with Westminster, but Unionist back-benchers gave their full support.

As could only be expected, the Unionist parliamentary party at Stormont continued the tradition of discrimination in favour of their own supporters. The patronage it could exercise through Public Boards was used twofold, in the appointment of members to the Boards as well as through those they employed, to maintain unionism and the dominance of the protestant sector of the population.[34] In the judiciary, too, favouritism continued. Unionists have often been accused of short-sightedness and lack of political grasp in not realising

34. *Ibid.*, p. 121.

that discrimination would lead to further alienation of the minority community. While this is certainly often, and particularly with hindsight, apt criticism, it tends to forget that the protestant siege mentality could not possibly allow catholics to be seen as fully equal. Even when more far-sighted unionist politicians attempted to follow Carson's lead, and even if some back-benchers were willing to support those policies, their electorate was liable to object. The 1950s was not yet a period in which prosperity and peace had endured and proved themselves sufficiently to allow protestants to relax their caution.

Yet if one does not employ hindsight, the 1950s looked very much like the foundation for rather promising developments. For the first time unionism was in a position to use the chances of postwar changes to improve life in the province substantially and thereby, however indirectly, make a positive case for Stormont rule. The political atmosphere was more relaxed, even though there was as yet very little visible change in unionist rhetoric. But the conditions seemed right for the beginning of a very gradual erosion of the religio-political divide in society. Unionism was not yet divided about how to preserve the Union, keep the party in power and appease the minority population, and some liberal unionist politicians had begun to remember the Carson inheritance of 'displaying . . . a tolerance, fairness, and a justice towards all classes and towards all religions of the community'.[35] Unionist conservativism, in its combination of the anglican landed interest and presbyterian radicalism, was flexible and undogmatic in all but the constitutional question. Elections were still won on the latter, but the population at large, and in the 1950s that included, generally speaking, the minority, was kept content by following principles arising from the former.

It has been said that relations between protestants and catholics in this decade resembled 'a cold war – each side profoundly conscious of the wrongness of the other, but neither being on the whole ready to carry condemnation to its limits'.[36] Indeed, relations continued much as before. Church attendance on both sides remained exceptionally high, probably by then the highest in Europe. Since politics, and hence existence, was so tightly related to belonging to a particular denominational group, secularisation did not have the same impact as in other industrialised or industrialising societies. By the same token theologies did not have to modernise and adjust their interpretations to changing living conditions and changing perceptions. In theological terms protestants were united only in their defence of the Reforma-

35. Quoted in *ibid.*, p. 31.

36. Barritt and Carter, *N.I. Problem*, p. 24.

tion and their political ascendancy, and therefore probably overestimated the unity of Irish catholicism which they always perceived as 'Roman' and monolithic, a world colossus against which they had to be on guard all the time. The political ambitions of the Catholic Church were taken for granted, justifying the participation of protestant clergy in the Orange Order and party politics and thus neatly closing the vicious circle that allowed catholics to accuse protestants of sectarianism and anti-catholicism. This general picture ought to be qualified by at least a mention of the non-bigoted tradition in unionism, probably growing during these years, which claimed and often implemented justice for and to catholics. But this was balanced, on the other hand, by a tradition which saw in catholics the followers of the anti-Christ in an almost literal sense.

Barritt and Carter in their description of the social class structure showed that protestants felt superior to catholics on all social levels.[37] Protestants clearly constituted the ruling classes, so that even an unskilled unemployed protestant worker could feel better and more powerful than his catholic counterpart. This goes a long way to explain why class politics in the socialist sense have never made any headway in Northern Ireland, or as Richard Rose put it, 'class appeal would imply that Protestant workers might have a common cause with Catholic workers – a proposition that Ulstermen have always found difficult to believe, though there has never been a shortage of native and imported idealists seeking to convince them that it is true'.[38] It also helps to understand why protestants assumed a natural connection between poverty and catholicism, and why in turn catholics blamed protestants exclusively for their lack of employment opportunities and assumed anti-catholic conspiracies in London and Stormont. There seemed to be confirmation, too, for both points of view in the Orange Lodges' insistence in marching their bands through predominantly catholic areas and towns.

The growth of catholic prosperity through educational and general economic improvements seems to have made urban protestants, and in particular the middle classes, more tolerant and liberal towards catholics, but the implied competition engendered fear of a 'catholic takeover' in rural areas, especially near the border.[39] Barritt and Carter found that 78 per cent of university students claimed friendly relations with members of the opposite faith, while 96 per cent rejected mixed

37. *Ibid.*, p. 57.
38. Rose, *Northern Ireland*, p. 47.
39. Barritt and Carter, *N.I. Problem*, p. 61.

marriages. However one interprets these findings, there seemed at least to be a promise of liberalisation from the top in the late 1950s and early 1960s. This may have been aided by the weakening unity in the managerial, commercial and technical protestant middle classes whose livelihood now often depended less on the old unionist network and more on the new firms which were run from Britain and operated under English supervision where more emphasis was placed on efficiency, thus bypassing the old patterns of discrimination and segregation.[40] This seems to suggest that further modernisation of the economy and continued prosperity might have led to a decline in sectarianism.

Even the trade unions could be seen as 'an important uniting influence' in which the religious differences were of secondary importance.[41] But while most unions took a stand against sectarianism, they had to avoid getting involved in real political issues which would have forced them to take sides. Unions could really operate successfully only by avoiding political issues. As there was little challenge for them to do otherwise in this period, they could easily have been seen as another promising element in the increasing stability and good fortunes of the province.

The party which had tried to remain neutral on the border issue and had instead considered economic issues of overriding importance, the NILP, had had to concede its position in 1949. Non-sectarian socialist political groupings had been in evidence in Ireland since the late nineteenth century but had never convinced many people that nationalism was of little importance. The NILP inherited this policy and therefore left the question of partition open. Given the limited size of the middle ground in the province, their election successes in the inter-war period were quite impressive: three MPs in 1925, one in 1929, two in 1933, one in 1938 and two in 1945. With the declaration of the Irish Republic in 1949 the party felt it had to make a choice and opted for Britain – with Labour in power and promoting welfare legislation there appeared to be hope for a socialist party in the province yet. The party and its support split over the decision and no seats were gained in either the 1949 or the 1953 elections. But the catholic votes they had lost over their 1949 decision appeared to return in the late 1950s and they won four seats in the 1958 elections and held them in 1962.[42] There seemed to be another indication here

40. Probert, *Orange*, p. 75.

41. Barritt and Carter, *N.I. Problem*, p. 142.

42. Elliott, Sydney (comp. and ed.), *Northern Ireland Parliamentary Election Results 1921–1972*, Chichester 1973.

that unionism could be liberalised, or at least that the Union with Britain was no longer a total anathema to catholic voters.

It can be concluded that for unionism the 1950s was a period of unprecedented strength and success in which the second generation of Northern Ireland politicians could overcome some of the difficulties that could not be resolved in the pre-welfare climate of the inter-war years. Towards the end of the decade there were clear indications that some small but growing sections of the protestant population were willing to adopt a more liberal attitude towards the minority population and, from a position of strength, possibly even offer them access to politics.

THE MINORITY POPULATION

As the decade was a period of assertion and a beginning of maturity for unionist rule, so the most important development in the minority community was the acceptance of this rule, or at any rate an acquiescence in the constitutional status quo. Very slowly but clearly catholic aspirations began to focus on Northern rather than a united Ireland. The reasons for this can be found in the economic and social developments in the North which arguably benefited catholics more than protestants and separated them from the South. This enlarged the catholic middle classes, even if it worked against the skilled and unskilled catholic working classes; it provided for better education, and more people began to have a stake in the existing system rather than aspirations to overthrow it. The rejection of militant republicanism, as apparent in the failed IRA campaign of 1956 to 1962, implied at least a conditional acceptance of the status quo, a beginning of the emergence of a so far absent consensus about the political system of the province. Very little of this was as yet articulated or politically formulated, since the minority population lacked any united political platform where these developments could have been transformed into demands for reformist politics. Not surprisingly, their tradition of non-recognition and non-participation made it difficult to form or find such a platform. The various shades of nationalism were divided and lacked unified support. But as there was promise in a liberalisation from strength on the unionist side, so there was promise of acceptance through economic and social developments on the catholic side: partition and the border had become less important than the improvement of their own economic, social and political standing in Northern Ireland.

The Nationalist Party was the second largest party at Stormont but refused the role and title of Loyal Opposition. It had no party organisation or headquarters (its first annual party conference was held in 1966) and hardly a policy beyond the end of partition. While this is not surprising, it was unfortunate in a period like the late 1950s and early 1960s, when some headway might have been made for the interests of the minority community. The party fought elections on the assumption of a community divided on partition and let its candidates stand predominantly in safe areas. Its general outlook on, in particular, social politics was conservative and close to the teachings of the Catholic Church. It did not object to the social legislation that benefited its electorate, but was quick to denounce perceived discrimination. Its role in parliament was generally a negative, though not necessarily a destructive one.

The majority of the support for the Nationalist Party came from the conservative countryside, where they were particularly pressurised to maintain their stand on the border issue by the existence of an anti- as well as un-constitutional republicanism. This often led to compromises, as in the tacit agreement of the late 1950s to concentrate on Stormont elections and leave Westminster largely to Sinn Fein. The constitutional dilemma seems to have paralysed the party politically; *de facto* it recognised the minority and second-class status of the section of the population it represented without, however, developing a programme that might press for improvements in the living and working conditions of catholics. There does not appear to have been any grassroots demand to change this. On the whole, the party found it comparatively easy to control its electorate, at least in the countryside. The failure of the IRA campaign in the second half of the decade confirmed its secure, if impotent electoral position. Yet, as in the unionist camp, there were signs that some nationalists were willing to accept partition and initiate cooperation in politics on that basis. The relative success of the NILP suggested that even sections of the catholic working classes were beginning to accept this. But it was not until the early sixties that these manifestations of catholics' changing attitudes towards Northern Irish politics began to bear fruit. The fact that the Nationalist Party never allied itself to either of the main parties in the Irish Republic is indicative not only of its growing difference from the South, but also of its inherent acceptance of the constitutional situation, irrespective of its rhetoric.[43] But in the mid 1950s it looked as if active nationalist interest in politics had almost ceased altogether.

43. Sayers, John E., 'The Political Parties and the Social Background', pp. 55–78 in Wilson, Thomas (ed.), *Ulster*, 70f.

The border issue was kept alive, however, not least in the border areas, by the renewed attempts of the IRA to remove it. The Irish Republican Army had had a difficult and ultimately unsuccessful time during the war. Its membership was decimated and its members demoralised by internment, and there seemed to be little chance of reorganisation after 1945. But attempts were soon made to create a new centre in Dublin and to rebuild the organisation throughout the country.[44] The revival of nationalism in the South in the late forties had brought new hopes to the republicans, as had the formation and activities of the Anti-Partition Association. The year 1949 brought a twofold setback: the proclamation of the Republic in the South and the guarantee for the Northern constitutional position from London. All that nationalist politicians from Dublin to Derry seemed to offer was 'pacifism, propaganda, and politics' which 'achieved nothing, no victory only words',[45] while the IRA still envisaged the establishment of a united Ireland by physical force; yet its attainment seemed to be as far away as ever at the beginning of the decade. However slowly its recovery came about, by 1951 the organisation was ready to consider a campaign in the North, to provide for training and the acquisition of arms.

In order to be able to concentrate its resources, the leadership had to renege on its fight against the Southern Republic which it had considered illegitimate, and 'to define quite clearly that the Irish Republican Army had only one enemy, England, no sanction will be given for any type of aggressive military action in the Twenty-Six County area'.[46] The political branch of the Republican movement in Dublin, Sinn Fein, had meanwhile developed a political programme which rejected the welfare state on the grounds that it was directed against the freedom of the individual. The late 1940s and early 1950s had also seen a breach in the IRA over methods to achieve a united Ireland: the older generation was willing to operate a policy of passive resistance in the North, but increasingly the cry for violent action from the younger groups had won out.[47] The movement was, however, not very strong or very widely spread, despite or perhaps because of a considerable turnover of membership. It was probably strongest in Belfast, but support there could not be trusted as the RUC was considered to be too well informed to dare start a campaign of violence in the city.

44. Bell, J. Bowyer, *The Secret Army. The IRA 1916–1979*, Dublin 1979 (3), 240ff.
45. *Ibid.*, p. 241.
46. Coogan, Tim Pat, *The IRA*, London 1970, p. 327.
47. *Ibid.*, p. 334.

In the run-up to the border campaign of 1956 a number of raids were initiated in order to provide the organisation with arms, reaching from the Ebington Barracks in Derry on 5 June 1951 to the Arborfield Depot in Berkshire on 13 August 1955. These met with mixed success but they showed that the organisation was active again, which maintained morale and, together with Sinn Fein's success in the Westminster elections of 1956 when two of their candidates were elected, improved recruitment. In late 1956 serious recruiting and training began in the North with the aim of building a guerilla force which would interrupt and subvert the 'enemy administration' and finally lead to 'liberation'. Civilian bloodshed was to be avoided; the campaign was to concentrate on the destruction of property.[48]

The grand military aims of the IRA, unachievable with their limited and inadequate manpower and resources, were not accompanied by any politics beyond the fight to end partition and the emergence of a new republican Ireland. Neither the question of how this new state would actually emerge from sabotage and piecemeal destruction, nor what exact form it should take, was made clear or even much thought about. The 1950s campaign's main function seems to have been to keep Easter 1916 and the republican spirit alive by instilling it into the new generation who had no personal experience of the earlier events. In that it appeared to succeed for a time; despite de Valera's renewal of internment which resulted in putting virtually the whole old leadership behind bars, the campaign continued, even though it often 'failed to rise much above the level of vandalism'.[49]

Wholesale internment in the North had started even earlier than in the South, and the RUC, in particular the B Specials with their local expertise, were far too formidable opponents for the poorly equipped and organised IRA. Even more demoralising was the fact that this violent fighting under adverse conditions appeared to have no political effect whatever, even though the leadership maintained that some sort of crisis was being engendered. But since both Dublin and Stormont governments had acted swiftly and efficiently, a military victory was clearly impossible. The campaign petered out in a steady corrosion of morale and ability, and was officially called off in February 1962. It had produced about 500 violent incidents and eighteen deaths, two-thirds of which were IRA men or their supporters.

The activities of the IRA during the decade, however unsuccessful, showed that the tradition of violence and physical force was still very

48. Bishop, Patrick and Mallie, Eamonn, *The Provisional IRA*, London 1987, p. 25.
49. *Ibid.*, p. 29.

much alive, as Liam Kelly, who won the seat for Mid-Tyrone in the Stormont election of October 1953, showed when he said in his campaign, 'I do not believe in constitutional methods. I believe in the use of force; the more the better, the sooner the better. That may be treason or sedition, call it whatever the hell you like.'[50] That he did not seem to offer any policy beyond his violent anti-partitionist stand does not appear to have worried the electorate. The failure of this policy, however, indicated even to the IRA leadership that it could no longer be sustained and that public support was insufficient, if due mostly to the politics of Dublin and Belfast. The lesson it drew was that if it wanted an end to partition, it had to evolve policies that would find support from the electorate, even though it has been estimated that there was a hard core of over 70,000 voters[51] who even in the early sixties voted for a policy of violence.

Thus by the early 1960s the IRA was defeated and with it ended the tradition of violent politics in Ireland, or so it was thought at the time. The *New York Times* commented: 'the Irish Republican Army belongs to history, and it belongs to better men in times that are gone. So does the Sinn Fein. Let us put a wreath of red roses on their grave and move on'.[52] And this was what most people felt at the time outside as well as inside the island.

The rejection of violence as a political means by the minority population of the province must imply a *de facto* acceptance of the political status quo, and particularly so since other means open to them were limited both through the constitutional structure of government and through the lack of positive policies from its political representatives. Barritt and Carter in their sociological survey of 1961 came to a similar conclusion when they described Northern Ireland as 'stable but deeply divided'.[53] How, then, had catholics come to terms with their role as second-class citizens?

The predominantly Irish and anti-unionist loyalty of the catholic community had clearly not changed, as can be seen in the election results. In parallel to this, however, there had grown up during the fifties an identification with the province which went beyond a mere regional or geographical allegiance. This development can be traced less in overt positive statements about the North than in the occasional derogatory reference to the South. Economic developments and social legislation, which compared so favourably with the South, had obvious

50. Farrell, Michael, *Northern Ireland: The Orange State*, London 1980 (2), p. 205.
51. *Ibid.*, p. 221.
52. Coogan, *IRA*, p. 418.
53. Barritt and Carter, *N.I. Problem*, p. 153.

benefits and had begun to pay dividends in terms of political acquiescence.

The changing and diversifying economy had enabled the catholic middle classes to grow and removed the worst excesses of poverty from the working classes, who did not otherwise benefit in this period; and social legislation gave equal educational opportunities to catholic children. Northern catholics, in other words, were generally better off than their Southern counterparts. The extent to which this changed attitudes is difficult to document or prove, but it can at least be argued that the 1950s saw the beginning of economic and social, if not yet political integration of the catholic middle classes, while the catholic working classes, if anything, declined in the social order even though they benefited economically through state aid.

The Irish catholic hierarchy had condemned IRA violence in a statement of January 1956 and declared that 'it is a mortal sin for a Catholic to become or remain a member of an organisation or society, which arrogates to itself the right to bear arms or to use them against its own or another state; that it is also sinful for a Catholic to co-operate with, express approval of, or otherwise assist any such organisation or society, and that, if the co-operation or assistance be notable, the sin committed is mortal'.[54] This may have assisted the case of constitutional nationalism, but as in the past, and perhaps more so in the North of Ireland in the 1950s, it created an ambiguity in practice, since many ardent catholics obviously disagreed with their bishops, as did some priests, as to the justice of the war they believed they were fighting; this might indicate yet another division between Northern and Southern catholics.

The Church remained the crucial integrating force for the minority community, however. It has been estimated that over 90 per cent of that community were active and regular church attenders who also participated in the various social activities connected with it.[55] The paternalistic nature of the Church and the importance of the parish priest in deciding on moral issues for his flock remained a vital bulwark against the challenge of a secular and heretical state. While there did not seem to be any fear of conversion (unlikely in any case, since all mixed marriages would have to bring up their children in the catholic faith), there was concern about the protestant dominance in virtually all major secular matters, political, economic and social, and, of

54. Whyte, J.H., *Church and State in Modern Ireland, 1923–1979*, Dublin 1980 (2), 320ff.

55. Barritt and Carter, *N.I. Problem*, p. 21.

course, the obvious involvement of protestant clergy in politics. The protestant 'right to rule' was, however, in practice accepted by most catholics, while rejected in principle. It was this dichotomy that made it so difficult for constitutional nationalist politicians to play a constructive role, since (very similar to the unionist case) any divergence from the principle would strengthen the extremists. It was only in 1960 that a new body emerged, the 'National Unity' group which was willing to act as a more constructive opposition and postpone the reunification until a majority in the province wanted it – much the same as the British parliament's attitude, if not accepted as such by unionists.

The 1950s also saw catholic segregation in towns very slowly beginning to break down, although this was noted with suspicion by protestants; mixed areas were regarded as socially inferior.[56] This was much more the case in working-class as opposed to middle-class areas, where there was less segregation in the first place. It has been noted that there was a very clear distinction between middle- and working-class social habits and that sectarian polarisation was much more pronounced in the working classes where there was less tolerance and stronger segregation in leisure activities, while protestant and catholic middle classes were increasingly joining the same social clubs and societies.[57]

Continued segregation in education, however, maintained the 'Irish' cultural identity of the catholic community with its political overtones of nationalism. Only at university level did this separation cease, and it was here that an increasing number of young catholics arrived who would make up the future new middle classes, and where they acquired a more tolerant social and political outlook. By the end of the decade about 22 per cent of students enrolled were catholics (in 1909 there had been about 5 per cent, but 25 per cent in 1915); they were not yet representative of their part of the population, but their numbers had greatly increased since the inter-war period. Perhaps as a reflection of a difference in the quality of teaching in different subjects in their schools, they were unevenly distributed among faculties, making up 35 per cent of all Arts students, 30 per cent in Law, 17 per cent in Applied Sciences and 14 per cent in Pure Science.[58] But it was here that social mixing in clubs and societies began.

As has been mentioned before, the social structure of the province was not a clear reflection of its economic base; for historical as much

56. *Ibid.*, 59ff.

57. Darby, John, *Conflict in Northern Ireland: The Development of a Polarised Community*, Dublin and New York 1976, 156f.

58. Barritt and Carter, *N.I. Problem*, 90f.

as economic reasons all protestants assumed a superior status over their catholic counterparts on the economic and social ladder. While resenting it, catholics appear to have accepted this as 'one of the unpleasant facts of life',[59] another indication of catholic acceptance of the general political framework in which they lived, perhaps the first step towards wanting to improve some of these 'unpleasant facts'.

Traditionally, for reasons of economic and social necessity, relations between catholics and protestants had been more cordial in the countryside than in towns. This appears to have begun to change in the fifties: as the larger towns grew more tolerant, so tension increased in rural areas, and not only near the border. The agricultural subsidies available from Westminster and Stormont were beneficial not only to protestants; the rural catholic community began slowly to grow more prosperous too, which resulted in competition and protestant fears of being swamped by catholics. These anxieties applied obviously much less in the comparatively prosperous climate of the towns where jobs, prosperity and advancement did not depend on land. Despite the fact that local authorities in towns, whether catholic or protestant, exercised their patronage, or discrimination, this did not seem to increase tension notably in these areas. In Belfast it was noted[60] that the arrival of larger or more impersonal firms led to a relaxation in shopping habits, since 'buying from one's own people' was no longer the best or most economic option.

Despite discrimination and secondary-citizen status, catholics in the 1950s were aware that their economic circumstances were better than they had been in the inter-war years and considerably above the average in the Republic. Out of this relative economic prosperity grew a relaxation of social and political tension which was accepted and encouraged. The political corollary of having a stake in the existing system was the *de facto* acceptance of that system and an unwillingness to see it destroyed by political violence, which implies at least the promise of further political relaxation and possible active political involvement in due course.

As the fifties drew to a close, many observers in and outside the province were cautiously optimistic about the future. 'One of the paradoxes of partition has been that while it has in some ways accentuated the cleavage between protestants and catholics within the six counties, in other ways it has tended to bring the two elements together,' wrote T.W. Moody, and added, 'The social consequences of

59. *Ibid.*, p. 57.
60. *Ibid.*, pp. 67, 76.

nearly forty years of "home rule" in the six counties are a historical fact of the highest importance, which, in the great debate over partition, has often been ignored.'[61] Out of the necessity to live together during that period had grown not only resentment but also, however cautiously, respect for the differences in each other's community and culture.[62]

In some respects and in very general terms the distribution of power in Northern Ireland in the 1950s was not dissimilar to the early to later nineteenth century in Britain: some social groups grew in importance due to economic changes and were given economic and social recognition accordingly, if not yet access to political power. It may be easier to understand the history of Northern Ireland in the framework of nineteenth- rather than twentieth-century democracy. The groups that actively challenged the existing system, both from the extreme conservative and from the extreme radical side, were small and of little immediate consequence, as the history of the decade appears to show. Looked at in this context, contemporary hopes for the eventual disappearance of the 'Ulster problem' were justified.

61. Moody, T.W., 'The Social History of Modern Ulster', pp. 224–35, in Moody and Beckett, *Ulster*, 234f.

62. Barritt and Carter, *Ulster*, p. 57; see also Murphy, Dervla, *A Place Apart*, London 1979.

CHAPTER FIVE

The Sixties: O'Neillism and its Failure

From the vantage point of the 1970s many observers and inhabitants of Northern Ireland looked back at the sixties as a period in which 'things would have got better and better',[1] or talked, as Cahal Daly, Bishop of Ardagh and Clonmacnoise since 1967, of 'the incipient growth of understanding and mutual acceptance which marked the ten years up to August 1969'.[2] While it is easy with hindsight to see that decade as a golden age of sectarian reconciliation and gradual improvement, it is even easier to blame the unionist politicians in charge for not having done more faster to reconcile the catholic community. After 1968 the province found itself in a revolutionary situation and the search for its causes can easily distort a historical assessment of the previous years.

In every respect the sixties grew out of the fifties – economically, socially and politically – and while there is little evidence of drastic or even very obvious change, there are clear indications of gradual improvements in all these areas. If one again uses the comparison with nineteenth-century democracy, this period saw attempted reforms from above, and a very gradual opening up of the system to admit the minority community. As on numerous other historical occasions, this raised expectations as much as it encouraged reaction against changes. When real or implied promises could not always be fulfilled or carried

1. Murphy, Dervla, *Place*, p. 126.

2. Quoted in Bleakley, David, *Faulkner. Conflict and Consent in Irish Politics*, London and Oxford 1974, p. 94.

through fast enough, it only needed the international atmosphere of the late sixties, with its improved and faster means of communication through the media, to encourage demonstrations for the principles of civil rights. As in other places around the globe, these then easily escalated into violence. Given the still fertile historical ground of sectarianism in the province, it is perhaps not surprising that the violence was soon difficult to contain or that the volatile political situation of 1968–69 was impossible to bring under control.

That is not to say, however, that the preceding years necessarily led up to the events of and after 1968. There is only limited evidence of growing tension or of an awareness that the system might not be able to cope. If anything, the reverse: unionism was as confident as ever it had been but now willing to reform gradually; catholics were increasingly reconciled to the political conditions in the province and began to support the planned reforms as well as to demand more; the economy was doing well. The frequently proposed interpretation which sees the 1960s as a test for the unionists which they failed is thus a retrospective explanation which requires a number of substantial qualifications.[3]

O'NEILL AND HIS POLICIES

Captain Terence O'Neill (created Lord O'Neill of the Maine in 1970) was appointed Prime Minister on 25 March 1963, after the ailing Brookeborough had finally resigned. As in the Conservative Party of Great Britain, the new leader traditionally 'emerged', whereas an election within the party might very well have chosen Brian Faulkner, the Home Affairs Minister, a professional and hard-line politician.[4] But in O'Neill's favour stood his landed background and the Unionist Chief Whip, William Craig, who, lacking the appropriate class or wealthy background himself, proposed O'Neill's appointment to the Governor (he was duly rewarded with the Home Affairs Office in O'Neill's first government). O'Neill not only came from a unionist landed family, but could claim Irish ancestry, through the female line, to the Celtic aristocracy of pre-British Ulster. Born in 1914 and Eton-educated, he

3. Buckland, *History*, p. 106; Harkness, *Northern Ireland*, 156f.
4. Buckland, *ibid.*, 106f; Harbinson, *Unionist Party*, 146ff; Farrell, *Orange State*, 228f.

served in the Irish Guards during the Second World War. In November 1946 he was elected unopposed as MP for the Bannside constituency in County Antrim and moved quickly up the political ladder: Parliamentary Secretary to the Minister of Health 1948–53, Deputy Speaker 1953–56, Minister of Home Affairs 1956, Minister of Finance 1956–63 and Prime Minister 1963–69. Although a member of the Orange Order, he was considered rather aloof from it and looked with disdain at most of its activities.

In his autobiography O'Neill had some harsh words to say about his predecessor, Lord Brookeborough: the Prime Minister without a desk whose preoccupations were fishing and shooting.[5] Clearly he intended to change this drastically. O'Neill not only wanted to work hard while in office, but he also wanted to break down the 'ancient hatreds' and 'to draw the sting of ancient sectarian bitterness'[6] to enable Northern Ireland politics to enter the twentieth century. His attitude towards catholics can perhaps best be described as late nineteenth-century paternalistic liberal. This was evidenced in the perhaps too much quoted and often misleadingly interpreted radio interview of May 1969: 'If you treat Roman Catholics with due consideration and kindness they will live like Protestants in spite of the authoritative nature of their church.'[7] While this certainly sounds condescending and undemocratic in twentieth-century terms, it was quite revolutionary language to some hard-line unionists, and has to be seen and read in the context of the backlash from militant protestants. The new leader of the Unionist Party clearly wanted reform, reconciliation and at least greater economic and social equality within the province.

As Minister of Finance O'Neill had built up useful relations with the Treasury in Westminster and with Labour leaders, which helped him to pursue the policies he considered vital for the province when he became Prime Minister. He aimed for a better planned economy based on the recommendations of the Matthew and Wilson reports. In order to facilitate the administration by means of developing a better infrastructure and better coordination of the social services, he set up two new ministries, of Development and of Health and Social Services. He had every intention of modernising the province's social and economic structure without changing the constitutional conditions. He relied more on professional advisers than on demands from the party

5. *The Autobiography of Terence O'Neill, Prime Minister of Northern Ireland 1963–1969*, London 1972, p. 40.

6. Cole, John, in Introduction to O'Neill, Terence, *Ulster at the Crossroads*, London 1969, p. 11.

7. Farrell, *Orange State*, p. 256; Gray, Tony, *Orange Order*, p. 226.

and eventually even succeeded in regulating ministers' business interests (an issue which had been debated since the 1920s) when he sacked Harry West, the Minister of Agriculture, over a disputed land deal in 1967.

The economic circumstances of the 1960s, based on and continuing the gradual improvements of the 1950s, were favourable for modernisation. The decade saw an expansionary wave in all Western industrialised economies; GDP and GDP per head in Northern Ireland continued to increase ahead of the UK as a whole, if now also in line with the much-improved economic performance of the Republic.[8] The major reasons for this were increased investment in manufacturing, a great deal of it coming from outside companies, and high levels of public-sector investment, while the natural increase in the population maintained the problems of unemployment and emigration.

By the time Brookeborough resigned, unemployment stood again at around 10 per cent. The Wilson Plan of December 1964 proposed the acceptance of the irreversible decline of the staple industries and the creation of a modern economic infrastructure with an initial £450 million and extra grants from government sources which would attract mostly foreign investment and new industries to the province.[9] This plan became the basis of O'Neill's economic policy and was implemented by Faulkner through the Ministry of Commerce. Under pressure from Westminster, which was worried about the ever-increasing bill for Northern Ireland, regional development policies were to be pursued. A new city, Craigavon, was to be created out of the adjoining towns of Lurgan and Portadown in County Antrim, and seven other towns were designated new industrial growth centres; massive road building was undertaken, including motorways, and a ring road was planned for Belfast. A second university was to be built in Coleraine.

O'Neill relied on the reports of the experts and quoted them frequently in his speeches; he looked back proudly on forty years of gradual improvement that would now enable him to 'transform the face of Ulster'.[10] In order to achieve this an economic council was to be set up in the province. For this he needed to gain the support of the trade unions, and he began by recognising the Dublin-based Irish

8. Johnson, D.S. and Kennedy, L., 'The Two Irish Economies Since 1920', in Moody, T.W., Martin, F.X., Byrne, F.J. and Vaughan, W.E. (eds), *A New History of Ireland*, VII, Oxford (forthcoming).

9. 'Economic Development in Northern Ireland' (Wilson Report), HMSO, Belfast 1965, Cmd 479.

10. O'Neill, *Crossroads*, p. 41.

Congress of Trade Unions which the Brookeborough government had consistently refused to do, so that its Northern Ireland committee could participate in the negotiations for the new council. This gave him full union cooperation for the advisory Economic Council and made possible an impressive labour training programme which now began. For the first time a unionist government appeared explicitly to care for the material well-being of catholics as well as protestants.

The new Ministry of Development, which included transport and local government, began its work under William Craig in January 1965. It was to direct and coordinate planning in the province and implement recommendations made by the Economic Council. Out of the abolished Ministry of Health and Local Government a second new ministry was created with effect from the same date: that of Health and Social Services. O'Neill's emphasis on planning and his belief in technocratic expertise extended the available incentives for incoming firms and eventually brought multinationals like Michelin, Goodyear, Du Pont, Enkalon, ICI and Courtaulds to Northern Ireland.[11] It could do little, however, for the rapidly declining staple industries. While the province became a centre for the artificial fibre industry, Harland and Wolff was kept in operation through money from official sources and was reorganised and re-equipped in the hope of making it more competitive. Unfortunately this was not achieved and the shipyards increasingly became dependent on government money for their survival.

There is some doubt as to the thoroughness of planning. Bew, Gibbon and Patterson have suggested that it did not go beyond cosmetic changes and was predominantly an exercise in extracting more money from Westminster which was no longer willing to support the staple industries.[12] They have pointed to the lack of detailed economic analysis and calculation in the economic planning, the lack of economists in the administration and the almost arbitrary choice of the new 'growth centres'. While this may all indeed have been of little use in laying a new basis for a restructured economy (and there may be doubts, too, about the ultimate possibility of that given the province's particular circumstances), it did provide the basis for a great number of large-scale public work programmes: housing, motorways, airport and improved port facilities. While it is as yet difficult to assess the success or failure of O'Neill's economic policies, industrial production did increase relatively more quickly than in Great Britain and diversification as well as new industries helped to modernise the economy while also

11. Farrell, *Orange State*, p. 229.
12. Bew *et al.*, *State*, p. 153.

changing the climate of business through international involvement. A review of the implementation of the Wilson Report explained that 'In manufacturing industry a total of almost 29,000 new jobs had been created by the end of 1969 compared with the target of 30,000. However the run-down in employment opportunities in the older industries was sufficiently large to offset this, and the net improvement in manufacturing employment was only 5000 jobs.'[13] While there was clearly no indication of an economic miracle, given the disadvantages of the province this was no mean achievement.

The many new British, American and continental firms also continued a trend, begun in the later 1950s, of changing the economic power structure: the old-established family firms, often the backbone of unionism and protestant privilege, had to give way to new firms who often employed catholics (and females) in semi-skilled labour. This eventually increased the discontent of the protestant working classes and the traditional power elite. It also made catholics more aware and more articulate about social and civil discrimination against them. Meanwhile, however, O'Neill made genuine efforts to improve community relations.

Whatever his motives – as has been pointed out, his public pronouncements on catholics certainly were ambiguous – O'Neill was the first Prime Minister of Northern Ireland who wanted all the population of the province to benefit from modernisation. In his attempts to find common ground between the divided communities, he not only visited catholic schools and other institutions but eventually tried to find accommodation for the civil and political ambitions of the increasingly better educated minority community. Perhaps there was some more or less indirect pressure, too, when Labour came to power in the autumn of 1964 (the Unionists retained their twelve seats at Westminster). Harold Wilson occasionally talked of a united Ireland and expressed his abhorrence of sectarianism and discrimination.

O'Neill's meeting with the Republic's Prime Minister, Sean Lemass, secretly arranged without prior cabinet approval, took place in January 1965 and served an economic as well as a political purpose – Lemass was more flexible and pragmatic than his predecessors, and O'Neill felt relations could be improved to their mutual benefit without 'touch[ing] upon constitutional or political questions'.[14] The interdepartmental and inter-ministerial discussions that followed had to be

13. Quoted in Wallace, Martin, *Northern Ireland. 50 Years of Self-Government*, Newton Abbot 1971, 128f.

14. O'Neill, *Crossroads*, p. 157.

careful not to weaken the unionist position on the constitutional status quo. They had to build on the *de facto* existence of Northern Ireland which the Southern government recognised by involving itself in practical cooperation.

Public opinion at large, including the chief of police, appeared to approve of this bold move from O'Neill. The cabinet, initially enraged about the secrecy, was, according to O'Neill, delighted to meet the Taoiseach, and the Unionist Party approved of the meetings a few weeks later.[15] After Eddie McAteer, the leader of the Nationalist Party, had visited Lemass in Dublin, his party became the official opposition at Stormont for the first time in its history. The policy seemed to be endorsed by the November elections in which the Unionists got the highest share of votes (59.1 per cent) since 1949.

In practical terms the new cooperation between North and South achieved an agreement about a connection of electricity supplies and the coordination of tourist promotions, and was favourably backed up by the Anglo-Irish trade treaty which came into effect in July 1966. Unfortunately this was also the period in which opposition from within the unionist camp against the Prime Minister's liberal policies forced O'Neill to tread more carefully, so that the new harmonious relations could not be carried on or extended as easily with Jack Lynch as with his predecessor.

O'Neill's overtures to the catholic population were clearly intended to integrate them further into the Northern Ireland state. In the face of opposition from within his own party it was more difficult to take tangible steps, so that, much more than in his economic planning policies, the Unionist leader's attempts at anti-sectarianism remained rhetorical. This has made it easy for some Marxist historians to dismiss these policies as part of mere class politics, an attempt to 'out-liberal' the NILP.[16] While O'Neill did not want to lose more working-class votes to the NILP, and the 1965 elections showed that he had succeeded in retaining their support, he did want to overcome the legacy of non-cooperation and lack of consensus in the minority population. A modern, industrialised system could not function to its full potential, he believed, without full acknowledgement and the participation of all its citizens. This was made clear in a speech he gave to open a joint protestant–catholic conference on Good Friday 1966 on the eve of the Easter Rising commemorations in which he touched on the issue which he had mentioned before and which might yet go to the root

15. O'Neill, *Autobiography*, p. 71.
16. Bew *et al.*, *State*, 155ff.

of the religio-political divide, namely segregated education, and concluded, 'let us at least be united in working together – in a Christian spirit – to create better opportunities for our children, whether they come from the Falls Road or from Finaghy'.[17]

O'Neill's aim was progress and liberal modernisation, which, he felt, the extremists in both camps began to fight. Looking back over 1966, which had seen the fiftieth anniversary of both the Easter Rising and the Battle of the Somme, he said in the House of Commons:

> From one side came the extreme Republicans, who sought to flaunt before our people the emblems of a cause which a majority of us abhor, and who once again refused to renounce violence as a political weapon. From the other side came those self-appointed and self-styled 'loyalists' who see moderation as treason, and decency as a weakness.[18]

He was fully aware that the animosities of centuries could not be set aside overnight and that a patient and very gradual approach was necessary if he did not want to alienate either of the communities. This can, and to some extent has to be seen as class politics, but even in those terms O'Neill's policies have to be understood as an attempt at modernisation which could be achieved only through social as well as economic reconciliation of the two communities.

While his autobiography gives only a limited explanation of why the 'lid blew off the pot' with the rise of the civil rights movement, it does express his conviction that he was successful in improving community relations:

> As the Party would never stand for change, I was really reduced to trying to improve relations between North and South; and in the North itself between the two sections of the community. In this respect I think I can truthfully say that I succeeded. During the period between 1965 and 1968 the Catholics came to realise that I was interested in their welfare. While the South began to take an interest in the North.[19]

To some extent at least this is borne out by the 150,000 signatures he got in response to a direct appeal to his moderate supporters in a television speech of 9 December 1968. Whoever these people were and from whichever side they came, there can be no doubt that they signalled support for his policies of moderation and gradual progress.

17. O'Neill, *Crossroads*, p. 116.
18. *Ibid.*, p. 123.
19. O'Neill, *Autobiography*, p. 137.

O'Neill's policies had for the first time generated some trust in unionist government from part of the catholic community, although it has been shown that this did not amount to anything like full allegiance or acceptance of the constitution.[20] It is a moot point historically, despite the available sociological and political theories on the subject, whether that objective might have been achieved given time.

O'Neill's attempts at modernisation embraced economic, social and foreign policy. In all these areas he can be said to have been moderately successful. There were limits to the extent to which the economy could be improved, but by keeping it at least from decline, further growth of an increasingly educated catholic middle class was promoted. For the first time in Northern Ireland's history reconciliation of the two traditions in the province became official policy, which aimed at the amelioration of the social and economic position of catholics. It could not reasonably be expected to lead to substantial results within a few years, but could only lay the foundations for future integration. While this helped to ease relations between catholics and protestants, on both social and political levels, it also began to show up the divisions within unionism. O'Neill's greatest failure was that he could not convince his own party and all of its supporters.

LOYALIST OPPOSITION TO O'NEILL

That O'Neill's liberal conservatism should have invoked opposition within the Unionist Party is not surprising. His most immediate opponent who, many felt, had been deprived of the leadership through O'Neill's succession, was Brian Faulkner. He maintained an ambivalent attitude toward the Prime Minister throughout. His transfer from the Home Office to the Ministry of Commerce in 1963, just before Brookeborough resigned, minimised the damage he might have done to O'Neill's policies and employed him in what he was best at in 'a good time to be Minister of Commerce'.[21] Faulkner believed firmly that political rights and responsibilities should come only through an economic stake in society which should not be state induced. While

20. Rose, Richard, *Governing Without Consensus. An Irish Perspective*, London 1971, 300ff.

21. Bleakley, *Faulkner*, p. 54.

he worked hard and successfully at improving the economic fortunes of the province, he was highly suspicious of O'Neill's reformist ideas and his overtures to the catholics, although he rapidly changed his views towards the end of the decade. Faulkner became deputy to O'Neill in 1965, and through his success in his role as Minister of Commerce commanded formidable support in the party. But personal dislike, possible resentment against O'Neill's landed power base, and a shrewd assessment of his own political interest made Faulkner withdraw into an at best ambiguous silence whenever the Prime Minister faced difficulties from hard-liners. The conservative unionism that Faulkner represented did not pose a direct threat to O'Neill's policies, at least not while these were reasonably popular with the unionist electorate, but certainly offered him no direct help.

The core of unionism remained conservative, and while a large number of protestant voters seemed to welcome some gradual change, constituency parties and the Orange Order remained wary of any reform that might endanger their predominant position. Their MPs therefore followed O'Neill's political guidance with the utmost caution. It was less the general policies of ameliorating the grievances of the catholic population than his plans for local government reform, however unspecific these remained, which began to worry the local organisations and drove them into articulate opposition. Potentially much more dangerous was the continued decline of the province's staple industries. It was in these contracting industries that the protestant working classes had their roots and identities, their assurances of superiority over their catholic counterparts: 90 per cent of jobs in the shipyards were held by protestants. Unemployment and housing problems had begun to afflict these groups, and the new growth industries were no longer the same centre of protestant patronage. That was why it had been necessary to prevent any further growth of the NILP. But this proved not to have been sufficient in the long run, although it is difficult to see how this particular Gordian Knot could have been cut; in order to halt any further economic decline the economy had to be radically changed, which could not be done without disturbing the protestant economic power structure.

By the mid 1960s a number of loyalist groups became increasingly worried about O'Neill and his policies. Their apprehensions appeared, ostensibly, to be based least on economic grounds but focused much more on the danger of modernisation in religious, social and political terms, while back-benchers frequently revolted against O'Neill's politics because their electorate had been promised jobs which did not materialise fast enough, or found themselves in competition with evidently and increasingly self-confident catholics. The new 'fashionable' spirit of ecumenism seemed to attack the protestantism of these groups directly; when it combined with political tolerance and even encouragement of catholics it appeared to endanger all they stood for, betraying their religious and political inheritance. Extremist and fundamentalist protestantism of this kind was not new, but it gained new support through the promotion of a clerical figure who became its representative political head: Ian Paisley. The equation of protestantism with unionism found its most forceful exponent in him. This followed two traditions in the North of Ireland: clerical involvement in unionist politics and the use of violent street rioting, not infrequently connected with each other.[22] To these people the ecumenical spirit of the time, Pope John XXIII and the Second Vatican Council offended protestantism and the principles of the Reformation.

Ian Richard Kyle Paisley was born in Armagh in 1926 as the second son of an independent baptist preacher and his Scottish wife. Raised and educated in fundamentalist Christianity he finished his theological college education in 1945 to become pastor at the Ravenhill Evangelistic Mission in protestant east Belfast where most of the inhabitants depended on the shipyards for their livelihood. In 1951 he established his own Free Presbyterian Church of Ulster over which he presided as moderator. His evangelical fundamentalism fiercely resisted any theological modernisation either within protestantism or towards friendlier relations with catholicism. It was from this religious position that he approached the politics of the province. He had joined the Orange Order in 1947 and became chaplain to the Junior Orangemen. Soon afterwards he began to appear on Unionist Party platforms.

In response to the IRA campaign of 1956 a protestant extremist group had been formed, the Ulster Protestant Action (UPA). Its constitution stated that 'Its purpose is to permeate all activities, social and cultural with Protestant ideas and in the accomplishment of this end it is primarily dedicated to immediate action in the sphere of employment.'[23] Paisley became a leading member of this organisation, which in the early sixties began to attract protestant workers as unemployment started to affect them. His fundamentalist evangelicalism appeared to provide a political as well as a religious answer; while the redundant protestant worker had probably little interest in the intricacies of protestant theology, ecumenism appeared to be supported by not only those people who had the jobs but also those who were offering more

22. Stewart, A.T.Q., *The Narrow Ground*, London 1977, *passim*; Boyd, Andrew, *Holy War in Belfast*, London 1969, *passim*.

23. Moloney, Ed and Pollak, Andy, *Paisley*, Dublin 1986, 81f.

to catholics. Thus, keeping their protestantism fundamentalist implied keeping catholics out and preserving protestant privileges in jobs, housing and political power.[24]

Paisley's rhetorical abilities soon made him the dominant executive member of the UPA. He thrived on confrontation and protest and succeeded in embarrassing unionist governments whenever they showed the slightest tendency towards moderation in their position. In the mid sixties the UPA was transformed into the Protestant Unionist Party and Paisley began to publish his newspaper, which was first fortnightly then weekly, the *Protestant Telegraph*. Before 1968 the party succeeded in some local government elections, but remained overall a street movement with as yet no important role in regional politics. No doubt some of Paisley's invective contributed to or started some of the street riots of the 1960s.

He defied the Special Powers Act with an impromptu loyalist march in June 1963 which demonstrated against the lowering of the Union Jack upon the death of Pope John. At this stage he was no longer concerned with the maintenance of unionist unity. Whether from religious or political motivation, and there is clear evidence for both, he tried to rally the anti-liberal elements in unionism behind himself in opposition to the increasingly moderate leadership which appeared to betray protestant values. 'Orange or Green', rather than any accommodation or compromise, was his political credo and he kept his followers on the streets and in the public eye throughout the sixties.[25] In 1964, on the eve of the Westminster election, serious sectarian rioting broke out in Belfast after he led a demonstration against the display of the Irish tricolours at the Republican headquarters, although this did appear to have helped the unionist candidate, Jim Kilfedder, to win the vote in West Belfast. Paisley's nineteenth-century rhetoric with its extremist and millennial vocabulary epitomised the siege mentality of an embattled protestantism for ever under threat from Rome which had now succeeded in converting the unionist leadership into dealing with the South, accommodating the catholics, and depriving the protestants of what was thought of as their rightful inheritance.

The year 1966 turned out to be a formative one in his struggle to put the proper protestant case: fifty years since the battle of the Somme which had wiped out so many of Carson's Volunteer Force, and the fiftieth anniversary, too, of the Easter Rising in Dublin. Dur-

24. Boulton, David, *The UVF 1966–73. An Anatomy of Loyalist Rebellion*, Dublin 1973, p. 27.

25. Moloney and Pollak, *Paisley*, p. 112.

ing that year Paisley founded his newspaper the *Protestant Telegraph* and the Protestant Unionist Party (PUP). He went to jail for three months after demonstrating against the General Assembly of the Presbyterian Church which appeared to him as too liberal and as appeasing protestantism's worst enemies. He insulted the Governor, Lord Erskine, and precipitated rioting in Belfast. There were also rumours of an IRA revival and when the new bridge across the river Lagan was called 'Queen Elizabeth II' rather than 'Lord Carson Memorial Bridge', as traditional unionists had demanded, Carson's son Edward briefly joined Paisley, intending to revive the Ulster Volunteer Force (UVF) to protect the RUC and protestant Ulster from the IRA.[26]

In an article published in *The Revivalist* shortly after the Lemass–O'Neill meeting Paisley summarised his political philosophy, showing its reactionary roots in the language and the interlacing of religion and politics:

> It is quite evident that the Ecumenists, both political and ecclesiastical, are selling us. Every Ulster Protestant must unflinchingly resist these leaders and let it be known in no uncertain manner that they will not sit idly by as these modern Lundies [sic] pursue their policy of treachery. Ulster expects every Protestant in this hour of crisis to do his duty.[27]

This was the rhetoric of national leadership, speaking on behalf of and for the country under threat, protestant Ulster.

The revival of the UVF took the form of the Ulster Constitution Defence Committee (UCDC) with Paisley as chairman, which was soon able to form an Ulster Protestant Volunteers (UPV) organisation. It adopted the UVF's motto 'For God and Ulster' and was open to born protestants but not catholics or RUC members, except for the exclusively protestant B Specials. Its organisation was modelled on the Orange Order and its hundreds of members and seventeen divisions throughout the province were to prove very useful to Paisley's future political career. As in his church, Paisley succeeded in gathering those discontented with established unionism, both those that felt deserted as well as those who felt official unionism was losing its protestant edge.

Paisley's appeal was clearly that of an extremist reactionary offering a scapegoat to the malcontent. The Roman conspiracy served this purpose very well, as it could easily build on the general ignorance of, and prejudice against, catholicism. The language and subject matter built on, and confirmed, hate, fear and sinister fascination. It dealt in

26. Harbinson, *Unionist Party*, p. 149.
27. Quoted in Moloney and Pollak, p. 121.

Old Testament parables and in seventeenth-century historical parallels to keep the protestants of Ulster vigilant against the sinister machinations of the Roman Church. Throughout the sixties Paisley exercised extra-parliamentary opposition and became an expert in the politics of the street. His first counter-march, soon the hallmark of his political technique and attracting utmost publicity, took place in response to the Easter Rising commemoration celebrations in 1966. The fact that one illegal parade was countered with another showed the government's weakness in dealing with extremist threats. Almost all Paisley's marches and demonstrations were designed to provoke and highlight sectarian conflict and intransigence, thus recruiting more support for himself but by the same token equally for nationalist extremists.

O'Neill compared Paisleyism, not entirely without reason, to fascism: 'The contempt for established authority; the crude and unthinking intolerance; the emphasis on monster processions and rallies; the appeal to a perverted form of patriotism',[28] and, one might add, a reactionary ideology which appealed to those frustrated by the existing political system and desiring a greater role for themselves within it. For many unionists O'Neill had gone too far: traditional unionism had used similar means as had Paisley to rally support and for some Paisley was perhaps indeed closer to the tradition of Carson and Craigavon, as they understood it, than to the Prime Minister, but Paisley had gone too far with his violent picketing of the Presbyterian Assembly: presbyterianism was at the heart of Northern Irish protestantism and not so easily spurned.

While the Presbyterian Assembly might have opened itself to liberal tendencies, the Orange Order had been uneasily debating the question of protestant membership of the World Council of Churches for years and finally came down against it. It condemned the Archbishop of Canterbury's visit to Rome and called for a return to the sixteenth-century rooted principles of protestantism. Sir George Clark, then the Grand Master, combined the introduction of this resolution with an appeal to ban Paisley from Orange Order platforms as an enemy of the Order and unionism. But it was too late; when Paisley was jailed on 20 July 2000 people turned up outside Crumlin Road Jail in Belfast, shouting for his release.[29] To undermine the support of the parliamentary NILP had been comparatively easy, but to counter Paisleyism appeared to be a much more difficult proposition for a government which through its politics of moderation and modernisation seemed to prove Paisley's points at every step.

28. Quoted in *ibid.*, 132f.
29. *Ibid.*, 134f.

The UCDC appears also to have had some links with the revived paramilitary UVF, under the leadership of the Spence brothers, which was made illegal by O'Neill in June. While Paisley denied any involvement to the Scarman Tribunal,[30] there have been convincing suggestions of a considerable overlap between UPV and UVF membership, although Paisley himself need not have been, and probably was not, personally involved. The UVF had taken it upon itself to ascertain protestant predominance by any means. A Belfast judge described them at the time as 'a seditious combination or unlawful association' whose activities were 'directed to asserting and maintaining the protestant ascendancy in areas of the city where there was a predominant protestant majority of the local population'.[31]

The year 1966 saw petrol bombings and intimidation of catholics throughout the year, which worried O'Neill and put him under considerable pressure not to go too far, while Harold Wilson and nationalist parties and groups pressed him to go further. Paisley's success, however, was as yet less in political than in religious terms. His prison term conveyed the stance of a true witness and follower of St Paul's example. While in jail, he began to write on St Paul's epistle to the Romans which earned him an honorary doctorate from the Bob Jones University in Greenville, South Carolina.[32] He won a great number of new converts who were attracted by both his fundamentalism and his political stand. The Free Presbyterian Church grew, supporting its Moderator in his 'O'Neill must go – O'Neill will go' campaign. A Lancaster University survey suggested that over 14 per cent of Northern Ireland's population supported Paisley, and his fundamentalism gained national as well as international attention. In November 1967 he introduced the motion 'that the Roman Catholic Church has no place in the twentieth century' to the Oxford Union.[33]

O'Neill tried not to take Paisley too seriously, while the latter made steady inroads into Orangeism. Repeatedly the unionist government had been forced to use the Special Powers Act against protestants in order to stop extremist marches which Orangemen increasingly joined. Growing protestant grass-root discontent could be seen in the 12 July celebrations of 1967, the yearly parade of the Orangemen to celebrate the victory in 1690 of protestantism in the battle of the Boyne, when

30. 'Violence and Civil Disturbances in Northern Ireland in 1969: Report of the Tribunal of Enquiry' (Scarman Report), 2 vols, HMSO, Belfast 1972, Cmd 566; Boulton, *UVF*, 37ff; Moloney and Pollak, *Paisley*, 140f.

31. Boulton, *UVF*, p. 40; see also Cusack, Jim and McDonald, Henry, *UVF*, Dublin 1997, pp. 15–18, 67.

32. Moloney and Pollak, *Paisley*, p. 143.

33. Smyth, Clifford, *Ian Paisley. Voice of Protestant Ulster,* Edinburgh 1987, 18f.

in many cases the conventional tribute to the Prime Minister and government of the day was omitted from the speeches. Under the influence of Paisleyism the attitude of the Orange Order had hardened, and liberal practices, as for instance the occasional indirect waiving of rules which forbade members to attend catholic services, were stopped and members expelled.[34] The leadership of the Order found it increasingly difficult to control its extremist members, and George Clark, overtly connected to O'Neill's liberal policies, resigned in October making way for John Bryans, a non-controversial master much less likely to be a target for Paisleyites.

In the government itself O'Neill faced the attempt of William Craig, the Home Minister, to place himself on the right of Faulkner to recapture attention lost to Paisley and to topple the Prime Minister, while local opinion polls suggested ever-increasing support for Paisley, who seemed to offer the certitudes of traditional unionism rather than the uncertainties of O'Neill's modernisation. The RUC even uncovered a plot of loyalist extremists to kill the Prime Minister.

With hindsight one can see the beginning of an explicit split in unionism between its upper- and middle-class sector, which was trying to come to terms with the changed economic climate, and its working-class grass roots who were most seriously affected by this change and felt most threatened by modernisation. At the time, however, this was not necessarily obvious, since no new extremist working-class party was emerging and unionists still felt they could contain the extremist element within the party by moving slightly to the right. The opposition within the party was looking for a replacement for O'Neill in case some of his policies should fail and he would become an easy target. Whether or not O'Neill survived and succeeded in modernising both his party and the province would depend largely on the catholic response to his reforms.

THE CATHOLIC RESPONSE

From the 1970s many catholics looked back to the almost golden age of the sixties: 'things would have got better for us – or anyway for our children'.[35] Continuing the development of the late 1950s, not only protestantism and unionism but also catholicism and nationalism were

34. Moloney and Pollak, *Paisley*, p. 148.
35. Murphy, Dervla, *Place*, p. 126.

liberalised. The failure of the IRA campaign, the attitude of the Church to the violence, and the arrival of a more liberal theology with Pope John XXIII had done their work. While each community had what was considered their 'lunatic fringe', the liberal groups on each side, it has been suggested, had more in common with each other than with their own hardliners.[36]

The openings made for catholics in Northern Ireland in the 1950s through education and economic diversification had by the mid sixties created a very much strengthened middle class who looked beyond serving their own community. These liberal graduates went mostly into teaching and the medical and legal professions, since public employment was dominated by protestants.[37] But they also wanted to change these limitations and liberalise, if possible, the traditional nationalist politics in order to be able to participate fully not only in the economic and social, but also in the political life of society; in other words, their growing economic and social confidence was transformed into the desire for full and equal political rights or citizenship.

For these groups the republican movement did not offer a promising policy at any time during the sixties. In the immediate aftermath of the 1950s campaign in 1962, due largely to lack of local support, the IRA suffered more than ever from factionalism and defeatism. For a time it even looked as if it might totally disintegrate. But it did survive, and the political arm of the movement began to consider the constitutional options and more left-wing policies to widen its one-issue appeal. By 1965 Sinn Fein representatives continued to sit in local bodies but to boycott Stormont and Westminster (as well as the Dail), while inside the organisation the debate went on as to how far a more socialist political philosophy could replace physical action. The new left-wing political line not only offended the traditionalists but proved a major challenge to its inherent sectarianism: the great majority of IRA members were devout catholics and not at all inclined to accept Marxist thinking. It also frustrated its new and younger members who had joined to fight a war and found themselves asked to participate in a political campaign. The option of violence was therefore kept officially open, but neither it nor the new policy attracted much support.[38]

If catholics wanted to take part in actual politics, they had to look elsewhere. Most middle-class catholics appear to have been willing to

36. Barritt, Denis, *Northern Ireland – a Problem to Every Solution*, London 1982, p. 6.

37. McAllister, Ian, *The Northern Ireland Social Democratic and Labour Party. Political Opposition in a Divided Society*, London 1977, p. 7.

38. Bishop and Mallie, *IRA*, 40f.

support O'Neill's policies or give him at least the benefit of the doubt. In 1967–68 Richard Rose conducted a major survey of political and social attitudes in Northern Ireland. This showed that most catholics (65 per cent, against 56 per cent of protestants) felt that community relations had improved since O'Neill had become Prime Minister, which did not, however, necessarily change their political outlook.[39] But nationalist politicians could therefore count on some support from their constituencies, when they accepted the role of official opposition in 1965. While a majority of catholics, even among those in public employment, still rejected the constitutional settlement, only 5 per cent of the population as a whole thought religion was a major obstacle to getting a job.

It is quite clear that the population of the province, if in unequal proportions, thought that community relations had improved and a very great majority of them (79 per cent protestants, 89 per cent catholics) wanted further improvements. There is not necessarily a contradiction between this and catholic feelings about the border or the constitutional situation. Since catholics' political attitude was generally conservative, it was not likely to change very fast in the terminology and imagery it used, even if the unity question was no longer of primary importance. The problem remained, however, that without constitutional changes which would allow them to participate in government, catholics would have no real political part to play in Northern Ireland; the continued use of the border issue symbolised that fact, rather than implying a continuing real desire for a united Ireland.

Another area where greater tolerance and relaxation have been noted was the Catholic Church. While the 'secularisation' of catholicism entered Northern Ireland unevenly, it was found that local priests, in particular in rural areas, acted much less as political guides and no longer took a lead on political issues. This in itself made catholic politicisation possible, and it was largely catholic middle-class laity that acted upon it. As early as 1958 a catholic speaker at a social studies conference had emphasised that the catholic community had 'to co-operate with the de facto authority' and to 'show a readiness to serve'.[40]

This new acceptance was reflected in the National Unity, a catholic middle-class movement which originated in Belfast in 1959 and at-

39. Rose, *Governing*, pp. 306, 297.
40. McAllister, *SDLP*, 9f.

tracted support there rather than in the nationalist countryside. It did not succeed in uniting all nationalists but did put some pressure on the Nationalist Party to develop a political programme. With this, catholics began to stake their claim for full political participation and ultimately a share in power. There remained, however, formidable difficulties in channelling this political awakening into effective organisation. From 1964 to 1969 the Nationalist Party was led by the politically moderate Eddie McAteer who accepted the role of official opposition for his party at Stormont. But the party found it impossible to uproot itself from its own anti-partitionist past and to develop a new political programme. It was not helped in this by the understandable reluctance of unionists at Stormont to embrace and welcome the new official opposition through the kind of consultation which would have been normal at Westminster.

A few other attempts were made to compete with the old nationalists; new parties were formed which tried either to displace or to replace the old one, but they all had only very limited success. Out of National Unity came eventually, in 1965, the National Democratic Party (NDP) which also organised largely in the Belfast area over the next five years without ever achieving electoral success. Its members were to have considerable influence in the newly established Social Democratic and Labour Party when it was founded in April 1970.[41] Another root of this later party can also be found in the sixties, namely the Republican Labour Party (RLP). The core membership of this republican, but non-violent, party came out of the split of the NILP in 1949 which left anti-partitionists stranded. Harry Diamond, MP for the Falls constituency and the leader of this new grouping, realised that a neutral Labour Party was not viable in the context of Northern Ireland. He was joined in 1964 by Gerry Fitt, the Irish Labour MP for Belfast Dock at Stormont who was elected for West Belfast to Westminster in 1966 and supported the British Labour Party there. As in the case of the NDP, the RLP depended for its support on Belfast and did not dare seriously to challenge the Nationalist Party for fear of splitting the catholic vote, but it was the first catholic party which actively participated in the system and tried to pursue the grievances of its constituents.

With hindsight it is easy to exaggerate the impact of O'Neill's politics on constitutional nationalism and catholic voters. There was clearly

41. *Ibid.*, p. 19, and McAllister, Ian, 'Political Opposition in Northern Ireland: the National Democratic Party, 1965–1970', in *Economic and Social Review*, 6:3, 1975, pp. 353–66.

a new tune in the Unionist government and the political atmosphere appeared to be changing, offering real economic, social and perhaps even political progress for catholics. But it is equally clear that catholic parties were not as yet ready or able to cope with these new developments. When asked what the Nationalist Party stood for in the spring of 1968, 48 per cent of catholics and 55 per cent of protestants thought a 'United Ireland', but 35 per cent and 31 per cent respectively said they did not know, even though the party had by then made efforts to adopt social policies and develop a higher profile.[42]

Perhaps it is not surprising therefore that some catholic voters began to drift towards moderate unionist parties. Middle-class votes seem to have moved towards O'Neill, while about two-thirds of the supporters of the NILP were catholic working class, even though some of that vote may also have to be counted as anti-unionist – in other words, it was still a religio-sectarian rather than an economic vote. Even more than in the 1950s catholics began to accept the status quo while at the same time maintaining their traditional view on the border issue, though very much moderated. Rose's survey showed that 81 per cent of catholics expected fair treatment from their local council, which appeared to contradict their concern about discrimination and their rejection of the constitution in response to other questions.[43] But again there might not be a contradiction here; catholic politics were in a state of flux, trying to find new issues while not yet daring to abandon the old ones. The rejection of the constitution (while also rejecting any violent act to remove the border and encouraging nationalist politicians to talk less about it) was part of traditional politics, as was the charge of discrimination. As has been seen, the former was in practice accepted, while the latter, too, seemed to diminish in practice. It can be seen from these moderations on practical issues, as expressed in Rose's loyalty survey, that most catholics were satisfied overall with the general political development in the province, and what they said about it in the 1970s was not necessarily nostalgic hindsight. One might also argue from this evidence that the cautious reformist approach of the Nationalist Party appears to have been very much in tune with its voters.

Those catholics who were impatient with traditional nationalist politics and wanted actively to improve matters politically for their community were, however, frustrated by their party representation and faced with a politically passive community. Out of this grew the press-

42. Rose, *Governing*, p. 228.
43. *Ibid.*, 283f.

ure groups and extra-parliamentary opposition of the mid sixties which originated from professional middle-class people and were encouraged by the rhetoric and promises of O'Neill's policies. The first of these was the Campaign for Social Justice (CSJ) which tried to collect and make public evidence of discrimination, particularly in housing and the gerrymandering of elections.

Public concern had been sparked off by housing of catholics in Dungannon, a town in County Tyrone, where the protestant-dominated council had refused to rehouse catholics from an overcrowded housing estate to unoccupied postwar houses of better quality. A Homeless Citizens League was formed which succeeded through protests and sit-ins. The lead had been taken by Mrs Patricia McClusky, the wife of a doctor in the town, who followed the success of the campaign by founding the CSJ with her husband a year later. They were joined by other professional people and began to distribute information about injustice in Northern Ireland while staying free from party politics. They contacted individual politicians who might be able to help them and lobbied a number of Labour MPs in Westminster.[44] In 1965 they affiliated to the National Council of Civil Liberties in London and with their help founded the Northern Ireland Civil Rights Association (NICRA) in 1967. The CSJ highlighted the impossibility of finding any redress for housing discrimination in the courts. It also realised very soon that O'Neill's rhetoric was not followed by decisive action and expressed its condemnation of this.[45]

By not taking a political stand and working as a pressure group within the existing system, the CSJ had collected a great deal of specific information about various forms of discrimination against catholics which was later confirmed by some of Rose's findings as well as by the Cameron Report. The main areas of injustice and discrimination were in the restrictive local franchise, the gerrymandering of local electoral boundaries and the exclusion of catholics from statutory bodies appointed by the government. While no pattern of systematic discrimination has been found, it would have been most surprising if there had been no discrimination at all in a society as divided on cultural and, more importantly, political grounds as Northern Ireland.[46] Each side would naturally attempt to preserve as much as possible of its influence. As the unionists formed the majority and

44. 'Disturbances in Northern Ireland: Report of the Commission Appointed by the Governor of Northern Ireland' (Cameron Report), HMSO, Belfast 1969, Cmd 532.

45. Bew *et al.*, *State*, 155f.

46. Rose, *Governing*, pp. 292–6; Wilson, Tom, *Ulster. Conflict and Consent*, Oxford 1989, pp. 98–133.

were in the dominant position, they could therefore exercise more successful patronage than the minority population. This had been expected and accepted by the population at large. It is borne out by Rose's apparently contradictory findings: that catholics were very sensitive about issues of discrimination, whereas in practice no more than 5 per cent expected to encounter it when applying for a job.[47] The CSJ had been active for about four years by the time most of Rose's survey was undertaken, and had been successful mostly through the various housing action groups that were set up throughout the province, but one is tempted to conclude that little of their information had penetrated beyond the more educated section of society.

What the CSJ tried to bring to the attention of a wider public, including, with the help of the British civil liberties organisations, the UK as a whole, was the existence of plural voting and residential and property qualifications in the local government franchise. They were thus trying to take O'Neill's drive for economic modernisation into politics, and attempting by demanding one person one vote to modernise the province's democracy and bring it into the twentieth century. The difference between the local and national franchise meant that by 1967 about one third fewer people had the vote in local government elections than in national ones. Since catholics were over-represented in the poorer sections of the population, this implied electoral discrimination against them. Added to this was the arguably more serious political discrimination exercised through gerrymandering of local electoral boundaries which ensured unionist majorities in some councils even when catholics were enfranchised and formed the numerical majority in a particular area. The most notorious example of this was Derry City Council where the electorate in 1967 consisted of 14,429 catholic and 8781 protestant voters, yet twelve unionists and eight non-unionists were returned in the local authority elections. On the government-appointed boards catholic representation varied but averaged only 15 per cent, although this particular figure has been disputed as being too high.[48]

The formation, at the instigation of the CSJ, of NICRA in 1967 widened the demands for social justice in terms of membership, support and issues towards the broader ones of civil liberties. The initial NICRA committee embraced trade unionists, communists, liberal politicians and academics, Labour representatives from both the Republican and the Northern Irish Labour Party, republicans as well as the

47. *Ibid.*, p. 298.

48. Darby, *Conflict*, pp. 51, 66; Wallace, *50 Years*, p. 117.

co-opted chairman of the Young Unionists at Queen's University. It continued to voice the concerns it shared with the CSJ – housing, one man one vote in council elections, gerrymandering of electoral boundaries – and attacked discrimination by public authorities. But it went one step further into the political field by demanding the repeal of the Special Powers Act and the disbanding of the B Specials. While it drew support from the moderate centre to which both communities contributed, it was predominantly catholic and concerned with the grievances of the minority, and it also received support and membership from the republican movement. From its inception this made it suspect in the eyes of the more extreme unionists.

Extra-parliamentary opposition aimed at reforming Western democracies (as well as some Eastern ones) was, of course, part of the international political scene in the late 1960s. Peaceful demonstrations, and the use of non-violent means to achieve ends which appeared impossible to gain through conventional channels of politics, were the tools they all had in common. But it was the first time that such international trends were taken up in Northern Ireland. The attraction was not only in the principles of civil liberties, which probably were taken up and supported mostly by students, but also in the social grievances that could be addressed by such means. While these matters were of immediate concern mainly to catholics, NICRA did not stand for any of the traditional nationalist issues. It did not want the border removed, but wanted to abolish the social and political borders within society. It could thus demand support from moderate unionists as well as from catholics. But because the grievances it wanted to see redressed were largely catholic gravamina, it could be, and was, seen by many unionists as yet another form of threatening nationalism, and this was not helped by the fact that a number of republican politicians were actively involved in the movement.

Helped by the economic and social developments of the 1950s, the catholic response to O'Neill's policies of modernisation can thus generally be seen to have been a positive one in almost every respect. The political traditions of both sides prohibited speedy changes, but the cautious offerings were cautiously accepted. While unemployment among the catholic working classes was proportionately much higher than among their protestant counterparts, they seemed to have seen some promise in the new policies and at least began to loosen their bond to their traditional nationalist political organisations. The catholic middle classes equally accepted, and perhaps more positively welcomed, the new more tolerant policies, its politically more active section beginning to ask for the rhetoric of O'Neill to be turned into tangible ends, though remaining very much in a minority. Both groups appeared to have been satisfied overall with the gradual and hesitant politics pursued by the Nationalist Party.

1968–69: TOO LITTLE TOO LATE, TOO MUCH TOO SOON?

The twelve months between the first civil rights march in August 1968 and the outbreak of serious sectarian disturbances in Londonderry and Belfast a year later have mostly been seen with hindsight as the watershed in Northern Ireland's history which proved the failure of O'Neill's policies and paid the dividends of the constitutional compromise of 1922. But even at the time, Professor J.C. Beckett, the recorder for the *Annual Register* of 1969, stated in his report:

> At the end of 1968 it seemed just possible that Captain O'Neill would succeed in leading Northern Ireland along the path of gradual and moderate reform. But this possibility, never very strong, was destroyed by various factors: the early renewal of violent agitation, the growth of sectarian bitterness, the lack of agreement within the Unionist Party. The tensions thus developed broke, in August, in a crisis that transformed the political situation in the province.

Yet by the end of 1969 he felt that 'There was some ground to hope that the two sections of the population might now come closer together.'[49] Should this year, then, be considered as a successful revolt or as a failed attempt at revolution which was yet never quite defeated by the governments of either London or Belfast?

For a proper understanding of later events in the history of the province it is obviously crucial to understand why things appeared to go so drastically wrong during these twelve months, since there had been little indication in the previous two decades that anything of this kind might happen. The best source for the events of the period is still the Report of the Cameron Commission which was appointed by O'Neill in March 1969 'to hold an enquiry into and to report upon the course of events leading to, and the immediate causes and nature

49. In Macadam, Ivison (ed.), *The Annual Register. World Events in 1969*, London 1970, pp. 51–5.

of the violence and civil disturbances in Northern Ireland on and since 5th October 1968; and to assess the composition, conduct and aims of those bodies involved in the current agitation and in any incidents arising out of it'.[50] Those giving evidence to the Enquiry were exempted from prosecution. While some people refused to give evidence, notably Major Bunting, William Craig and Ian Paisley, Faulkner resigned over the commissioning of the report, and Cameron has been accused of not throwing his net even wider, there is as yet no better summary and disposition of the available contemporary evidence. The report began its interpretation of the year by indicating the 'failure in leadership and foresight among political leaders on all sides',[51] an assessment which suggests a wider criticism than has often been allowed for since. This raises the question to what extent the leading figures in the events were fully aware of the implications of their actions and what might follow from them; it might be suggested, following the exposition on the previous pages, that they may not have been able to foresee the consequences that their actions turned out to have.

The first civil rights march in the province, from Coalisland to Dungannon in August 1968, was sparked off by a housing dispute in Caledon, County Tyrone, where in June catholics had been evicted from a council house while a single protestant woman had been allocated a neighbouring house. The Nationalist MP Austin Currie occupied the house and it was the publicity generated by this action that directly led to the first large-scale demonstration of NICRA in August. The CSJ had led the way towards greater awareness of injustices in housing and there had been a number of sit-ins and smaller demonstrations, particularly in Londonderry. This march passed off peacefully.

The difficulties began with the second large march which was proposed for 5 October in Londonderry. It was initially banned by the Minister of Home Affairs, William Craig, under the Public Order Act of 1951, since it threatened to disturb the public peace as a march of the Orange Order was planned to take place at the same time. The demonstration went ahead, however, and while held under the auspices of NICRA, it was organised largely by local groups, led by the Derry Labour Party, which tried to defy the rerouting. The march thus ended in violent clashes with the police and was followed by rioting throughout the catholic Bogside area of the city. This event

50. Cameron Report, p. 3.
51. *Ibid.*, p. 12.

attracted worldwide publicity[52] and was followed by reciprocal accusations of police brutality from one side and of deliberately provoked violence by the other. There were almost constant protest marches in Derry during the following two months, as well as counter marches organised by the Reverend Paisley and Major Bunting, who had emerged as a leading loyalist activist during the year, while a ban on all marches within the Walls of Derry remained ineffective. A new organisation, the moderate Derry Citizens' Action Committee, under the leadership of John Hume and Ivan Cooper, had emerged which orchestrated the demonstrations, while the Nationalist Party announced its temporary withdrawal from the role of official opposition.

The attention these events attracted in the UK and abroad put pressure on the government, not least through Prime Minister Harold Wilson who, however, also assured O'Neill that the British government stood by its commitment of 1949, and that the end of partition 'as a cure for unrest in Northern Ireland',[53] as apparently advocated by the Republic's Prime Minister, Jack Lynch, was not contemplated by Westminster. O'Neill obviously did not dare to propose universal adult suffrage in local elections, but his government did announce a number of reform proposals for Londonderry in November. As non-unionist opinion began to rally behind the civil rights activities, the spiral of fear had begun: moderate protestants were worried, if still willing to concede, while Paisley's and Bunting's support grew. These ultra-loyalists blocked the path of a civil rights march in Armagh in November and were both jailed as a result.

There was now also pressure on O'Neill from within his own cabinet. The reform measures announced in November made a number of unionists feel uneasy, foremost among them Craig, who had held throughout that NICRA was a front organisation for republicanism and publicly said so. Encouraged by the response to his unprecedented popular appeal on radio and television of 9 December, O'Neill felt strong enough to dismiss his Home Minister on 11 December and appoint Captain William Long, previously Minister of Education, in his place. Given the apparent popular support for O'Neill, Unionist MPs at Stormont endorsed his policies with only one abstention. This did not, of course, stop, and indeed arguably increased, the support for more extremist protestant politics as advocated by Paisley and his supporters. But it did help to moderate the attitude of the government to civil rights demonstrations.

52. This was sparked off by a single RTE camera present; the saturation coverage of later days had not yet begun (personal information from Kevin Boyle).

53. *Annual Register*, 1968, p. 52.

The seeming success of NICRA drew the support of more groups broadly sympathetic to its aims, but also resulted in the first disagreements and splits in the movement. Since October students at Queen's University had responded to and organised in support of the civil rights movement. Up to then the almost worldwide wave of student protests and demonstrations appeared to have made little impact on them. But students were involved in and among those arrested in the Derry march of October, and it was largely out of moral protest against police activities – reported from all over the world, but now happening in the province, too – that People's Democracy (PD) was born, initially a mere body of protest which was politically uncommitted.[54] PD proposed a march from Belfast to Derry in January 1969. This was nominally supported by NICRA but opposed by the Derry Citizens' Action Committee (DCAC) which was reconsidering its views on direct action since the government seemed to be answering its demands. The majority of PD fell in with this advice and decided to cancel the march. But within PD a radical group had emerged which was not willing to concede any victory to the government and did not mind abandoning the hitherto ultra-democratic structure of PD or embarrassing DCAC by defying its wishes.

The march took place on the first four days of the new year and was naturally accompanied by counter demonstrations and violence. On arrival in Londonderry it engendered sectarian rioting and violence and led to some police misconduct. This in turn seemed to prove the left-wing and republican assertions about an authoritarian government and encouraged further marches over the next few months, notably in Derry and Newry, with very similar results.

These activities of the now more politicised civil rights movement weakened O'Neill's standing within his party. By the end of January his leadership was under attack once again; Brian Faulkner had taken the opportunity to resign and been followed by another minister and a back-bench revolt. O'Neill dissolved parliament and announced a general election for late February. The elections showed the confusions and divisions within both communities: eight anti-unionist parties and groups stood for election but did not gain more than about one third of all votes, while on the unionist side local party organisations varied greatly in their support of the Prime Minister who himself won only on a minority vote, while 40 per cent of his constituency voted for the Reverend Ian Paisley. The wider significance of this election was that it showed the weakening of the traditional parties on

54. Arthur, Paul, *The People's Democracy 1968–1973*, Belfast 1974, 23ff.

both sides. Unionism was split into pro- and anti-O'Neillites as well as Paisley's Protestant Unionists who were as yet unsuccessful, while the Nationalist Party lost substantially to the new civil rights activists. Yet the underlying sectarian division was still as obvious as ever, if anything reinforced by the recent violent events.

Thus O'Neill emerged overall weakened by the elections, but continued his reform programme, which now included the granting of universal adult suffrage in local government elections, one of the main demands of NICRA. Meanwhile civil rights activities continued. In their wake violent attacks on public buildings and utilities reached such a level that the army had to be called in to guard them. The Prime Minister's position had become too weak, however, and his continued reforms allowed traditional unionists to gain support within Stormont. At the end of May he had to resign and was succeeded by his cousin Major Chichester-Clark who brought Faulkner back into the cabinet and appointed two leading anti-O'Neillites to junior offices, but left the rest of the government unchanged. He declared himself committed to the continuation of O'Neill's policies and went even further by promising the redrawing of local government boundaries by an independent commission and the postponement of local elections, due in 1970, until the boundaries were redrawn a year later.[55] This suggests, at any rate, and without considering the juggling for power within the Unionist Party, that the government did not dare to go back on the reforms it had started for fear of escalating agitation and violence. But it also found itself in an impossible balancing act: these very reforms increased fear among protestants and certainly gave extremist politicians like Paisley renewed support.

The weeks immediately following the change of prime ministers were quiet as NICRA suspended all demonstrations, but sectarian tension remained high. By then many protestants identified civil rights with republican and nationalist politics and this renewed the fear of being swallowed by a united Ireland, while most catholics indeed saw NICRA as the champion of their rights. This situation rendered government ultimately impotent as the summer season of marches approached. Rioting in July and early August was contained by police, but on 12 August, the date of the traditional Apprentice Boys' march in Londonderry, it erupted there and spread quickly to other towns, including Belfast where thousands of people were made homeless by fire; four-fifths of these were catholics. Two days later Westminster authorised the use of troops to contain the sectarian clashes and, in the

55. *Annual Register*, 1969, p. 53.

first instance, to protect catholic areas against further attacks, first in Derry and then also in Belfast.

The Scarman Tribunal which was set up to investigate these events concluded that both communities displayed similar fears and similar distrust of lawful authority and had similarly acted in self-help to defend themselves. There was no planned revolution or plot to overthrow the government, but some speeches by anti-government politicians, specifically the Reverend Ian Paisley's, had contributed to heighten fear and tensions.[56] Like Cameron, Scarman found the police guilty of some misconduct, but equally recognised this to be exceptional rather than the rule. The RUC was not trained in crowd or riot control and easily broke under the strain. Some of them clearly and explicitly did side with protestants, but more important was the fact that catholics did not trust them and at least doubted their impartiality. The Hunt Committee, appointed in August 1969 'to examine the recruitment, organisation, structure and composition of the Royal Ulster Constabulary and the Ulster Special Constabulary and their respective functions',[57] reported in October and recommended that the RUC should be disarmed and relieved of any military duty, and the B Specials be disbanded. It thought the police force understaffed and with low morale which was in part to be explained by its isolation from the rest of the UK, but more important was the need for greater public confidence in the RUC. It recommended the setting up of a new part-time force which, it hoped, would particularly attract catholic recruits, and the establishment of a police authority the membership of which should proportionately reflect the different groups in the community. In the context of August 1969 all the deficiencies of the RUC worked against them and they could thus easily be seen as a protestant force which was part of a unionist attempt to crush catholics once and for all.

From this brief review of the events of 1968–69 it can be argued that Northern Ireland found itself indeed in a revolutionary situation; as the initially reformist civil rights movement became more politicised, the traditional issues of the province's history surfaced and soon gained the upper hand in most people's awareness, rather than the radical democratic ones that NICRA proposed. For very many people politics thus reverted to the old power question of which should be the disadvantaged minority: catholics in Northern Ireland or

56. Scarman Report.

57. 'Report of the Advisory Committee on the Police in Northern Ireland' (Hunt Report), HMSO, Belfast 1969, Cmd 535, p. 2.

protestants in a united Ireland.[58] While for many activists, particularly among the students, this was a fight for a better democracy, for the majority of the population and the extremist leaders on both sides it was not. This weakened the position of the government, which could respond only in a measured way to the civil rights demands for fear of losing its own support, and might well have collapsed totally but for the intervention from Westminster and the British army. So that while no revolution or even revolt was intended or attempted, the different forces working against the governmental status quo so undermined Stormont's authority that civil war might easily and would probably have resulted if London had not intervened.

'We had all the benefits of belonging to a large economy, which were denied to the Republic of Ireland, but we threw it all away in trying to maintain an impossible position of Protestant ascendancy at any price'[59] wrote O'Neill with hindsight in his autobiography. But this is clearly too simple an explanation. Given the history of unionism, it could probably never have sustained and supported O'Neill's economic and social reforms without breaking apart. With growing prosperity and the diminution of the constitutional threat, the need for at least an appearance of the monolithic unity of unionism had diminished; a liberal fringe could be tolerated and so could an extremist one. It was by no means clear before 1968–69 that resistance to liberalism within unionism had grown at almost the same speed with which expectations rose in the catholic community. It was the civil rights marches of late 1968 and 1969 which sparked off the latent violent sectarianism, providing the background against which Paisley and the left-wing republicans could step up the tension; and it was the fear generated by the increasingly violent clashes which made it impossible for the established traditional parties of both communities to renew their influence over the population or get their support for speedy reforms. The mutually dependent extremists engendered their own momentum. They interpreted everything that happened in the old language of sectarianism, while in the process the radical democratic demands also became part of the sectarian vocabulary.

The limits of modernisation must therefore be seen in the clash between nineteenth-century political values and a twentieth-century international reality: what could grow gradually and slowly on the basis of a developing economy in the nineteenth century had to be

58. Stewart, *Narrow Ground*, London 1977, *passim*, in particular: Part Five, 155ff; O'Malley, Padraig, *The Uncivil Wars. Ireland Today*, Belfast 1983, p. 138.

59. O'Neill, *Autobiography*, p. 67.

accelerated under internal as well as international pressure in order to accommodate the rising expectations of the catholic community, while by the same token the expectations of conservative unionism were frustrated and did not have time to adjust gradually. It needed the spark of the civil rights movement and international student demonstrations to destabilise and interrupt the 'natural' modernisation process. With the intervention of Westminster a new chapter began in the history of Northern Ireland.

PART III

1969–1998: The Problem Exposed

Introductory

Since 1969 the governing of Northern Ireland has been concerned with the establishment of consensus politics. At various points during the following two decades this appeared to outside and moderate inside observers to be achievable and in reach, but it has always failed owing to challenges from within the province's society. The basic reason for this is not difficult to find: to construct consensus artificially, or to impose it, is a contradiction in terms. Ironically, it is probably true to say that the majority of the population for most of this period, and with the exception of only occasional, very heated moments, would have been able to find an agreed form of government. But it was always pulled back, for various reasons and mostly by the respective political leaders, for fear of what the other side might do and how it might misuse its power. Some interpreters of the province's difficulties in finding an agreed form of government have talked of the 'mythology of moderate values'[1] which is both accurate and misleading. There was a great deal of middle ground in terms of pragmatic common sense on the basis of what one might call humanitarian values, but these became secondary, as in a war, when an existential challenge arose in the form of the other side's claim to power.

Once the regional government could no longer cope with the volatile politics of the province and the national government took over in a semi-colonial fashion, that is without giving Northern Ireland's voters direct access to national power (none of the national parties existed within the province until the arrival of the Conservative Party in 1989), the need for political unity on each side grew ever less urgent, though it was, paradoxically, often stressed by local politicians. In essence each side broke into a moderate and an extremist wing out of

1. Darby, *Conflict,* p. 14.

which grew often new, vested political, social and economic interests. The continuity with the sixties was broken. Yet the search for a new stability had to be based on a society which had been transformed in the previous two decades. On the catholic side, at any rate, this was also a generational conflict: the younger generation did not want to go back to the values of the sixties which they perceived as humiliating and demeaning for their community, but this once again confirmed protestants' fears that catholics wanted to lord it over them.

Once the British government began to get involved, it had to learn about the region which it had neglected politically since its inception. Its involvement prevented the escalation of violence into a civil war, but as it took on more responsibility, it also became the target of political opposition from both sides. A solution short of military means, be that a civil war or the use of the British army, was impossible to find. By stages Whitehall learned to deal with the problem by keeping violence under control and political options open. A precarious balance and a certain amount of stability were eventually achieved. 'Conflict management rather than conflict resolution'[2] became the practice until the last decade of the century, when most of the paramilitary groupings finally realised that violence alone could not achieve their aim and a political compromise became the more viable option.

2. Hayes, Maurice, *Minority Verdict. Experiences of a Catholic Public Servant,* Belfast 1995, p. 320.

CHAPTER SIX

The Last Years of Unionist Government, 1969–1972

The violence accompanying 1969 escalated during the following years. It drove the protestant population into greater fear and more hardline politics, encouraged the growth of paramilitary groups on both sides, made catholics accept the IRA to a large extent as their legitimate defence force, and urged governments to find reform policies which would eradicate the perceived source of the unrest: the lack of equal civil liberties. Very soon it emerged that Stormont's frantic desire to find consensus and some cooperation with the catholic community, which was shared by the constitutionally inclined opposition, was at odds with the politics of the streets which had reverted to the old issues: from civil rights to political rights, to demands for a united Ireland on the one side, and the protestant corollary of fighting reunification. It was Stormont which represented and tried to widen the middle ground in the province's society in those years, whereas the population at large lived in a crisis which demanded the reduction of their political views to the essentials.

The British government was at first at a loss as to what help to offer beyond the sending of troops when required. Misunderstandings about the division of responsibility between the army and the RUC were frequent, and it was over these issues that Stormont finally collapsed. As the B Specials were replaced by the Ulster Defence Regiment (UDR), and a major RUC reform was undertaken, the army expanded its role in security matters, while Stormont retained a major share in the policies of law and order. It was when these were taken over by Westminster that Faulkner resigned.[1]

1. Arthur, Paul and Jeffery, Keith, *Northern Ireland Since 1968*, Oxford 1988, 11f.

What need to be investigated are thus two increasingly separated layers of politics: the politicians officially in charge who quickly tried to learn the lessons of 1968–69, encouraged by London, and the extra-parliamentary groups who drew quite different conclusions from the events of that year and could therefore no longer be appeased by the granting of the initially demanded reforms. Each side had a military dimension with which it could attempt to enforce its policies, the RUC and army on the one hand and paramilitary groupings on the other. The following brief, and by necessity somewhat congested, chronological outline of the major events during these three years will facilitate the analysis which follows.[2]

As already indicated, Major Chichester-Clark's government constituted a compromise, pursuing O'Neill's reform policies with an only slightly changed cabinet personnel. In April 1969, when he took over, Bernadette Devlin was returned as an Independent at a by-election for Mid-Ulster. A final year student at Queen's University, Belfast, and a political activist from the earliest days of PD, she had participated prominently in most of the marches of NICRA.

The events of the summer have already been mentioned. Peace was temporarily restored when British troops were sent in, much to the relief of catholics, some of whom had hoped for military intervention from the South; and the Dublin government had indeed called up reservists and stationed troops along the border. While this appeared to support extremist protestant fears of a planned overthrow of Northern Ireland, there is little evidence to suggest that the Republic was either able or willing to intervene in the North. The Scarman tribunal was appointed by the Northern Ireland government to investigate the events of the summer in late August. Rioting and tension, however, continued into the autumn; barricades remained in the Bogside of Londonderry and the Falls Road in Belfast, and military patrols attempted to keep the rival sides apart.

With control of the military in Westminster, pressure on the Stormont government to implement further reforms increased. The Home Secretary, James Callaghan, had visited the province in late August and discussed the proposed reforms.[3] Following the recommendations of the Hunt Report the B Specials were disbanded in October and recruitment for a new force under military control, the UDR, began. A

2. The *Annual Register* 1969, 1970, 1971, 1972. There is a slight but perceptible shift in emphasis as A.T.Q. Stewart takes over from J.C. Beckett as contributor for Northern Ireland from 1970.

3. Callaghan, James, *A House Divided. The Dilemma of Northern Ireland*, London 1973, 67ff.

month later the RUC was disarmed. Two senior British civil servants were appointed to Stormont as liaison officers, and at the end of the year the government established a Community Relations Commission under a minister.

In December the IRA split over the decision of its council to grant token recognition to the three parliaments at Stormont, Dublin and Westminster, and the Provisional Irish Republican Army (PIRA) emerged as the major descendant of the physical force tradition in the movement. This was formalised in January when the new provisionals walked out of the official movement which had drifted towards Marxist politics. The provisionals were better placed to attract support in the catholic ghettos of Belfast and Derry and could therefore effectively assume the leadership of Northern catholics who had felt let down by the movement during the violent protestant onslaught of the previous summer (IRA = I Ran Away, read a slogan on walls in catholic West Belfast). The first aim of PIRA was therefore to win back support from catholics.

The year 1970 saw increased and ever more violent rioting which was countered by the army's use of CS gas. The provisionals, PD, and occasionally NICRA as well, had tried to persuade the catholic population that the army was there not so much to protect them but to maintain the Unionist government. By April they had succeeded; when the Orange Order was allowed to march through catholic areas in Belfast, the provos provoked attacks from the population and a riot resulted. This was put down by the army, but not without injuring many an innocent bystander in the process. As a result catholics began to turn against the troops, at first in catholic working-class estates in Belfast, but soon throughout the province. The commander of the British army in Belfast, General Freeland, announced that the army could not stay for ever and that Northern Ireland would have to solve its own problems. Perhaps not altogether surprisingly, Paisley and a colleague won by-elections for Stormont, reaping the benefits of ever-increasing protestant fears.

In Dublin Jack Lynch had to dismiss two members of his cabinet, Charles Haughey and Neil Blaney, who were under suspicion of being involved in gun-running for the North. Another member resigned out of sympathy, and the government considered the introduction of internment and sent its Foreign Minister, Patrick Hillary, on a tour of the Falls Road, which was considered a most undiplomatic act by Stormont and Westminster.

As the summer progressed, rioting in Belfast and Londonderry took on a more organised form and focused primarily on the army, while snipers not only operated against military forces but also caused a number of sectarian incidents. The army was increasingly seen by catholics as their major enemy, representing the military arm of Stormont and no longer just protecting them from protestants but actively helping to suppress them. With the resulting increase of IRA activities the troops felt compelled to operate predominantly in catholic areas and against catholics. The vicious self-fulfilling circle of ultimately blaming Britain for what was happening to catholics in Northern Ireland had begun.

The government did not only use troops for riot control, but tried to ban marches and passed a number of Acts intended to restrain demonstrations by introducing mandatory prison sentences for rioting and making incitement to hatred a criminal act. Little of this had much impact, however, and the traditional Orange march was guarded by 11,300 troops as well as 3000 RUC and UDR men, which succeeded in preventing any major clashes. While all public processions were banned from July 1970 to January 1971, sporadic rioting continued into the autumn and then began to decline.

By the end of the year twenty-five people had been killed, all but two civilians, and well over a hundred bombs had gone off, while Chichester-Clark's government tried to continue introducing reforms that might calm the situation. The continuing disorder in the region, however, did not favour only Paisley and his supporters, but also unionists like Harry West and William Craig who wanted much tougher law and order action. Meanwhile not only Paisley but also Gerry Fitt were returned to Westminster. The government succeeded in forestalling further civil rights marches by granting universal adult suffrage without qualifications in council elections immediately and promised to consider proportional representation for the future.

In keeping with the political developments of the previous eighteen months, two new parties were founded in 1970: the Alliance Party (AP) in April and in August the Social Democratic and Labour Party (SDLP). Alliance was trying to capture and maintain the middle ground, hoping to realise O'Neill's promises; it deliberately set out to get support from both sides of the community. Its original membership and support came from the middle classes of both sides, but it soon also began to attract former NILP supporters.

The formation of the SDLP, too, helped to weaken the appeal of the NILP. It was a coalition of Republican Labour (with Gerry Fitt who became leader of the new party), independent MPs who came out of the civil rights movement, and the old Nationalist Party. It eventually absorbed the supporters of most of these groups as well as the National Democratic Party. A radical, left of centre, labour party in programme and outlook, it embraced the aims of the civil rights movement and promoted friendship between North and South in the hope that a united Ireland could eventually be achieved through the consent of the majority on both sides of the border.

The following year saw the continuing competition for the support of the population between the government and moderate politics on the one hand and extra-parliamentary activities and violence on the other. Violence escalated throughout the year and the ghetto borders were redrawn as catholics and protestants burned each other out of their respective areas. Various attempts by government to reverse this trend were unsuccessful or even counter-productive. It looked as if moderation had lost touch with the politics of the streets. What the extremists wanted could by definition no longer be delivered by the powers that were in charge, because their aim was the overthrow of these powers.

Yet the government had also to defend itself against attacks from extremist unionism while trying to cooperate with and woo the constitutional opposition and to speed up the implementation of its reform programme. At the same time it tried to defeat the ever-increasing power of the IRA by keeping the army in the forefront of the confrontation. It passed the Northern Ireland Housing Act early in 1971 making one central housing organisation responsible for all public housing in the province. But the IRA was no longer very interested in civil rights; while engaged in internal fighting between the official and provisional wings, it succeeded in making the British army appear to be the true enemy of the catholic population, not only to an increasing number of frightened catholics particularly in Belfast and Derry, but also to many observers in Britain and abroad. The government used the Special Powers Act to curtail these activities, but with little success, because all government activity could now be interpreted as further attempts at imperial suppression. Not surprisingly the attitude of both the Dublin government and the catholic hierarchy remained ambivalent, condemning the violence on the one hand, yet by maintaining their sympathy for the catholic section of the population appearing to many protestants to condone everything the IRA stood for.

As the IRA succeeded in establishing 'no-go areas' in Belfast and Derry, pressure on the Prime Minister grew to implement tougher security measures and to employ internment. Despite attempts by the British Home Secretary, Reginald Maudling, to support him, he had to resign in March, handing over to Brian Faulkner who defeated William Craig for the leadership and widened his cabinet by taking in

Harry West from the right and David Bleakley from the NILP. Faulkner still could not fully use the RUC which had not yet recovered from its reorganisation, and the UDR, while recruiting well, was used mainly for guard duty, so that he had to rely on the army, which drew yet further accusations of British imperialism. But he was equally attacked by sections of the Orange Order and Paisley's DUP. As the summer marching season approached, violence and street battles were joined by armed robberies, while rubber bullets and water cannons were used for crowd control. The bloodiest day occurred on 9 August with battles between the IRA and the army in the streets of Belfast and Derry which left ten people dead. Internment was introduced and 300 people were arrested, a quarter of whom were released after a few days.

The introduction of internment was an act of desperation which could soon be seen to have been a mistake; police and army intelligence was not good enough to make it effective, and it increased support for the PIRA as many of the old IRA were interned who had previously not had much sympathy for either the methods or the declared aims of the new version of the movement. As a result violence increased dramatically: of the 173 people killed in the province that year 143 were killed after the introduction of internment. While the army thought it had defeated the IRA, its leaders held a press conference. The political repercussions, however, were as serious; the Unionist government could be seen to have acted with the army against the catholic population at large, breaking any remaining good will of catholics towards unionism. The SDLP refused any political cooperation while internment lasted, and even Paisley was against the measure, as it might be applied to loyalists too. David Bleakley, the only representative of moderate unionism, resigned from the government.

In Dublin the Taoiseach, Jack Lynch, felt obliged to denounce internment and called for the abolition of Stormont. This inspired a rebuff from his British counterpart, Edward Heath, that he was interfering in British affairs. But London did set up an enquiry into the alleged brutalities by the police and the army during the implementation of internment. It reported in November that a certain amount of physical ill-treatment had occurred. With increased attention from Dublin the division between moderates and extremists grew wider and changed, as constitutional nationalism was forced into supporting anti-internment and more unionists called for tougher law and order measures.

Civil disobedience campaigns (non-payment of rates and rents) and hunger strikes by internees proceeded in parallel with a continued campaign of bombings and shootings by the PIRA. The UDR, though under the command of a catholic, continued to recruit protestants, but catholic interest declined after internment. As the geographical lines between catholic and protestant working-class areas became ever more rigidly drawn, the PIRA had its most successful recruiting campaign ever.

Tripartite talks between the three prime ministers were held in early autumn 1971 in which the British government proposed to find a way of accommodating the catholic minority in a broader government of Northern Ireland without alienating the extreme protestant wing of unionism. The Irish government suggested United Nations observers and promised to try to control the movement and production of explosives, while the province's Prime Minister was trying to find further ways of defeating the PIRA. These talks continued into the autumn. Eventually Faulkner produced a Green Paper proposing proportional representation and increased numbers of seats in both the Stormont Houses. Soon afterwards he had to rearm the police as they were frequently attacked, while police stations were no longer protected by military guards.

In November William Craig founded a new political group, Ulster Vanguard, in direct response to increasing rumours of Direct Rule. He hoped to reunite unionism by taking a strict loyalist line and gained support from, and cooperation with, a number of protestant paramilitary groups. Some of Vanguard's rallies attracted tens of thousands of supporters, but it did not appear to succeed in either substantially diminishing support for Paisley or spelling the end for the traditional Unionist Party.

By the end of the year the PIRA offered a programme for peace after a series of pre-Christmas attacks on the centre of Belfast. Its major points were demands for the end of violence by the British army, the abolition of Stormont, free elections for a regional government, the release of political prisoners, and compensation for those who had suffered from British violence. While these demands could be described as anti-imperialist and directed against Britain, they were by implication sectarian, because protestants were portrayed as being in support of the imperial power.

Thus by the end of 1971 the sectarian division in the province's society was firmer in place than probably ever before in its history. The civil rights demands of the previous years had increasingly, and ironically, become the politics of a moderate centre which had begun to fall apart under the onslaught of violent street politics. The government, while still trying to pass as much reformist legislation as possible, had begun to use the very suppressive control measures of which its worst enemies on the catholic side accused it.

The new year continued the general pattern of the old one. The army reported ever more successes in breaking down the structure of the IRA, while this did not appear to diminish in any way the bombings and shootings. Faulkner said that internment could end only once terrorism was defeated, but there was little new legislation he could bring forward. The ban on marches was renewed for another year, and civil rights leaders who had participated despite this, three MPs among them, were prosecuted and were given the mandatory, if suspended, six-month prison sentences. The pressure on the British government increased and reached breaking point when an illegal civil rights march in Derry on Sunday 30 January 1972 resulted in the killing of thirteen people by the army. Lord Widgery's report on the events of this 'Bloody Sunday' was probably too sympathetic to the government forces. The army, and in particular the paratroopers employed, seem to have been tense and unable to survey the situation calmly. When they felt threatened they over-reacted. What exactly happened that day remains controversial, except that thirteen unarmed people were killed (see also below, p. 146f.). The IRA retaliated and allowed its members to shoot at any British soldier. The events of 'Bloody Sunday' in Derry attracted worldwide attention and London felt compelled to consider its options, as pressure from Dublin and the USA (see next chapter, pp. 152f, 191f.) mounted. A committee under Lord Widgery was to investigate the Derry events. As there did not appear to be any improvement in Stormont's handling of the situation and Faulkner was unwilling to give up his ultimate control over security, Heath announced Direct Rule for the province as from 1 April. William Whitelaw was to become Secretary of State for Northern Ireland, responsibility for law and order would be transferred to Westminster, the Stormont parliament and government were to be suspended for one year, periodic plebiscites on the border would be introduced, and internment would be phased out. The intention and hope was clearly to continue where Stormont had failed and bring catholics more responsibly into policy planning and making.

With this, even the most ambitious civil rights aims had been achieved and both the Provisional and Official IRA hesitated before they rejected Direct Rule. Their ideology had already changed to accommodate this eventuality, but they obviously had to consider their supporters. More immediate protest came from unionism: Faulkner and Craig succeeded in establishing a united front and organised a two-day strike by the protestant workforce. But once Whitelaw was installed, this unity petered out. Direct Rule, like its predecessor, had thus to face the mistrust of both communities and would have to do well by both in order to be successful.

Throughout these years of violence and destruction the economy overall was little affected. A government White Paper of December 1971 painted a rather gloomy picture; new investment from outside, it suggested, had dried up as a result of the violence, the private sector was beginning to lose the momentum developed in the sixties, and investment in the new industries was also drying up.[4] But the overall performance of the economy did not confirm this forecast. There was an obvious and immediate impact in selected areas, namely tourism, pubs and some retail business: 200 pubs were damaged in 1970–71 and most of these closed for good; there was an initial decline in retail trade; thirty buses were damaged, and about 22,000 households participated in the rent and rates strike (see above, p. 124). All of this was a drain on public revenue, but the general economic patterns of the 1960s continued. Unemployment remained high as the old staple industries continued to decline, but while investment was briefly interrupted, it soon picked up again. Manufacturing output rose by 7.2 per cent in 1970 and 6.1 per cent in 1971; industrial productivity in 1972 rose twice as much as in Britain, about 7000 new jobs were created through expansion of existing firms in 1972, and even Derry again began to attract new industries and outside investment.

CIVIL RIGHTS, PEOPLE'S DEMOCRACY AND SOCIALISM

Among the extra-parliamentary groups, PD and NICRA and their link to socialism and left-wing organisations need to be investigated first, since it was their insistence that the province ought to have more democratic social and political structures which set the ball rolling by antagonising the less liberal elements in unionism.

As indicated before, People's Democracy emerged out of students' moral outrage over the violence against the civil rights march of Oc-

4. *Review of Economic and Social Development in Northern Ireland*, HMSO, Belfast 1971, Cmd. 564.

tober 1968 in Londonderry.[5] Its most prominent members were Kevin Boyle, a law lecturer, Bernadette Devlin, an undergraduate, and Michael Farrell, a postgraduate and college lecturer, all of whom later contributed to interpretations of the events they were involved in (see bibliography). As has also been pointed out, initial student enthusiasm to support civil rights, encouraged by similar worldwide activities, was politically idealistic and in support of the principle rather than particular politics and certainly not in support of any particular political parties. A number of these students, Boyle and Devlin among them, were eventually converted to socialism through the response they seemed to receive from the state: the apparent unwillingness of the Unionist government to concede civil rights and social justice for all; instead the state seemed to suppress the public expression of justified grievances. Others, prominent and most important and influential among whom was Farrell, who had been a supporter of left-wing politics since the mid sixties, were socialists who hoped to convince and educate PD towards New Left policies which embraced anti-partitionist and united working-class politics. Their social and political analysis was idealistic rather than pragmatic, their aim to expose the fraud of the unionist system regardless of practical political consequences. They urged the Revolution, and radical change was to come through their exposure of unionism by marches and protests and (by implication) the provocation of the state's violence in response. As has also been previously related, the PD march of January 1969 from Belfast to Derry, which resulted in ugly scenes and violent clashes and which became the 'Burntollet march' (the place in County Londonderry where the march was ambushed by militant protestants) of left nationalist mythology, had been instigated by the left, although most of the marchers still appeared to follow American civil rights examples. Following different, notably French, student examples, the march could, however, also be seen as an attempt at a student–worker alliance, but it was certainly in the first place a rejection of the existing government and any compromise it was willing to offer.[6]

In terms of the left's expectations the march succeeded, with a sardonic twist: it not only hardened the government's attitude, but it polarised the community to an extent that the events of autumn 1968 had not done. However well intended and idealistically motivated these students were, Stormont and the protestant community could

5. This whole section is indebted to Arthur, Paul, *The People's Democracy, 1968–1973*, Belfast 1974, and to additional information from Kevin Boyle, now professor of law at Essex University.

6. Arthur, *PD*, p. 40, and information from Boyle.

easily see them just as nationalists and focus on the issue of a united Ireland. Cameron was probably not far wrong in concluding that PD wanted to polarise society with that march, since it did not trust or could not believe in any success of reform or moderation.[7] While these attitudes and expectations were not uncommon among students and their leaders in 1968–69 – in France and Germany, too, it appeared to many as if 'revolution' might be about to happen – against the background of Northern Ireland's history and its specific political conditions, these ideas were even less likely to lead to revolution than elsewhere. By aiming for the overthrow of the system, by not accepting any compromises, and by appearing to ally itself with left-wing nationalism, PD helped to create a revolutionary, chaotic situation without being able actually to supply that revolution itself. Even more important, it helped to create political conditions in which polarisation became the main feature of the province's political life.

The lessons PD drew from the events of the summer and autumn of 1969 led it into policies of ever greater irrelevance; it grew more consciously socialist and tried to reorganise and discipline itself, thus turning its attention from students to workers and running straight into the problems that such approaches had always faced, namely the sectarian working class of the province. The revolutionary socialism that PD developed over the following year was not explicitly sectarian, but since it could not shed its anti-partitionism and adopted the catholic working class as its agent, it could never hope to appeal to much of the protestant working class. With the loss of its student base and with little support even from among catholics, PD soon lost any impact on, or importance in, the province's politics.

A not altogether dissimilar fate befell NICRA. It, too, was caught in the maelstrom of forces it had helped to release but could no longer control. The Burntollet march divided the association. Its more radical members drifted towards socialism and eventually supported violent measures against the state, while its more moderate majority tried to maintain the function of a radical democratic pressure group. As the reforms passed by the Unionist government fulfilled most of their demands, they turned their attention eventually to passive resistance and helped to organise the civil disobedience campaign against internment.

As has been mentioned before, NICRA was seen by many unionist politicians as a front organisation for the IRA. This was certainly not the case during the earlier campaigns, although some republican members participated and often functioned as stewards.[8] But as time went

7. Cameron Report, para 100.
8. *Ibid.*

on, its membership changed and there appears to have been a growing number of official republicans within it.

NICRA's politicisation – its constitution proclaimed it a non-political organisation – began during its clashes with PD, which was most obvious in their disagreement over the organisation of what became the Burntollet march. This also highlights the generational conflict that is part of the events of 1968–69. As has been shown, the civil rights movement grew out of social concern by the catholic middle classes and tried to remedy social injustice through lobbying and public demonstrations. While this involved the principles of justice and democracy, it also implied a reformist principle. The original NICRA members had too much at stake in the existing system to want to overthrow it. Not so the students whose stake was in the future, not in the past or present. They, too, started from similar principles but carried them to their logical, if abstract and revolutionary conclusions, unhampered by pragmatic political considerations. As time went by they could understand less and less how their parents' generation could have put up with and even accepted discrimination and second-class citizenship for catholics as a price for gradual economic improvement. Nor did they stop at criticising and applying their ideals to the standards of the North: the South, too, was judged illiberal, conservative and oppressive. Their united Ireland would achieve economic, social and political equality for all.

Not surprisingly 'PD's youthful exuberance'[9] helped to split NICRA into moderates and extremists, and this happened to a large extent on generational lines. Its younger members joined the socialist and more idealistic faction of the anti-moderate and anti-reformist extra-parliamentary opposition. The rift ran through the whole movement, from the executive down to branch level. While NICRA as an organisation was willing to cooperate with PD, it found its decision to support particular marches and demonstrations often pre-empted by that body's leadership, thereby supporting ventures which could only confirm protestants' doubts and fears about them. Thus, while remaining officially non-political, NICRA's name was increasingly associated with radical and revolutionary political demands.

Ironically it was the republican movement which was given a clean bill of health by civil rights officials themselves, rather than the radical students, for not interfering in NICRA's principles of peaceful demonstrations and abstention from any party political alliances, and for not pushing its own policies on to the agenda.[10] Naturally the IRA was

9. Arthur, *PD*, p. 61.
10. Bishop and Mallie, *IRA*, p. 53.

very interested in using the civil rights movement, but for tactical reasons wanted to keep a low profile. NICRA appeared to offer a unique opportunity for the left wing of the republican movement to achieve the cross-sectarian working-class unity which could lead to a revolution for the whole island. But NICRA's leadership was aware of the IRA's aims and did not allow them to obscure the short-term civil rights objectives they hoped to and then did achieve. Because of these successes, civil rights having become a government preoccupation, the movement soon became irrelevant and surfaced only briefly again in opposition to internment. Government reforms thus ironically helped to reduce moderate extra-parliamentary groups, which left the streets to the extremists.

Another group with at least working-class, if not necessarily socialist aims was the NILP, and it, too, suffered the fate of all moderate groups in these years: it lost out to the extremists. David Bleakley's brief participation in Faulkner's government and its reform programme came to an end when that government felt compelled to use non-moderate means to handle the spiralling violence. Some of the party's members joined the SDLP or Alliance, repeating the split of 1949 into moderate unionism and moderate nationalism.

In the 1960s O'Neill had succeeded in making inroads into the NILP electorate, which made it difficult for the party in the later sixties to develop policies in sufficient contrast to those of the Unionist Party, when the extremist protestant vote began to drift to Paisley.[11] While fully in support of the civil rights campaign, the party decided against active involvement in it, whereupon Paddy Devlin, one of their two MPs, left in protest, soon to be one of the founding members of the SDLP. In addition Eamonn McCann, who had become a full socialist, had to be expelled. The decline of the NILP continued, as it stood in the British Labour Party's and trade unions' tradition rather than a socialist one and support for reformist, moderate aims went either to unionism or to NICRA until it found its new alignment somewhere between the Alliance and the SDLP.

The left wing in the province's politics can therefore be seen to have been part of the increased polarisation that took place under the impact of growing violence between 1969 and 1972. It was part of the forces that accelerated polarisation by denying the possibility of reform and at least in part condoning violence, which either forced the less revolutionary sections out of politics altogether or pushed them into the new alignments of constitutional opposition parties that emerged during these years.

11. Darby, *Conflict*, p. 101.

THE REVIVAL, SPLIT AND GROWTH OF THE IRA

To a large extent the IRA was part of the left-wing section of the extra-parliamentary opposition during the last years of the old Stormont, but it went further than others in two respects: it did not just condone violence under specific circumstances or use it solely as a defensive measure, as many students did, but employed it as a deliberate policy, following its own tradition of a violent overthrow of the existing system; secondly, it combined the nationalist and thus sectarian bias with its, at least in part, socialist theories to an extent and at a level that many of the members of the other groups wanted to overcome. Without simplifying too much, it can be said that the IRA successfully tried to exploit the clash between the radical democrats of NICRA and PD on the one hand, and the protestant backlash on the other. It used its old republican nationalist tradition of violence against the state and had now reinforced it with a left-wing ideology which made cooperation and collaboration with the new forces of radical democracy and socialism that much easier.

As related before, in the late sixties the IRA seemed to have lost its rationale; catholics had fewer grievances, relations between the North and the South on governmental level had never been so good, and the Unionist government grew more explicitly tolerant towards the catholic section of the population. While violent protestant backlashes against this new liberalism began in the mid sixties, they were small in scale, and the catholic community appeared to accept the constitutional status quo, thus depriving the IRA of its rationale. Yet the emergence of NICRA, with its combination of catholic middle-class members and protestant trade unionists, appeared to provide a new approach towards the province's politics. But, as has been shown, while NICRA used the IRA, it did not allow it to play a prominent role within the movement. Apparently the Dublin leadership of the movement was content with this minor role and willing to support civil rights issues only for the time being. The reason behind this acquiescence seems to have been the need to widen its appeal in the North again and remove the legal ban on Sinn Fein (dating from 1964) and the Republican Clubs (banned since 1967) by demonstrating with NICRA for the repeal of the Special Powers Act under which they had been outlawed.

The IRA thus provided stewards for most of the civil rights demonstrations and marches. Both the police and the protestant extremists were aware of their presence, which reinforced the backlash from the state as well as from protestant organisations. What the radical left had hoped to achieve was accomplished: protest against police brutality mobilised more and more people, but it also pushed the IRA on to the sidelines, since the civil rights movement was swamped by traditional and newly emerging catholic politicians and activists. Yet, as the IRA leaders realised, it helped to do their job for them by weakening the structure of the unionist state. Disregarding the implications of the observable split in unionism, they argued that 'the nationally minded people would be in a much better position to push forward to ending partition and winning independence' once unionism had collapsed, and would also be able to 'win the friendship and respect of members of the Protestant and Unionist community who were not utterly blinded by bigotry and hatred'.[12] The escalating violence that started with, and continued after, the Burntollet march had thus little to do with the IRA's intervention or even intention, which was as yet concentrated on revolutionary strategies involving the civil rights movement rather than active and/or leading participation. The leadership of the new violence on the catholic side came not from the IRA but from radical students and working-class youths, although these soon availed themselves of military protection from the old IRA.

It was from some of the old IRA members, who had not been able to swallow the new left-wing policies or accept passive resistance as a valid form of political activity, that demands were made to Dublin headquarters in May 1969 to supply them with arms which would enable them to counter the build up of military strength among the protestant paramilitaries, in particular the UVF.[13] But in the late sixties the IRA had no funds, and through its emphasis on politicising the movement had in real terms become virtually demilitarised. When the catholic population needed protection that summer, the IRA was not able to give it. They had lost prestige on political grounds, since a few years of civil rights agitation had achieved social reform for catholics on an unprecedented scale; now their image as the protectors of the community was equally seriously damaged.

What was left of the IRA at this stage still drew its membership from all social sections of the catholic population and the views expressed in it were thus diverse and contradictory. The 'cross-fertilisation of revolutionary socialism and romantic nationalism'[14] made for endless debates and disagreements. A split was avoided at the annual

12. Bishop and Mallie, *IRA*, 56f.
13. Coogan, *IRA*, p. 422.
14. Bishop and Mallie, *IRA*, p. 60.

convention in June 1968, but by January six prominent Tyrone republicans had resigned from the movement, pointing out that Dublin was out of touch with what was happening in the North: the impact of NICRA had made abstentionist policies totally unattractive to Northern catholics. Yet at the same time the IRA in Belfast had been one of those least willing to give up its policies of violence. They had been under-represented on, and neglected by, the Dublin council. By 1969 there were said to be at most sixty members of the IRA in existence in Belfast and at least half of these were inactive or lapsed. There was no longer any military activity. Nothing much changed in this respect during that year, which was to a large extent because the focus of civil rights attention was in Derry, not in Belfast.[15]

It was the violent events in Derry which led to increased criticism of the inactivity of the Belfast IRA. But Dublin refused to change its policy and would not even grant better protection for civil rights marches, even if the violence against them continued. The political logic behind this refusal was quite sound: military involvement would reveal a sectarian stand and the official policy of the movement was the reconciliation of and cooperation between the catholic and protestant working classes. But the underlying political analysis was clearly faulty; by the summer of 1969 a reconciliation of the sectarian communities was obviously as far away as ever. On the other hand, the leadership in Dublin had neither money nor armaments at its disposal and was thus in no position to order a renewal of the military campaign. What they advised instead was the setting up of defence committees in the catholic areas, so that the people could defend themselves. But in Derry by then 'the "hooligans" had taken over, and the stage was set for a decisive clash between them and the forces of the state'.[16]

A Derry Citizens' Defence Committee was, however, set up in July, under the leadership of republicans, to defend the catholic Bogside of the city against the expected onslaught by protestants at the annual Apprentice Boys' march on 12 August. While they were largely successful with the organisation of the committee, the 'battle of the Bogside' did not endear them to the population who felt rescued from the B Specials and violent protestant youths only when the British army marched in. It did, however, provide them with a fertile field for recruitment.

It was during the severe rioting that happened in Belfast in the days after the Derry events that the IRA first appeared as an armed defence

15. *Ibid.*, p. 67.
16. McCann, Eamonn, *War and an Irish Town*, Harmondsworth 1974, p. 58.

force again, though poorly armed and using mainly petrol bombs against the RUC and protestant mobs. Their presence and involvement were, however, limited and made little impact; in Belfast, too, the IRA was not ready to fulfil its long-propagated pledge to defend the catholic population. As the army was called into Belfast, the IRA once again asked for arms from Dublin, was promised them but received none. But the burning and looting of August 1969, from which catholics suffered substantially more than protestants, provided the atmosphere in which a catholic paramilitary force could thrive, while it also showed that there was as yet no such force.[17]

It was as a result of these events and in order to be able to play an active part in the North that in December the Army Convention in Dublin decided to abolish abstentionism, to recognise the three governments in London, Dublin and Belfast and to work towards a united national front of liberation which would include the left as well as the men of action. But the men of action walked out and formed the Provisional Army Council, declaring military action as more than ever important in order to defend 'our people in the North and the eventual achievement of the full political, social, economic and cultural freedom of Ireland'.[18] They formed a Northern Command in Belfast to counter the existing official Command and began rapidly to organise, drawing support from the 'purist' section of the IRA in the whole of the island, but as yet little in the North. When the convention met in January the split was finalised and the PIRA formed their own Army Council and a separate Sinn Fein committed to abstentionism which soon began to publish its own paper, *An Phoblacht*. Support came largely from the activists of the 1940s and 1950s, many of whom had been interned and all of whom had been and were suspicious of left-wing politics. In policy as well as in membership it was a return to the inter-war years, but it now had a better rationale: the catholic population of the province needed to be defended, and volunteers found it at last easy to recruit and collect money and weapons. This policy appeared particularly urgent to the provisionals, since it was obvious that the catholic population generally accepted the protection of the 'enemy', the British army, and began to take the barricades down in exchange for army patrols against attacks from protestant mobs.

In this they even found a tacit ally in the Southern government, at

17. Bishop and Mallie, *IRA*, 81ff.
18. Bell, *Secret Army*, p. 367.

least until the arms trial of April 1970, by which time the claim of the provisionals that they knew what the North needed, and the officials did not, had apparently been proved right. Ironically, in the widening gulf between 'backward' extremists and 'forward' moderates, the provos had a side to fight on, while the officials fell between two stools with their socialist revolutionary policies that would support the use of the gun only on rational grounds. They were rightly afraid that the policy of violence would lead to increased sectarian warfare, but their alternative, the revolutionary unity of both working-class sections of the community, was less an option than ever.

It took the PIRA most of 1970 to build up its organisation and acquire sufficient arms to control their own movement as well as the rioting. Active service units rather than a militia emerged, numbers swelling eventually to over a thousand in Belfast by early 1971. The officials did not grow as fast in the city overall, but did increase steadily in limited areas. In Derry there was and remained, however, direct competition for recruitment between the two and they did not do equally well. Outside the urban areas, the officials kept their old supporters and the provos had to start their organisation from scratch, often from the basis of the 'old men' of the 1940s and 1950s. The frequent mishandling of ritual minor riots, through over-reaction and out of ignorance by the British army, however, provided them with continuing growth in the urban areas. The government reforms had little impact on the catholic ghettos in these areas and the continuing confrontation with the army began seriously to erode the acceptance of legitimate authority. The professional approach of the army to riot control and the perceived attempted insurrection provoked the provos from a defensive, if often provocative approach to open offensive action. They declared war on the British army, which was without political guidance from London and acted as in previously encountered colonial situations.

As the violence escalated, and internment was introduced as the last desperate attempt to halt it, those sections of the catholic ghettos and working classes who might still have held some trust in the legitimacy of law and order lost it in the sweeps of the army and police and were joined by many of the as yet neutral catholic middle classes. Internment was neither militarily nor politically a success for the government, but proved to be just that for the IRA; they found most of their older members and many sympathisers interned, but many of their young activists still on the ground and free. They now also recruited new supporters from finally alienated ever larger sections of the catholic population. As has been said: 'Internment did not crush the Provos but unleashed them';[19] it enabled them to create no-go territories in Derry and to some degree in Belfast too, while the supporting population refused to pay rates or rents to the state. The British army's frequent resort to brutality since internment generated further support and recruits.

By the end of 1971 the British government conceded for the first time that the guerilla tactics of the provos could not be defeated, that instead the violence would have to be reduced to an acceptable level.[20] This guaranteed the continuation of the provos, whose rather confused aims had hardly congealed into even a military strategy but had often become just terror from which the civilian population suffered most. They appeared to believe that somehow this ill-coordinated use of tit-for-tat violence would bring about a united Ireland. It was the continuation of this terror which neither police, nor army, nor politicians seemed to be able to stop which brought both an increased protestant backlash and the end of the Unionist government. But at least the IRA had no need to blame the protestants as the lackeys of an imperial power; they could now have their war, ideologically at any rate, directly with Britain.

PROTESTANT MILITANTS AND EXTREMISTS

Like the IRA, the protestant extremists wanted to bring the Unionist government down. Their aim, a mirror image of the IRA's united Ireland, was the return to a strong, conservative and protestant Stormont that would keep the threat of Rome and Dublin at bay by suppressing everyone who was not loyal to both the Crown and protestantism. Their response to the civil rights marches, which they saw as threatening their very existence, generated the same kind of fear among catholics and therefore succeeded ultimately also in reviving the IRA. Between them, they did indeed bring Stormont down.

The protestant politician who benefited most from this was Ian Paisley, whose influence and power grew despite the decade-old rejection of both his Church and his politics by the unionist establishment. His hard work at the grass roots of unionism at long last paid off.

19. *Ibid.*, p. 382.
20. *Sunday Times* Insight Team, *Ulster*, Harmondsworth 1972, p. 163.

With every violent clash between civil rights marchers and militant protestants and/or the police, he saw his policy vindicated and O'Neill's appeasement of catholicism proved wrong. In response to the Derry riots of October 1968 he wrote in his *Protestant Telegraph*: 'There is no doubt we have been betrayed by his [O'Neill's] policies. He takes every opportunity to smear the Protestants and to eulogise and condone the actions of the Roman Catholic Church and her puppet politicians and her puppet priests, cardinals, monseigneurs and canons.'[21]

Continuing the tactics they had developed in previous years, Paisley and his followers staged a counter march whenever there was the smallest civil rights march, and, much like the emerging 'socialists' of the PD, wanted and provoked confrontation. His political analysis was not any sounder than that of his idealistic student opponents, but his assessment of the political mood of his followers was better. While PD eventually lost the initiative to the reactionary nationalism of the PIRA, Paisley developed into an astute politician who could not easily be overtaken on the right, without ever getting close to his political aim. If his aim was power, he was caught in a vicious circle of his own making: the politics he offered to his supporters can only be described as very conservative and backward looking, and this was the one option that neither Stormont nor Westminster could ever consider again.

Apart from Paisley's evident religious motivation, what all commentators agree on is his desire for power, either sparked off or reinforced by his repeated experience of rejection by unionism's established organisations. It remains unclear, however, whether he was aware that the very fundamentalism, rhetorically embracing both religion and politics, which created his support would also prevent his supporters from accepting any change or moderation in his political views. Only by pursuing a more conciliatory. line could he ever have hoped to achieve real power.

With hindsight it is not difficult to perceive Paisley's strategy and the reasons for its easy success: with every reform that the government announced, its appeasement policy towards catholicism could be denounced and protestant fears of a catholic take-over revived. Once NICRA was identified as a catholic pressure group, the enemy was in clear sight, and the emergence of the IRA was only an expected and much-predicted phenomenon. Like the PIRA, he also soon focused on the British government as at least part of the enemy as a result of

21. Moloney and Pollak, *Paisley*, 158f.

its support for O'Neillism and its appeasement of the catholics. Similarly he provoked the police, but with the advantage of occasionally leaked information to counteract or pre-empt police moves to block some of his attempts at violent counter marches.[22] Furthermore, he availed himself of the help of hardliners within Stormont, like William Craig, to support his anti-government drive.

This raises the question of the extent to which Paisley's success depended on the emergence of NICRA. There can be little doubt that his political prominence grew through his involvement in street politics. His tactics needed supposedly catholic activity to react against: if there was no march, there could be no counter march and no publicity. When O'Neill succeeded in calming the waters in December 1968 and civil rights marches were called off for a month, it looked as if he had won a victory over all, including Paisley's, street politics. But the PD march of January changed conditions again and handed the torch back to Paisley. Even a cautious assessment would thus suggest that while Paisley's drive for power would probably have kept him in politics as head of an extremist, fundamentalist and conservative unionist party, his real chance for support came with the growing activities of NICRA and then PD. Once the student movement opted for deliberate provocation and against reform and compromise, he could not have wanted a better target; his supporters could easily see the threat to their beliefs, political standing and perceived constitutional rights. His followers' assault on the catholic population at large – which was both metaphorical and real – brought first the army and then the IRA to their defence, thus separating politics at the Stormont and Westminster levels from those of the streets, helping to drive a permanent wedge between the moderates of compromise and the achievable on the one hand and the extremists of no-surrender and not-an-inch on the other.

Paisley's and the UPV's political platform, as eventually that of the DUP, has been described as 'a mixture of uncompromising, traditional unionism and social and economic populism'.[23] It stressed law and order and the suppression of civil rights demonstrations, but equally demanded improved housing, employment and living standards for all. With his close defeat by O'Neill in the February 1969 elections, Paisley had become a political force, no longer just a street politician. His Protestant Unionist Party (PUP) came of age. In April 1970 he and the Reverend William Beattie won the Bann Side and South Antrim

22. *Ibid.*, 163ff.
23. *Ibid.*, p. 173.

by-elections. Shortly thereafter he was elected to Westminster in the 1970 general election. In the autumn of the following year the DUP was founded to replace the PUP. According to Desmond Boal, an anti-O'Neillite and first chairman of the new party, it was 'right wing in the sense of being strong on the Constitution, but to the left on social policies'.[24] This conservative populism proved a successful and potent recipe, particularly since it was based on religious fundamentalism, the fear of catholicism thus knitting it into the cultural background of protestant workers.

During the last months of Stormont rule, however, it did not look as if the DUP could stand up in the face of William Craig's success in rallying unionist hardliners against Faulkner and the British government with his Ulster Vanguard Movement. It is difficult to say when and why Craig, who, according to O'Neill, 'had gradually changed from a forward looking person, interested in continental and international affairs, into a narrow-minded sectarian',[25] made that change. It was the reversal of Faulkner's development and it might well have had its main basis in the perceived chance of power, as hardline unionism appeared to be in the ascendant. If so, he miscalculated as badly as Paisley in the long run, and was further disadvantaged by not having developed firm grass-roots support. His belief in the IRA as the motivating force behind NICRA seems to have been genuine, and shared by many protestants, and he certainly assessed the mood of unionism better than O'Neill when he openly denounced the financial pressure put on Stormont in order to implement reforms which, he said, amounted to blackmail. His flirtation with UDI for Northern Ireland seems also to have been rooted in this assessment of the province being let down and ultimately abandoned by Westminster. His opposition to both governments' security policies grew, as the B Specials were disbanded and Faulkner succeeded Chichester-Clark. Craig was head of the Ulster Loyalist Association from 1969 to 1972, which was prominent in those years in organising rallies against any tampering with the province's constitutional position. Vanguard, launched in early 1972, briefly gained even more support by opposing the imposition of Direct Rule and by helping to organise a forty-eight-hour strike against it. But Vanguard was meant to be, and in the end was, no more than an umbrella organisation which for a short time attracted a wide field of protestant followers but fell apart when it did not succeed in preventing Direct Rule.

24. Flackes, W.D., *Northern Ireland: A Political Directory, 1968–83*, London 1983, p. 76.
25. O'Neill, *Autobiography*, p. 104.

Vanguard's and Paisley's party's membership overlapped with those of various protestant paramilitary organisations. Foremost among these was the UVF which had emerged in the mid sixties in opposition to O'Neillism and with the declared aim of fighting the IRA. After a number of murders of catholics in Belfast, the UVF was made illegal by O'Neill and was generally equated with the IRA. With the emergence of NICRA and O'Neill's apparent appeasement of catholics the UVF gained support and began to organise in protestant working-class districts, attracting principally ex-soldiers. Through its search for explosives in the quarries of the countryside it eventually also succeeded in forming units in protestant areas there.[26] Its violent anti-catholicism and anti-republicanism expressed itself in assassinations of catholics, and bombings and burnings of catholic houses, but it also could be called upon to swell the ranks of anti civil rights counter demonstrations, marches and riots. The overlap of membership in illegal and legal organisations made it very difficult to draw very clear lines between their various activities and by the same token enabled legal organisations and leaders to deny any connection with violent and/or criminal activities and denounce them when they happened.

As rioting and violence increased during the last years of Stormont rule, the UVF reformed itself and developed a military-style organisation whose hit-squads increasingly found reasons to pre-empt and counter IRA violence. From the autumn of 1971 it began to become part of, and was eventually absorbed into, the Ulster Defence Association (UDA) which was then formed to coordinate the various protestant defensive organisations which had been set up in protestant areas of Greater Belfast, often as vigilante groups. The UDA wanted to be seen as a working-class organisation excluding the middle classes from membership. It has been estimated that at its peak in 1972 its members amounted to 40,000.[27] Ironically the protestant workers were clearly becoming more class-conscious, but they did not, as the idealistic left still hoped, drop their sectarianism in the process; if anything, anti-catholicism was part of their rationale and identity, as anti-protestantism, if to a lesser extent, was part of their catholic counterparts' creed. Later there were to be attempts from some protestant working-class leaders to overcome the sectarian divide and achieve working-class co-operation.[28] But in these years the UDA, as the IRA, and as its name suggested, was less directly concerned with politics and meant to oper-

26. Moloney and Pollak, *Paisley*, p. 136.
27. Flackes, *Directory*, p. 229.
28. Bell, Geoffrey, *The Protestants of Ulster*, London 1976, p. 137.

ate primarily as a defence force for its community, by setting up road-blocks, evacuating threatened protestant families and intimidating catholic ones. It was to show its strength as well as the ambiguity of its politics in the years to come.

Protestant extremism can thus be seen to have fed on the emergence of the civil rights movement which was perceived as a threatening catholic organisation. Once the left wing took over within that movement and welcomed confrontation, politics, as has been shown, moved from parliaments and governments to the streets, and Faulkner soon lost all initiative. With the inability of the RUC to cope with what increasingly looked like a threat of civil war, the British army was brought in to stop further deterioration. But the army's handling of the situation, despite the initial purpose of their intervention as the protectors of the catholic community, did not prevent the growth of the IRA which quickly succeeded in re-establishing itself as the true defenders of its people. What, then, was the role of British politics in Northern Ireland in the ensuing escalation of violence?

THE ARMY AND BRITISH POLITICS

As pointed out in a previous chapter, Northern Ireland at Westminster came under the responsibility of the General Department in the Home Office and the convention established in 1922, whereby Northern Ireland affairs were not discussed on the floor of the House of Commons, lasted until 1969.[29] 'Benign neglect' worked satisfactorily until the Unionists began to lose control and their difficulties with law and order became an infamous international spectacle on every television screen. Thus the need arose to send in the army in August 1969 and put pressure on the Unionist government to reform its institutions to meet the demands for equal citizenship for catholics.

The British government had been reluctant to get involved. 'The advice that came to me from all sides was on no account to get sucked into the Irish bog,'[30] wrote James Callaghan, then the Home Secretary, about the summer of 1969. O'Neill's rhetoric and plans for reform had sounded promising enough to the Labour government and

29. Callaghan, *House*, 1ff.
30. *Ibid.*, p. 15.

his policies had appeared to be quite successful. The British government could not have foreseen the historical accident which brought worldwide student and civil rights agitation to the attention of some groups in the province and under its impact allowed the old divisions to surface again, wiping out O'Neill's limited achievements. Nor could it have prevented the succeeding events, even if it had had such foresight and a fuller understanding of the ultimately still fragile state of the province's politics.

Demands for Direct Rule had come from prominent left-wing civil rights activists soon after O'Neill's resignation, but the British government apparently used this only as a threat to keep Chichester-Clark in line and force him to agree to its changed security policy involving the use of the army.[31] According to Crossman the cabinet considered that its policy would be a failure if it led to Direct Rule: 'The Protestants are the majority and we cannot afford to alienate them as well as the Catholics and find ourselves ruling Northern Ireland directly as a colony. We have also to be on the side of the Catholic minority and try to help and protect them against their persecutors.'[32] By the autumn the military take-over was considered to have been a success, but it was feared that the troops would have to stay for at least two years.

While fully aware of the possible need for a political take-over as a consequence of the military move, the British government was conscious of being poorly informed about the political situation in the province and uncertain as to how the army would be received by either community or whether the civil servants would remain loyal. But it also felt very strongly that if the Stormont government had to depend on troops for its survival, it would have to accept some control and pressure to change its policies, and was quite unimpressed by what appeared to be a veiled threat by Chichester-Clark that the UVF would stage a rebellion if Britain took over.[33] The Northern Ireland Prime Minister had therefore to accept the recommendations of the Hunt Committee to reform the RUC and phase out the B Specials, while Britain provided the money for new job creation schemes and an emergency building programme, but also pressed for a new central housing authority to build and allocate public housing and a number

31. Bew, Paul and Patterson, Henry, *The British State and the Ulster Crisis. From Wilson to Thatcher*, London 1985, p. 19.

32. The Crossman Diaries, *Selections from the Diaries of a Cabinet Minister 1964–1970*, London 1979, p. 645.

33. Callaghan, *House*, 21ff.

of other measures designed to deal with discrimination in public employment.

Initially this programme seemed to be successful and the British government thought it had succeeded, by hastening Stormont's reforms, in re-establishing the traditional relationship between Belfast and London. This soon proved to be an illusion, however, when the army encountered its first clashes with catholics in the spring of 1970. But Westminster tried its utmost not to get involved any further. The next two years saw various attempts to help unionism come to grips with the problems by offering more reforms to the dissatisfied sections of the population. This clearly overlooked the political reality of the emerging extra-parliamentary politics which no longer related in any direct way to Stormont or Westminster. It is very unlikely, however, that this reality would have substantially changed if London had introduced Direct Rule at an earlier stage. The politics of fear and confrontation were running in parallel with official politics, taking from the latter anything that might be useful to pursue the former.

These general lines of policy changed little when the Conservatives took over in 1970. By then the emergence of Paisley's PUP in Stormont and Westminster forced the government to accept Chichester-Clark's concessions to the right wing of unionism. If they could possibly avoid it, they would not get directly involved beyond the control of security, but would try to push the Unionist government towards civil rights and more democracy. However, a duly elected extremist protestant representation could be only appeased, no longer suppressed, and reform could be successful only if street politics could be brought under control. This left the army to fight the IRA and increasingly, by implication, the catholic community. This was all that Faulkner could have hoped for; if the IRA could be defeated, reforms would be successful and Stormont could be saved. This thinking was encouraged by the provisionals' open declaration that their first aim was Direct Rule, which not only gave Faulkner the more reason to prevent it, but also made Britain that much more reluctant to employ it.[34]

The army's initial role, to maintain the peace and, in the first instance, protect catholics from the onslaught of protestant mobs, came to an end during the marching season of 1970. The GOC 'announced much tougher retaliatory policies warning that in future petrol bombers were "liable to be shot". The Provisionals retaliated by saying that they would shoot soldiers, if Irishmen were shot. The Protestant Ulster

34. Bew and Patterson, *British State*, p. 35.

Volunteer Force . . . quickly joined in, offering to shoot a Catholic in return for every soldier shot by the IRA.'[35] While the army was thus employed in upholding security, its presence as well as its actions had political implications beyond its control and often understanding; like the British government, the army was only gradually beginning to comprehend the politics of the province. It was the publicity generated by the army's activities in January 1972 which would ultimately lead to the imposition of Direct Rule.

In 1969 there were just over 6000 soldiers in the province; a year later this figure had risen to 7500 plus well over 3000 of the newly formed UDR; by 1972 the highest number ever was reached with 16,867 regular army and 8728 UDR. The counter-insurgency methods which the army had developed in a number of colonial campaigns after 1945 were, as it turned out, of only limited use in Northern Ireland.[36] The political objectives of the activists in the province appeared to be clear enough when the troops first moved in, but soon grew confused and often contradictory. Not only was the enemy not easily identifiable, but he also changed frequently. Once PIRA's terrorist tactics became clear, the army tried to concentrate on keeping the level of violence low by focusing on the gunmen and bombers. But even this was not a straightforward task; the good will of the catholic population had to be maintained or recreated if the political aims of Westminster and Stormont were to be achieved. The 'pig in the middle' role of the troops, accused by extremist protestants of not being tough enough and by catholics of doing the protestants' job, made success ultimately difficult, and it very soon emerged that a 'military solution' was not possible. The army could only replace the police while it was reformed into a force better trained to deal with the civil violence and more acceptable to both communities. As a result the army maintained a very low profile in terms of military security operations, trying to preserve the balancing act the politicians required and benefiting from their own previous experiences.[37]

While the incoming Conservative government was a little less cautious than Labour had been and inclined to give the army more freedom to act, the problem remained the same: the tougher the army action, the more support for the catholic extremists which endangered the success of reformist policies; but if the army behaved with more

35. Hamill, Desmond, *Pig in the Middle: The Army in Northern Ireland, 1969–1984*, London 1985, p. 32.

36. Faligot, Roger, *Britain's Military Strategy in Ireland. The Kitson Experiment*, London 1983.

37. Hamill, *Pig*, p. 34; for the soldiers' perspective see Arthur, Max, *Northern Ireland Soldiers Talking*, London 1987.

restraint, the IRA was allowed to grow and protestant extremists were further alienated from reform. Increasingly the army could therefore be seen, and this was at least in part a conscious decision of policy by the British government, as fighting predominantly the IRA – that is, catholic extremists rather than protestant ones, which, while giving reassurance to sections of the protestant community, helped to alienate catholics ever further. This was not helped by the army's lack of intelligence sources and, for instance, its apparent inability to distinguish between official and provisional IRA strongholds, while civil rights consciousness and traditional sectarian sensitivities made people particularly aware of the brutalities involved in searches, arrests and interrogations. Any military success thus often turned out to be a political disaster, making for more IRA recruits and deepening the divide between the communities.

Relations between the army and the RUC were at best uneasy, as the latter was reformed following the British model and was thus in no position to challenge the policy of the army. The RUC blamed the army for being a catalyst for the IRA, offering an ideal enemy-image as alien occupiers as well as an easy and obvious target. Cooperation was therefore kept to an absolute minimum, although this did not hinder the army much, as specific RUC intelligence at that stage appears also to have been very poor.[38]

The most difficult and confusing task for the army lay in the fact that they were not in the province to fight a war but to function as a police force; in other words, a semi-military task had to be combined with diplomacy, politics and staying within the peacetime laws of the country. Under the circumstances the army did very well, but it is not surprising that blunders and mistakes were often made in attempts to reconcile contradictory demands. Ultimately the army had only very limited freedom in its operations and could do only what it was told to by the government and learn about Northern Ireland as it went along. That is not to say that either an easy military or political solution was on offer. As has been shown, the politics of the province were complex, had developed their own momentum, and were speedily moving back to the entrenched positions of earlier decades if not centuries.

The whole problem of the use of the army to control law and order in the province during those years came to a head with 'Bloody Sunday', 30 January 1972. Between 2000 and 5000 people joined an illegal march, demonstrating against internment. The march was in-

38. Hamill, *Pig*, p. 51.

tended to be provocative and show that Stormont could not effectively impose its ban in Derry. The army intended to maintain a low-key approach as long as possible, watch for expected IRA snipers and arrest any hooligans who would attack them with stones, bottles and nail-bombs. When the paratroopers were sent in to effect these arrests they thought they were fired at and returned the fire: 108 rounds of ammunition were fired and killed thirteen people, seven of them under nineteen years old, and injured nineteen. The marchers and NICRA leaders always maintained that the army had not been shot at. No soldier was killed or injured. At the official inquest the coroner concluded that 'it was sheer, unadulterated murder'. Even the comparatively sympathetic Widgery Tribunal concluded that some soldiers' actions during those events 'bordered on the reckless'.[39] It was the culmination of the army's ambiguous role in the province, having to listen to two masters, being wedged between two opposed extremist groups, while being asked to clear the way for the politics of reform and moderation. With the world's media showing the mistakes of the military at every step in its impossible role, the British government had little choice but to simplify the matter of government at least by introducing Direct Rule.

It can therefore be argued that British politics in Northern Ireland and the employment of the army to curb civil disturbances, while preventing an outright civil war and a total collapse of law and order, could not halt, and arguably contributed to, the drift into greater instability, coupled with increasing violence and an ever-deepening division between the politics of compromise and moderation and those of confrontation and physical force. When Westminster decided at long last to bring the province into line with its own ideas of twentieth-century democracy, it had to side with those forces that were opposed by both protestant and catholic extremists who believed in and relied on popular support for nineteenth-century modes of politics.

CONSTITUTIONAL NATIONALISM AND DUBLIN'S POLICIES

British involvement in the province did provide space for one important new grouping which emerged out of the upheavals of those years:

39. Hamill, *Pig*, p. 93, and (second quotation) 'Report of the Tribunal appointed to inquire into the events on Sunday 30 January 1972, which led to loss of life in connection with the procession in Londonderry on that day by the Rt. Hon. Lord Widgery, OBE, TD', HMSO, London 1972, p. 38.

the new constitutional nationalists. These consisted of those, largely catholic, members of the civil rights movement who disagreed with the confrontational policies of the left and had learnt from the 1960s that an equal place for catholics in Northern Ireland was a possibility, no longer just in economic and social but now also in political terms. What needs to be investigated more closely here is why their impact was not greater and why they, too, were swamped by the left, IRA violence and nationalism.

As has previously been pointed out, the Nationalist Party had lost most of its active support during the civil rights campaign of 1968–69 which had moved catholic middle-class interest away from anti-partitionism and into the specific field of redeemable economic and social grievances, even though it thereby implicitly recognised and accepted partition. The gap between the ideological aim of a united Ireland and the reality of Northern Ireland, which most of them had long come to accept in practice, appeared to have become clearer and more explicit to many catholics during those years. The party had watched NICRA with approval as a result of its success but with great reservations as to its tactics: 'we must not allow ourselves to be goaded into precipitate action'.[40] This lagged behind popular catholic opinion on demonstrations and street protests which were approved by almost 50 per cent and thought politically helpful by 70 per cent. In the Stormont elections of February 1969 this was brought home to the party: it lost three of its nine previously held seats to Independents – John Hume, who took Eddie McAteer's Derry seat, Ivan Cooper and Paddy O'Hanlon, all of whom had been active in the civil rights movement. This effectively indicated the demise of the NP; the Independents functioned as a focal point for a new parliamentary grouping in Stormont which would accept partition and concentrate on limited and specific demands on behalf of their disadvantaged constituents, taking politics from the streets back on to the floor of Stormont's House of Commons.[41]

The various opposition groups were forced to cooperate against the Public Order (Amendment) Bill, introduced by the government in March 1969 to curb street protests and counter demonstrations, which they succeeded in having debated for over 100 hours until it finally became law in February 1970. This experience facilitated a common basis from which a new opposition party could be formed. But this

40. Quoted in McAllister, *SDLP*, p. 21.
41. *Ibid.*, 27f.

was by no means easy to achieve. The alliance of opposition parties which emerged to shadow government ministers represented the differences in expectations and outlook of the NILP, the RLP, the NP and the new Independents. This explains the partly contradictory origins of the Social Democratic and Labour Party as well as the complex structure which this coalition imposed upon it and the difficulties involved in developing coherent policies. But as the focus of politics shifted ever faster from Stormont to the streets, the formation of a well-functioning opposition in parliament became an overriding consideration.

Finally the SDLP emerged under the leadership of Gerry Fitt, formerly of the RLP, in August 1970 with leftist socio-economic policies, an open membership, a democratic organisation and a policy on nationalism that envisaged the reunification of the island only by majority consent. It was supported by five other opposition MPs: John Hume (Independent), Ivan Cooper (Independent), Paddy O'Hanlon (Independent), Austin Currie (NP) and Paddy Devlin (NILP), and the NDP merged with it soon afterwards. This was a clear attempt to bring the civil rights opposition off the streets and into parliament and to establish a catholic parliamentary tradition to be balanced against that of physical force and a refusal to cooperate. Under the circumstances of the time it was probably possible to form a united opposition party to represent the catholic community only on a parliamentary level and to hope that it could be developed into a mass party afterwards. The mandate to do so appeared to be there and it looked as if the formation of the SDLP would focus catholic discontent on parliamentary remedies.

The complex origins of the SDLP were to have an impact on both its policies and its structure. It never succeeded in getting the mass membership it had hoped for and was therefore financially often dependent on sources from the South; on the other hand, its institutional organisation did provide a focus for active catholic constitutional politics and ended the ineffective, disparate and incoherent politics of the past. In the first two years of its existence, however, it did not succeed in reconciling the dilemma of recognising the constitutional position of Northern Ireland and effecting change through participation in a system that refused them participation, or to develop a coherent socio-economic policy. The dynamism of the new party, which existed predominantly as a party in parliament, came to a large extent out of the new style of leadership which differed substantially from the old NP: its leaders were younger (the average age of the six in 1970 was thirty-four), more than half had higher education (compared with less than one third of the Nationalists), and most had been born in their constituencies.[42]

The SDLP had been formed in the hope that catholic desire for reform would thus find a new focus in parliament. As the party could not agree on a programme while the violence on the streets continued, large parts of the catholic community could find little confidence in the new party and increasingly turned to the IRA for protection. But optimism within the party grew when it was offered participation in the committee system by the government. At long last cooperation seemed possible and catholic grievances and demands could be discussed and made part of the process of government. Like the parliamentary Unionists, the SDLP thus began to operate on a level which appeared to bear little relation to the politics of the street, and pressure was soon put on its MPs to withdraw from cooperation. When it did withdraw in July 1971 after the renewed violence in Derry, it did at least solve the dilemma of appearing to support a system which looked increasingly oppressive to its supporters. But by removing itself from the position of official opposition, it lost the only access moderate nationalism had to power. While not wanting to support them, it had none the less been forced out of the system by the politics of confrontation.

The introduction of internment in the following month justified the SDLP's abstentionism once again; its counter-productive effect on the catholic population of the urban areas could not possibly allow a nationalist party to cooperate with the government that had introduced it. But it also put the party in an awkward position: abstention made it politically impotent, while it had to condemn internment without appearing to lend support to the violence of the IRA. An answer was found in the call for catholic withdrawal from public life and the organisation of a rent and rates strike to force the collapse of Stormont through civil disobedience. Of these the latter was more successful than the former, but not sufficient to bring the government to its financial knees. It did, however, highlight the increasing alienation of many catholics from the state (at its height in late 1971 the strike attracted the support of just under a quarter of all catholic council householders).[43] Even this small success misfired for the SDLP, though, as they soon lost control of the strike, which was taken over by local committees, often run by republicans, and cases of intimidation increased; the strike could be associated with violence as much as

42. *Ibid.*, pp. 53, 67.
43. *Ibid.*, 97ff.

with the party. The SDLP found itself thus complementing the IRA's methods in bringing Stormont down, even though, when this aim was achieved, it was through violence rather than civil disobedience.

In its policy of abstentionism the party had found only limited support from the South. Jack Lynch, Taoiseach and leader of the ruling Fianna Fail party, had grave reservations about the policy of non-cooperation and at one stage suggested that it gave him a mandate to negotiate with the British government on behalf of the catholic population of the North. But although Lynch was cautious about the policies of the SDLP, he certainly had given them moral support throughout. 'Bloody Sunday', with the concomitant burning of the British embassy in Dublin, however, made him publicly commit money to 'finance through suitable channels for political and peaceful action by the minority in Northern Ireland, designed to obtain freedom from Unionist misgovernment'.[44] This raises the wider issue of Dublin's interest and involvement in the politics of the North.

Relations between North and South had generally been constrained on two grounds: firstly, by the fact that the province was constitutionally a region of the UK, albeit a unique one in terms of self-government, and did not have a sovereign government; and secondly, by the constitutional compromise of 1920 which neither part of the island had wanted but which embodied hostility between them, at least until the Republic would drop its constitutional and political claim to the six counties of Northern Ireland. While friendlier relations, and perhaps greater economic cooperation, may have been desirable for every Southern government, the border issue continued to provide votes, even though the active popular interest in the North declined increasingly as time passed. A 'united Ireland' grew therefore into mere ideology and became part of the national identity, much used in political speeches and manifestos, but not something that was thought in practice attainable or even politically desirable.

The Republic of Ireland had emerged as a conservative state with an established Church which represented one of the most conservative forms of catholicism in Europe. The end of partition was in the interest of neither the state nor the catholic hierarchy. Even if the North could be incorporated into a united Ireland without a civil war, this would raise questions and problems of liberalisation that neither church leaders nor politicians could feel easy about; it would turn an almost totally homogeneous culture into one in which a substantial minority of 20 per cent would most certainly want to make their

44. *Ibid.*, 108ff.

influence felt, not to mention their expectation of social welfare. 'Partition has won acceptance in the 26 counties,' wrote one historian, 'and it has won it at the hands of Irish nationalists.'[45] While both communities in the North, if for different reasons, paid a great deal of attention to any utterances by Southern politicians, most of the population of the Republic soon lost all practical interest in the North, except for that part of the national identity that required the end of partition and hence could be evoked by politicians without the need to do anything about it. It has been convincingly argued that Southern politicians, while rhetorically stressing anti-partitionism, did in effect pursue policies that strengthened the continuation of the division.[46]

It should therefore not come as a surprise that the Irish Prime Minister faced difficulties with the demands from Northern catholics who were ultimately anti-partitionists. The civil disorder that followed the civil rights march of October 1968 certainly revived Southern popular interest and this required some response. But it took a year before the Irish parliament had a full debate on the situation. Lynch appeared to steer a much more conciliatory course than the British government, trying to reassure the North of its 'own great tradition'[47] and suggesting some vague federal solution in which the rights of the protestants would be guaranteed.

> Mr Lynch's strategy seems to have been to permit his party faithful to blow the dust off the anti-partitionist harp and strum it noisily enough to drown any Socialist comment and exhaust themselves; if anti-partitionism was to be reinvoked in any new contest for power, he himself would occupy the righteous high ground and leave the quagmire of interventionism to his rivals.[48]

The form the North's debates took was indeed rather worrying; the increasingly socialist sounding civil rights politics would definitely not be welcome in the South. When McAteer, who appeared to represent the safe conservative nationalism of the past, strong on hostile rhetoric but without any real policies, lost his political influence, John Hume was briefly taken up. But he also soon appeared to be rather left-wing, and while the Southern government had to respond to revived public interest at home and increased demands for intervention, it does not appear ever to have contemplated crossing the border.[49] Lynch suc-

45. Edwards, Owen Dudley, *The Sins of our Fathers. Roots of Conflict in Northern Ireland*, Dublin 1970, p. 286; see also Wilson, *Ulster*, in particular Chapter 21.

46. Edwards, *Sins*, 186ff.

47. Quoted in Wallace, *Northern Ireland*, p. 178.

48. Edwards, *Sins*, p. 311.

49. Downey, James, *Them and Us: Britain, Ireland and the Northern Question 1969–82*, Dublin 1983, 100f.

ceeded in persuading Heath that Dublin had a legitimate interest in the province, and that it ought to act as guarantor with Britain to protect the rights of the catholics there. He often also suggested a tripartite arrangement, and both these suggestions changed the traditional anti-partitionist stand of Southern governments by at least half-officially recognising the independent existence of Northern Ireland.

The SDLP found favour with Dublin because it aimed at power sharing within the province and an institutionalised link to the Republic, while not threatening immediate unification. Lynch's rhetoric not only tried to appease the official Unionists in the North as well as his own supporters, but also offered hope for constitutional nationalism while being sufficiently ambiguous even to encourage IRA support. However, it equally raised fear among the protestants of the North. In the newly emerging division between extremists and moderates, the SDLP arrived too late to be able to halt the drift towards extremism and violence and thus take reforming catholic interests to Stormont. Its roots, as those of reforming unionism, were in the upheavals of these years, but political, social or even economic reforms were no longer tools that could be usefully employed to restore stability. In the end they had to recognise that the abolition of Stormont, which the extremists from all sides called for – if with different expectations and aims – had to be accomplished before they could hope to realise any of their aims. By ceasing to cooperate, however, they sided with the extremists, and from a protestant perspective that meant the IRA. This in turn left Faulkner's reforming unionism without any support from catholics. Its end became very likely.

CHICHESTER-CLARK AND FAULKNER: FIGHTING FOR SURVIVAL

When O'Neill gave way to Chichester-Clark in the spring of 1969, it still looked as if reform and moderation could halt the slide into extremism and civil war. Only with knowledge of subsequent events can it be argued that 'the middle ground was being swept away, those who tried to occupy it were destined to be swept away as well'.[50] Before the events of Londonderry and Belfast during the summer of

50. Farrell, *Northern Ireland*, p. 257.

1969 the problem appeared to be difficult but solvable: to make concessions on civil rights and to do it in such a way as not to offend protestant extremists any further. The test for the new Prime Minister was thus whether he could prevent any further escalation of the violence.

The period 1968–69 had been a shock to unionism, and the election of February 1969 publicly showed divisions that had never appeared so openly before. As long as the Unionist Party had been undisputedly in charge in the province, it could maintain control over its own rank and file comparatively easily, but as soon as that political inheritance appeared to be under renewed threat, the various factions within the party began to disagree about the ideal answer to this threat. As has been shown, some sections of unionism even grew more interested in bringing down their own moderate leadership than in maintaining the unity of their party – with the assumption, of course, that only by so doing could they preserve their political dominance. Perhaps the unionist leadership was too far removed from its largely working-class grass roots to perceive the accelerating drift towards confrontational street politics which was soon impossible to reverse. This turned out to be a class war of sorts; indeed, there were two class wars going on side by side in Northern Ireland – the working classes of each community taking up extremism against the moderation of their own middle classes, but fighting each other by proxy rather than their respective middle classes.

The first two weeks of Chichester-Clark's premiership looked promising enough. He ordered an amnesty for all those convicted or charged with political offences since the previous October, and the civil rights activists were at first willing to wait and see whether he would deliver the promised reforms. But the spiral of demands for reform, accompanied by confrontational demonstrations and counter demonstrations demanding an end to reform and the repression of those who wanted them, had begun to move. The Prime Minister soon found he had to ask Britain for troops in order to maintain the peace. He accepted the strings attached and tried to pre-empt future demands from the British government by offering to hand over security control to the army and to set up an enquiry into the police.[51] Throughout his brief period in office he found himself under constant and often contradictory pressures: Westminster wanted fast reforms, while moderate unionism preferred gradual reforms; constitutional nationalism favoured fast reforms, while increasing numbers of catholics

51. Bew and Patterson, *British State*, p. 194.

wanted very fast reforms. But the latter also wanted to bring the government down, which was also the wish of extremist protestants who themselves wanted no reforms at all. This isolated the Unionist Prime Minister and increasingly polarised his party.

Law and order in the province and the survival of Stormont depended on the British army, and therefore the good will of Downing Street, as never before. Chichester-Clark could thus be seen as weak, and the peculiar British tradition which allows strong (rather than democratic) government to be considered ideal enabled all groups to see him in that light. A large section of the UP, and certainly the DUP, saw him as having handed over responsibility and therefore having entrusted the fate of protestants and protestantism to Britain. From their point of view this was heightened by Jack Lynch's interference through his speeches and the erection of Irish army field hospitals along the border. Given the caution with which the British army had to operate in the North, the Prime Minister could neither regain control of the republican 'no-go' areas nor stop the increasingly violent protestant backlash which mutually reinforced each other and weakened his position ever further. The emergence of PIRA brought this to a head and its activities against the army precipitated his resignation. He resigned, he said, 'because I see no other way of bringing home to all concerned the realities of the present constitutional, political and security situation'.[52]

The relationship between Stormont and Westminster had changed drastically under his premiership: decisions were taken out of his hands and manoeuvrability was restricted. No incoming government would be able to turn the clock back, but would have to work with Westminster and according to its wishes if it wanted to survive. Thus weakened and not able to fall back on more rigorous use of the RUC and the B Specials, unionist government faced the worsening dilemma of not being able to control the violence on the streets and thereby losing more and more credibility even among its own supporters, while constantly trying to persuade the British government that harsher tactics and measures were required.

It was under these circumstances that Brian Faulkner was elected Prime Minister (with twenty-six votes against four for William Craig) in March 1971. Born in 1921 into presbyterianism, he was the first prime minister of the province who neither came from a landed background nor had had a military education. His was thus potentially a suitable social background for a reformed and reforming unionism.

52. Flackes, *Directory*, p. 153.

The war had interrupted his education and propelled him straight into his father's manufacturing business, as well as into farming the family's land, both of which he had gradually relinquished after the war to become a politician. At O'Neill's suggestion he fought and won James Craig's old constituency of East Down in the election of 1949.[53] He had been active in the Young Unionists and had helped in creating the new party structure in 1954. He was made Chief Whip in 1956 and became Minister of Home Affairs in 1959. His success in the latter post, by quelling the renewed IRA campaign through efficient use of the RUC as well as internment, affected both his view of the IRA and his reputation among unionists and his political opponents. It made him popular with the constituency associations while establishing his reputation as a hardliner among his opponents.[54]

Of equal importance for his future career was his experience as Minister of Commerce when he pursued the economic policies that prevented the further economic decline of the province with such success that even some of his political opponents found it difficult not to pay him some tribute. His commercial experience and 'inherited business instincts'[55] stood him in good stead as he initiated the restructuring of the economy with financial help from Westminster. After his resignation in January 1969, Chichester-Clark brought him back into the cabinet as Minister of Development in the following May.

When he assumed the office of Prime Minister, Faulkner was very much aware of the pressure for Direct Rule and believed that the only way to maintain Stormont and parliamentary government in the province was through renewed control of law and order; what was needed, he said, were 'not new principles, but practical results on the ground in the elimination not only of terrorism and sabotage, but of riots and disorder'.[56] His aim was thus to defeat the IRA yet retain unionist unity and avoid at all costs any further dependence on Britain. Given the split in unionism, the spiral of sectarian working-class violence on the streets, and the British search for a compromise solution that would in the first instance appease the catholics, it becomes clear with hindsight that his chances of succeeding with this approach were minimal. Faulkner's attempt to reunite unionism resulted in a cabinet that represented as many shades of it as possible: from David Bleakley of the NILP as Minister for Community Relations to Harry West, a consistent opponent of all reforms. While this created a facade of unionist

53. Faulkner, Brian, *Memoirs of a Statesman* (ed. John Houston), London 1978.
54. Harbinson, *Unionist Party*, p. 159.
55. Faulkner, *Memoirs*, p. 13.
56. Harbinson, *Unionist Party*, p. 160.

unity and of a renewal of protestant supremacy, it also alienated the various grass-roots sections which thought that either the left or the right, respectively, ought to have been excluded; and it did little to disperse catholic suspicion of Faulkner as a hardliner. The result was that he reinforced the very divisions he was trying to overcome.

This was, however, only part of the problem. The growth of the PIRA, which was responsible for most of the 304 explosions between January and July 1971, appeared to affect the economy, or at least trade in central Belfast, severely. Despite increased army efforts and the partial rearming of the RUC, the death toll grew and forced Faulkner to adopt internment in August 1971, for which there had been increasing pressure from extremist unionism but which he also believed to be a viable option that would serve as well now as it had in the 1950s. While this guaranteed him support from his own part of the House and thus maintained unionist unity, it also united virtually all catholics in opposition to him for the first time. Under the circumstances of the time, internment without trial under the Special Powers Act had to be condemned by every catholic politician, be he ever so moderate.

Even before internment, his attempts at making Stormont government at least appear more democratic by setting up new committees – some of which were chaired by members of the opposition – had been shattered after his refusal to have the army shootings of July in Derry scrutinised by a public enquiry, a refusal which led the opposition parties to walk out of parliament. Two members of his own party subsequently crossed the floor to function with the DUP as opposition. The 'Green Paper' for government reform that he produced in October did not offer any real participation for catholics either. Faulkner did not appear to have any ideas on a resolution of the stalemate. Even his hardline law and order politics did not stop the growth of extremist unionism and the emergence of Vanguard, while it united the catholic opposition and encouraged support for the IRA. But with hindsight it is difficult to blame him for this; there does not appear to have been a solution available.

'Bloody Sunday' and its aftermath epitomised the paralysis of Faulkner and Stormont; it could be only a matter of time before Britain, however reluctantly, took over, even though Faulkner appeared to believe that his special relationship with Heath would prevent this. When Faulkner was faced with the abdication of all security and legal control in March, he threatened his and the cabinet's resignation, whereupon Heath prorogued Stormont for one year and William (later Viscount) Whitelaw took over as Secretary of State. Faulkner has been blamed for his lack of 'foresight, forthrightness and statesmanship'[57] which may indeed have damaged his party and Stormont rule. His greatest mistake was the introduction of internment, but even without that the spiral of violence would have continued, albeit probably less quickly. The mutual fears of the province's communities were still growing and with this grew their defensiveness and willingness to use force, and there were no policies any government could have employed to change this.

It can, in retrospect, be argued that the most important period, the 'watershed' in the province's history, was not the year 1968–69 but the subsequent three years. While there was, of course, no complete break with continuity, these were the years in which the ground was laid for the political developments and frustrations of the following two decades.

As sectarianism had prevented the development of cross-sectarian class politics, so it also held liberal democratic forces in check. Northern Ireland's geographical isolation and the sectarian nature of its politics thus helped to preserve an essentially nineteenth-century mode of politics. In the late 1960s this was challenged by the most radical democratic ideals, and, perhaps not surprisingly, the uneasy equilibrium which had emerged during the previous years was shattered. As the government and moderate politicians tried to forestall any further clashes between the communities by moving faster into twentieth-century politics, the backlash from both protestant and catholic extremists forced most of society back into tribal certainties and clear enemy images. The civil rights movement probably could have helped to overcome the sectarian fears given time, but because it unluckily coincided with worldwide student protests it became radicalised, thus initiating the turn to explicit sectarian politics it had attempted to overcome.

The events of these years also help to explain large sections of their historiography. Leaving aside the literature prejudiced by the sectarian divide itself, journalists and political scientists, particularly from outside Northern Ireland, find it difficult not to assess these years by some ideal standards of twentieth-century democracy, often comparable to the early PD ideals, thereby identifying with the causes of civil rights and PD. This invites judgement, inhibits historical empathy and frustrates historical understanding, and is made worse when this view is then also projected back into the previous decades. These, very often unconsciously, prejudiced attempts at understanding the 'Ulster Prob-

57. *Ibid.*, p. 164.

lem' in their own way aid the continuation of sectarianism, as they are perceived to have a catholic bias. The language itself has become part of the sectarian debate: 'discrimination', 'equal rights' and 'power sharing' are easily assumed to be part of a 'catholic' terminology.[58] More often than not the writing on this period is therefore at best political analysis set against ideal standards rather than history.

58. And it has remained so: 'Reconciliation is a Catholic word for unification.' O'Malley, *Uncivil Wars*, p. 127.

CHAPTER SEVEN

Stormont Suspended: The Search for New Forms of Government

In October 1972, after the Darlington conference of the previous month, the British government published a paper, 'The Future of Northern Ireland', which outlined 'proposals and possibilities' for a settlement in the North.[1] All the province's parties had been invited to contribute and all except the DUP (it and the SDLP had not attended Darlington either) did so. While their proposals revealed the traditional reservations and prejudices, some agreement might in time have come out of discussions between these groups, but it would have required the initiative to return to the government, or rather the Northern Ireland Office and the established parties of the region. The fact that the DUP did not cooperate was a bad omen: it looked as if the division of the province into extremists and moderates was to continue under Direct Rule. This indeed remained the major problem for the British government throughout the seventies: to what extent a compromise and consensus could be achieved by wooing the alienated extremist sections of both sides of the community. Mistrust of, and bitterness towards, each other appeared to have ossified. Extremist organisations had grown in influence and power and had begun to develop vested interests. As during the previous three years, constitutional parties had thus continually to be aware of pressure from their grass roots which may not have allowed them to compromise even if they had wished to do so. By then, there was also a propaganda war to be fought: Northern Ireland and its problems had been propelled into worldwide headlines and this international attention could, and had to be, used and exploited by all sides. Yet the security

1. 'The future of Northern Ireland', a paper for discussion, HMS0, London 1972.

situation remained uncertain, its ups and downs dictated by the changing policies and strategies of the paramilitaries, not by the government or moderate politicians. The basic political division established during the three years of 1969–72 thus remained the same and hindsight suggests that all attempts at 'solving the problem' were doomed to failure.

The economy, after the rapid growth and buoyancy of the sixties, reached its highest point in industrial output in 1973, after which it went into reversal and into 'a prolonged industrial crisis'.[2] While it is difficult to offset the cost of violence, be it in terms of law and order, compensation or lost investment, there can be little doubt that its effect on economic developments overall was detrimental (although this should not be exaggerated). Employment in agriculture, if not its output, continued to contract and industrial employment fell sharply throughout the 1970s, but total employment continued to rise. The latter was due to the continuing trend of rapid increases in the public service sector, especially in health, the civil service and education. This paralleled the 1960s but now with new opportunities in the law and order sector of the police, prison and security services. In both communities the effects of these developments were felt: a general steady increase in living standards for those in employment, and in particular for the middle classes, and a concomitant polarisation between the better off and those in unemployment and poverty. Unemployment among manual workers was more marked among catholics than protestants.[3]

The downturn in economic fortunes followed the slumps that occurred in Great Britain in 1974 and 1979–80, which were more severe in the province and recovery was much slower. This was offset to some extent by the ever-increasing government spending: Direct Rule continued the principle of parity with Great Britain over and above the extra spending on a per capita basis.[4] By 1978–79 government spending per capita was 50 per cent higher in the province than for the UK as a whole. It was only under Direct Rule that public spending rose to a level appropriate to the specific needs of the region. This helped to overcome the sharp overall contraction of the econ-

2. Rowthorn, Bob, 'Northern Ireland: An Economy in Crisis', in Teague, Paul (ed.), *Beyond the Rhetoric. Politics, the Economy and Social Policy in Northern Ireland*, London 1987, p. 111; see also Simpson, John, 'Economic Development: Cause and Effect in the Northern Ireland Conflict', in Darby, John (ed.), *Northern Ireland. The Background to the Conflict*, Belfast and New York 1983, pp. 79–109.

3. Gafikin, Frank and Morrissey, Mike, 'Poverty and Politics in Northern Ireland', in Teague, *Rhetoric*, 149f.

4. Simpson, 'Development', in Darby, *Background*, p. 93.

omy, yet it still left the province as the least prosperous region in the UK. The underlying trend of the declining staples could not be halted, and to this was now added the contraction of many of the international and new industries that had been attracted to the province in the 1960s. Economic developments thus underpinned the political stalemate: declining living standards in the lower social strata and rising ones in the middle and upper layers were mirrors of the continued division between those who wanted their prosperity guaranteed by a political compromise and those who hoped to change the system, either back to a protestant-dominated Stormont or to a romantic nationalist and 'socialist' united Ireland. This is not to say that the middle classes on either side were not willing to support more radical solutions provided these did not interfere with their economic and social interests.

WOOING THE UNIONISTS: FROM DIRECT RULE TO SUNNINGDALE

The year 1972 witnessed the highest death toll to date: 467 people were killed, 143 of them in explosions, and almost 5000 injured; there were 10,628 shooting incidents, 1382 explosions and 1932 armed robberies (see Tables II.1 and II.2, pp. 256 and 257).[5] If the imposition of Direct Rule, while risking protestant rebellion, was intended to break the vicious circle of violence by giving catholics what they were supposed to want and gaining their cooperation against terrorism in return, it certainly had not succeeded. Protestant rebellion was kept in check largely by protestant political leaders themselves, and the IRA could now concentrate on British 'imperial' might as its real enemy.

It is as yet unclear how soon the British government changed the purpose of Direct Rule from a stop-gap measure to a deliberate policy of changing the Northern Ireland system of government.[6] It appears reasonable to assume that the two intentions began to go hand in hand when it became clear in the early 1970s that the IRA could not be defeated by straightforward military or political means. Arguably, Brit-

5. Flackes, *Directory*, 320ff.
6. Utley, T.E., *Lessons of Ulster*, London 1975, p. 89.

ish intervention damaged unionism considerably. With direct access to power gone, unionist politicians in the province could concentrate on inter-party friction and use Britain as a focus of their discontent rather than think constructively about future politics for the region. This helped to put the final stamp on the fragmentation of unionism.

Whitelaw's reputation as a conciliatory and personally charming politician, given to compromise and pragmatism rather than theoretical positions, was perhaps less promising in the Northern Ireland context. His declared policy of phasing out internment started with some immediate releases as a gesture of good will and therefore worried most unionists. It probably helped to persuade the IRA to agree to secret talks, while it achieved little towards his aim of reconciliation. The IRA grew stronger on the ground and began to introduce its own system of 'war law' in the areas it controlled, while it also had to concede a brief ceasefire, following the officials' example in May, to take its supporters' response to the British government's gesture into account.

What appeared to be a deal between the British government and the IRA brought the protestant paramilitaries into the forefront again, and it was probably at this stage that Whitelaw decided he had to cooperate with the moderate forces if he wanted to achieve democratic government in the province. He regained some protestant confidence through 'Operation Motorman', the re-occupation of the no-go areas by the army in Belfast and Derry in July, and he followed this up with the Darlington conference on political options for inter-party agreement on government in the province. This was attended by the Official Unionists, Alliance and the NILP, and even though they could not agree on future forms of government for Northern Ireland, it did give the Secretary of State some indication about the scope of their disagreement. This was followed in March 1973 by a referendum on the border to ascertain whether the province's citizens wanted to remain within the UK or join the Republic. This was of psychological importance, to reassure the unionists and opinion further afield, rather than of immediate political significance, as the outcome was predictable and even though many catholics boycotted the poll.

Two weeks later Whitelaw published his White Paper proposing an assembly elected by proportional representation. It envisaged a legislative assembly with large powers over domestic policy, the eventual emergence of a Council of Ireland, and measures to guarantee civil rights. It remained ambiguous about control over security, and legislative powers were to be devolved step by step by the British government as it became satisfied that the assembly had established a working system. The executive was to be drawn from representatives from both communities. Whitelaw clearly hoped that this would appease the SDLP while not offending at least the Official Unionists who could hope for cooperation with the Alliance Party. On the moderate level, Whitelaw's ability to compromise had produced a promising opening; even the fact that control of security would remain with Westminster for the time being, while appeasing the SDLP, could not offend the Unionists unduly. The only serious flaw for unionism in the new constitutional proposal, which became law in June 1973, was the withdrawal of the office of Governor, which severed the constitutional link with the Crown and increased the powers of the Secretary of State.

But Faulkner proved flexible enough to accept this, since Paisley and Craig and their supporters would have been outraged in any case and unwilling to give the proposition even qualified support. But he may have made a mistake when he tried to force his confused and demoralised party into supporting his liberal, compromising unionism.[7] The results of the Assembly election gave the Official Unionists only about one third of the vote, while another third went to the much-divided right wing of unionism. It also signified the arrival of the SDLP which captured 22 per cent of the total vote, thus clearly representing the majority of the catholic population. But in order to keep its more republican-inclined support the party had to stress its ultimate anti-partitionist stand which deprived it of any possible protestant votes. The Unionists, too, had lost the moderate catholic middle-class vote; the Alliance Party captured that middle ground. So even on the moderate level, unionist and nationalist parties had drifted further apart.

These three groups represented about 60 per cent of the electorate in the Assembly when it opened in July amid interruptions and much noise from extremist loyalists. Paisley appeared to support full integration into the UK, although he also flirted with Craig's suggestion of further devolution and ultimate UDI for Northern Ireland. By November a power-sharing executive had been agreed between the Official Unionists, the SDLP and Alliance. In his efforts to retain his own role and unionist representation on the executive, Faulkner even accepted the Council of Ireland at the conference at Sunningdale, Berkshire, where representatives of the Northern Ireland Executive designate and of the British and Irish governments met under Edward Heath, with Francis Pym, the new Secretary of State, in attendance, to find a framework for the future government of Northern Ireland. Bri-

7. *Ibid.*, p. 104.

tain agreed not to stand in the way if the majority of the population in the North ever agreed to a united Ireland. Dublin accepted that unity, if it were to be achieved, could be reached only through peaceful means and the agreement of the majority in the region. A Council of Ministers would be set up to facilitate further cooperation between North and South which would eventually be able to exercise executive functions. Similar to the organisation of the EEC, of which both parts of Ireland were now members, a consultative assembly would also be elected. There was a promise of transferring internal security matters back to the Northern Assembly at some future stage. The present priority, however, was to be cooperation between Belfast and Dublin in order to suppress terrorism. The ratification of Sunningdale was to happen at a future conference.

When the new power-sharing executive took office in January 1974, it looked on the surface as if twenty months of Direct Rule had been successful: the protestants appeared to have accepted a compromise, the catholics seemed to have voted for constitutional politics, violence had declined considerably since the previous year and there appeared to be a prospect of working out a political solution. Almost a third of the electorate, however, had given its vote to non-Faulknerite unionism and, though divided, this was a larger section of loyalism than Faulkner commanded unequivocally. Neither protestant nor catholic paramilitaries had been or could be defeated, and new fuel was added to the sectarian smouldering by the introduction of the 'Irish Dimension', which enraged loyalists but did not appease extremist nationalists. Given the developments of the previous years the British government had little choice but to try to push a political compromise which, it was hoped, would eventually produce effective government for the province. With hindsight it is clear that it could not work, but that was perhaps rather less apparent at the time.

THE POWER-SHARING EXECUTIVE AND THE ULSTER WORKERS' STRIKE

As soon as the executive took office in January 1974, the Ulster Unionist Council rejected the Sunningdale agreement and Brian Faulkner resigned as leader of the Unionist Party. He was replaced by Harry West. Unionism at Stormont split into two groups, the reformist Faulknerite Ulster Unionist Party and the United Ulster Unionist Coalition (UUUC) which embraced all anti-power-sharing sections. In the Westminster general election of 28 February the UUUC won all eleven unionist seats, while the SDLP held its seat for West Belfast. The election returned a Labour government and Merlyn Rees became Secretary of State for Northern Ireland.[8] While the UUUC had made a proposal in April for a federal UK in which the province would have its own regional government, the power-sharing executive won an Assembly vote (by forty-four to twenty-eight) on the Sunningdale agreement in May. The loyalist Ulster Workers' Council (UWC) immediately called a strike which very soon caused widespread disruptions and led to the resignation of Faulkner on 28 May and the collapse of the executive. These five months require further investigation, since they throw light on unionist as well as catholic politics.

Faulkner's main concern in politics, and the one area where he had been singularly successful, was the economic fortune of the province. With a majority of fifty-one to twenty-seven the executive could confidently build on the economic successes of the previous years. A new Department of Manpower Services was to provide better training for the labour force, and the reactivisation of the house-building programme was considered another priority. Thwarting pessimistic popular expectations, the executive cooperated well and work in all departments commenced with great enthusiasm. There is almost a feeling of euphoria in the various reports from participants: the solution had been found, cooperation between the two communities was possible, they could govern the province together.[9] From the beginning, however, the problem was that even within the Assembly the anti-Faulknerites could and did argue a case that the executive was imposed by Britain and was not democratic because it did not represent what the majority of the Northern Ireland electorate wanted. These arguments were reinforced by the success of their proposers in the Westminster election.

What worried and finally infuriated the majority of the province's protestants most was the proposed Council of Ireland. It was easy to suspect a London–Dublin conspiracy which was aiming at an ultimately united Ireland. Even the executive appeared to them to be dominated by the SDLP and catholics: the most visible offices were held by Currie, Devlin, Hume and Napier (a catholic Alliance member), and

8. See his own account of his experience in Northern Ireland in Rees, Merlyn, *Northern Ireland. A Personal Perspective*, London 1985.

9. Faulkner, *Memoirs*, 240f.

even Faulkner's deputy, Fitt, seemed to make more official statements than his chief.[10]

Grass-roots unionism had been as confused during the previous two years as its leadership was divided. The leader who was to gain most from Faulkner's fall, Ian Paisley, had changed his mind from full integration into the UK, and the concomitant support for the Secretary of State, to various forms of an 'amalgamated' or federal Ireland. Opposition to the power-sharing executive gave him his chance: the DUP had returned the second-largest unionist grouping to the Assembly and this gave their leader equality with Craig and West in their attempts to bring down the executive. All three sat on the UWC's coordinating committee which ran the strike. This got off the ground only with the help of Andy Tyrie and intimidation from his UDA, but then generated its own momentum manifesting general protestant hostility to the 'Irish Dimension' of Sunningdale.[11] All loyalist leaders had been reluctant to approve the strike, remembering the lack of success of the 1972 strike which had been intended to stop Direct Rule. But once it began to be successful, Paisley mobilised the world media. He succeeded in re-establishing his dominant role as a loyalist leader and took a prominent part in calling off the strike, after the executive had collapsed.

The UWC strike highlighted the potential strength of the protestant grass roots and its paramilitaries who seemed to be able under certain circumstances not only to challenge the unionist establishment but to take over from the most extremist political leaders. Arguably, it was only the greater political experience of Paisley which enabled him, with Tyrie's support, to stop the strike against considerable pressure from the UWC.[12] But it ascertained the UDA's importance and Tyrie's role within it. One way or another protestant politicians would have to take this into account in the future.

The executive, and especially the SDLP representatives within it, was urging the Secretary of State to take a stronger line and have the barricades taken down. But the British government was obviously reluctant to confront the UWC and let the army take over. The army itself had made it clear early on that it considered the breaking of a civil strike the responsibility of the police.[13] Its power derived from the Emergency Provisions Act, 1973, which did not concern itself with civilian disputes unless a state of emergency was declared. Fur-

10. Barritt, Denis, *Northern Ireland – a Problem to every Solution*, London 1982, p. 28.
11. Moloney and Pollak, *Paisley*, 325ff and p. 357.
12. *Ibid.*, p. 362; see also Smyth, *Paisley*, 92ff.
13. Hamill, *Pig*, p. 145.

thermore, the police could operate freely in protestant areas, which would not have been the case if the strike had affected the catholic areas of Belfast. While the army's apprehension that their involvement would lead to violence and escalation of the trouble was probably right, its non-involvement reinforced catholic impressions that the British army supported the protestant case. With hindsight it can also be argued that firm action by the government at the beginning of the strike would probably have put an end to it, while not necessarily guaranteeing the survival of the power-sharing executive for very much longer. This had been doomed since the February election.

Different groups learned different lessons from these five months. The British government realised that an 'external attack had been successfully made on the authority of Parliament' and therefore 'No solution could be imposed from across the water. From now on [they] had to throw the task clearly to the Northern Ireland people themselves.'[14] Faulkner lost his standing and power within unionism for not having paid enough attention to grass-roots opinion. Anti-Faulknerite protestant politicians began fully to appreciate the potential power of the UDA which could mobilise working-class support. The protestant workers who had supported or had been made to support the strike realised that the 'spirit of 1912' was not dead and that they could still successfully rebel against British politics. The SDLP leadership recognised with its first taste of power that Northern Ireland was a viable unit and power sharing within it a desirable aim which perhaps could be achieved again in the future. The catholic population, provided with essential services largely by the IRA during the strike, felt once again intimidated and doubtful about the possibility of reform and compromise from the unionist community.

THE WAR OF THE PARAMILITARIES

After the failure of the power-sharing executive the British government, realising the difficulties of imposing an 'Irish Dimension', re-established Direct Rule with the Northern Ireland Act, 1974, and offered the Northern Ireland Convention which was supposed to

14. Wilson, Harold, *Final Term. The Labour Government 1974–1976*, London 1979, p. 78.

negotiate the future of the province through elected representatives. This was duly elected in May 1975, only to confirm once again what the success of the UWC strike had suggested: unionists were not willing to share power, and the SDLP would not cooperate without some legislative say by right. Rees had to accept the indefinite continuation of Direct Rule.

For the British government the 1970s was a decade in which they tried to find a political compromise in the province while keeping the violence to an 'acceptable level'. In the latter they did eventually succeed, but this was none the less predominantly the period of the paramilitaries of both sides, during which they began to stake their social, political and economic claims. Internal feuds within their respective organisations indicated power-political and to some extent ideological conflicts. But by the end of the decade they had been successful in maintaining the status quo established in 1972: a compromise could not be achieved for the politicians' fear of grass-roots violence – arguably a case in which the working classes dictated politics, or the lack of it.

In the wake of their success with the UWC strike the UDA became more politicised, to the extent that they at least contemplated discussions with the provos and certainly met SDLP representatives. But little came of these, largely, one would have to assume, because the ultimate political objectives of the protestant working classes did not and could not include an 'Irish Dimension'. During the first half of the decade the UDA considered supporting Craig and his ideas of UDI for the province as against Paisley and West. By 1977 they supported Paisley and Ernest Baird, the leader of the UUUP, in their United Unionist Action Council strike against the government's security policy. When this did not command sufficient support, Tyrie seems to have hoped to develop his own political stand with the foundation in 1979 of the New Ulster Political Research Group which developed a plan for negotiated independence. Rees had been trying to encourage a more political approach from the protestant paramilitaries by lifting the ban on the UVF in April 1974, but had to impose it again eighteen months later after the organisation claimed responsibility for various violent and murderous attacks. In the subsequent army and police operations which were followed by trials in the courts, the strength of the UVF was much diminished. As with the UUUP, political attempts by the UDA failed because they could not offer a proposal that incorporated power sharing of some kind and were ultimately defensive about the position of protestants in the province's society and politics. While maintaining and strengthening their social importance and political potential throughout the decade, the protestant paramilitaries, both the legal as well as the illegal varieties, remained politically a passive force.

For the revived IRA, and in particular the provisionals, however, the 1970s were overall, and despite sometimes contrary appearances, a period of consolidation, achieved through in-fighting, increased social control in the areas it dominated and even occasional attempts at a more coherent policy. This is not to say that there were obvious and continued increases in its power – rather the reverse often appeared to be the case – but it succeeded in establishing itself as a force that could not be defeated, either by the British army or from within the catholic community, as the case of the 'peace people' showed (see below). But its violence remained largely without coherent political targets beyond the general one of overthrowing the system. It never grew strong enough to attain this by the violent means it used, while at the same time it increased its social, political and even economic power. As a political force it thus remained negative and destructive. It is not easy to understand 'the political sterility and intransigence of the leadership'[15] in rational terms, except by assuming that their aim was less immediate or even long-term power, but rather the continuation of the romantic, rebellious tradition of Irish politics which did not necessarily entail attainable political ends.

From 1973 and throughout the decade PIRA was under pressure from the increasingly efficient RUC and army. Its military fortunes were in steady decline and it had to change its tactics several times in order to meet successful RUC and army inroads. Its initial tactics – the car bomb, which was supposed to have hit economic targets, and riot encounters with the army – were replaced by the sniper, a tactic which was initially successful but had lost its punch by the late 1970s and was replaced by ever more sophisticated incendiary devices. The bombing campaign in Britain, which was aimed at 'economic, military, political and judicial targets'[16] in order to create popular support there for military and political withdrawal from Northern Ireland, had to change its tactics from quick excursions of bombing teams to the mainland to sleeper teams which could be activated when required. This did not appear to have been successful either: popular opinion in Britain seemed to favour withdrawal but did not link this to the bombing campaigns of the IRA, while the British government could use these campaigns to justify its policy in the province.

15. Bishop and Mallie, *IRA*, p. 180.

16. Dathi O'Connaill (a leading strategist in the provisional movement) quoted in Bishop and Mallie, p. 197.

The feud between the official and provisional IRA which had involved street battles in the period 1970–71 became less apparent, as OIRA declared a ceasefire from May 1972 and began to pursue a much more political approach, eventually largely dissolving into the Republican Clubs (the Northern equivalent of the Republic's Sinn Fein [The Workers' Party]). A new group broke away from OIRA in 1974, the Irish Republican Socialist Party (IRSP), with its military wing, the Irish National Liberation Army (INLA), probably the most ruthless of all paramilitary organisations in the province. There was serious feuding between OIRA and IRSP in 1975 with a number of assassinations on both sides. The proscription of the Republican Clubs was removed in 1973, and they followed the increasingly Marxist political line of Official Sinn Fein.

PIRA responded to pressures from church leaders and conciliatory remarks from Rees and declared a ceasefire from Christmas 1974 which lasted, with interruptions, throughout 1975. While it gave breathing space to the organisation, it could not last, since the provisionals had no policies to offer that the British government could accept. Its minimal demands always included a declaration by Britain of its intended withdrawal from the province. The end of the ceasefire began with the death of an IRA hunger striker in a British prison, and the statistics of violence flared up again. But Roy Mason, Callaghan's new Secretary of State, brought the SAS in officially and the undercover operations that followed seemed to affect PIRA seriously. When in the summer of 1976 the Peace Movement (see below, pp. 173f) got under way, it lost even more support. By the late 1970s PIRA thus had reduced support from the ghettos in Belfast and Derry, and morale was lowered through feuding within the organisation. The leadership had turned away from the middle-aged Southern controls, and the new leaders were younger Northerners who were looking for new ways to gain ground and take the initiative again. In the late 1970s they began to regain support through the 'dirty protest' in the prisons which was to demand 'special category status' for the prisoners and function at the same time as an international propaganda effort (see next chapter).

In many respects the 1970s must be seen as a decade in which the British government succeeded in curtailing the paramilitaries of both sides. The fact, however, that they could only be curbed, but not eradicated suggests a slightly different picture: government and security forces on the one hand, and paramilitaries of both sides on the other, found a *modus vivendi*, accepting each other's continuing existence without ever publicly conceding it.

THE 'TROUBLES' AND THE PEOPLE: A SOCIETY UNDER STRESS?

The effects of the disturbances on the population of Northern Ireland have been much researched and speculated on. A good deal of this work confirms what common sense would suggest. Even the most sophisticated of it is hampered by the unavailability of data prior to 1969, so that proper conclusions about the impact of 'the troubles' cannot be drawn.[17] It is indeed the continuation of social and general behavioural patterns which is most likely to be the more important, rather than any changes. Social science research has also found it difficult to find general patterns, since conditions varied greatly between areas and communities, and case studies often turn out not to be typical of anything but themselves.[18] Frequently surprise is expressed at how little change there appears to have been, which allows us to revert to the general historical pattern.

As has been shown in previous chapters, society in Northern Ireland was generally conservative, rural and religious. Belfast and Dublin have been described as the two largest villages in the Western world, that is to say both Irish societies were under-urbanised.[19] As has been suggested before, in Northern Ireland, where some economic modernisation had taken place, the lack of concomitant social and cultural modernisation was due to a complex mixture of causes: geographical remoteness, sectarianism and the conservative political structures resulting from this. The conventional nature of society was reflected in a socially much more stable framework than elsewhere in the UK: marriage stability and general family cohesion were higher than in similar industrial communities; there was less child abuse, less alcohol consumed per household, more children continued education after the statutory leaving age, a greater proportion took A levels, and more went on to further full-time education.[20] While the crime rate rose by 150 per cent in the ten years after 1968, it was still much lower than in England and Wales. This is similarly true for juvenile crime: by 1978 the rate of juveniles found guilty of indictable or other offences was half that of England and Wales.

17. Harbinson, Jeremy and Joan (eds), *A Society under Stress. Children and Young People in Northern Ireland*, West Compton House, Somerset 1980.

18. Darby, John, *Background*, p. 7.

19. Harbinson, *Society*, p. 12; see also Heskin, Ken, *Northern Ireland: A Psychological Analysis*, Dublin 1980, p. 130.

20. Harbinson, *Society*, p. 4.

The murder rate had remained low and has to be seen against the background of the 1960s when it never rose to annual double figures. Even within the changed circumstances of the 1970s direct political crime was only a small proportion of the overall increasing crime figures. It is well to be reminded of the much-quoted fact that in only one year during the 'troubles' were more people killed by them than in road accidents. Violence, furthermore, never affected the whole population directly and as its nature changed with time, different groups and people were targeted and subjected to fear of it. The quick dissemination of unrest and disturbances through the local media often helped to create an atmosphere of threat, even though the direct impact of violence on people's lives was small.[21]

Another factor that needs to be taken into consideration was the general economic 'backwardness' of the province and the level of unemployment (back to the high levels of 1940 by 1978) and poverty, since it was in the urban areas and among the working classes that most violence took place. Furthermore, the high and increasing level of youth unemployment made paramilitary recruitment easier, and frequently promoted even rioting to a 'leisure activity'.

Against this general background, and ultimately as no more than part of it, the Peace People emerged in 1976. This was initially a women's peace movement, inspired by the death of three children in West Belfast when they were struck by a gunman's getaway car. The children's aunt, Mairead Corrigan, and Betty Williams, a housewife who had witnessed the accident, were its founders. They were soon joined by Ciaran McKeown, a journalist who took the political initiative and named the movement the Peace People. It organised peace rallies and marches throughout Belfast and other centres in the province, attracting tens of thousands of people (though never as many as a 12 July parade).[22] Similar sympathetic events were soon held in London, Dublin and abroad. As a mass movement in support of peace and an end to violence, the Peace People obviously generated enthusiasm and appealed to the war-weariness of those from the most affected areas as well as to the well-meaning middle classes on both sides. The hope and enthusiasm that seemed to be expressed by the movement soon spread abroad and Williams and Corrigan were awarded the 1976 Nobel Peace Prize. Generally Christian and humanitarian overtones of reconciliation gave it cohesion as long as it did not try to translate its search for peace into a political programme. As was to be expected,

21. Murray, Dominic, 'Schools and Conflict', in Darby, *Background*, p. 150.
22. Barritt, *Problem*, p. 110.

the movement attracted abuse and opposition from the catholic paramilitaries. But it was its venture into politics which aligned it with the moderate middle ground in Northern Ireland politics and thus made it politically as ineffective as all other groupings in the centre. General good will and revulsion of violence were not enough to break through to the existential fears, and by now also vested interests (see next chapter) that could be called upon and were catered for by the extremists of both sides.

Yet the Peace People's failure to break the mould of a polarised society highlights the extent of support for moderation and anti-violent sentiments. This is confirmed by surveys which show, for instance, the large number of people who would have preferred some form of integrated education (over 80 per cent of both protestants and catholics).[23] Ten years earlier only about two-thirds of the population had favoured integrated education. This change in attitude seems to indicate the realisation by many people in the province that only long-term change could spring the trap of cultural conditioning. The most interesting findings on the impact of ten years of violence on people's attitudes in Northern Ireland, however, show how little change there was. Moxon-Browne's study of changing attitudes in the ten years since Rose's survey of 1967–68 (see above, pp. 92, 101) comes to the conclusion that 'there was an almost negligible change in the polarisation between the two communities. . . What we seem to have is a crystallised society, crystallised into polarisation, but not torn apart by strife.'[24] As did Rose, he found that outside the immediate political issues, people felt more divided by class than by religion, which is confirmed by studies into social attitudes of children across the religious divide who appeared to share the same general value system irrespective of their cultural backgrounds.[25]

In conclusion it ought to be emphasised that, contrary to expectation, Northern Ireland's society does not suffer from any more stress than most Western societies, and in most areas of daily life probably less. The historically conditioned social and political attitudes of its people had only marginally changed by the end of the 1970s. Arguably there was a change in awareness in the two working classes: catholics feeling more worried than they had in the 1960s that their middle classes were selling them out to Britain, and protestants that their

23. Moxon-Browne, Edward, *Nation, Class and Creed in Northern Ireland*, Aldershot, Hampshire 1983, p. 134.

24. *Ibid.*, p. 167.

25. Heskin, *Analysis*, pp. 126–52; McKernan, James, 'Pupil values as social indicators of intergroup differences in Northern Ireland', in Harbinson, *Society*, pp. 128–40.

middle classes were selling out to the catholics. However, this was as yet only beginning to be reflected in voting patterns on the protestant side.

UNIONISM DIVIDED

The continuation of Direct Rule after the failed attempt of the power-sharing executive had left unionism divided and at a loss about future developments. Throughout the decade unionism was fragmented: as there was no longer direct access to majority rule, so there was now no longer any need for even superficial unity. The divisions within unionism reflected both class interests and, mostly closely connected, different answers to Westminster's rule.

Only a small minority of unionists under Faulkner remained in favour of power sharing and these founded the Unionist Party of Northern Ireland (UPNI) in September 1974. But its appeal to voters declined steadily, from 7.7 per cent of first-preference votes in the Constitutional Convention election in May 1975 to 0.6 per cent in the 1979 European election. Faulkner (Lord Faulkner of Downpatrick in 1977) withdrew from politics after the failure of the Convention in 1976 and died in a hunting accident a year later. But his name, as that of his party, was associated with cooperating with those forces that most unionists now considered their greatest enemy: Britain and the catholics of the province.

It was as much in opposition to Faulknerite unionism as to show Westminster protestant unity that unionist parties formed the United Ulster Unionist Council (UUUC). This coalition came together originally to fight the Sunningdale agreement and succeeded in winning eleven of the twelve Northern Ireland seats in the Westminster election of February 1974. It comprised the Official Unionists under Harry West, the DUP under Ian Paisley and the Vanguard Unionists under William Craig. It operated as a parliamentary coalition at Stormont, where its support of the UWC strike was crucial, and it carried on into the Convention. The parties within the coalition, however, maintained their separate identities, and the cooperation began to falter as soon as the unifying factor, that is opposition to any policy that might lead to a united Ireland, was no longer in clear evidence. Craig was expelled from the UUUC when he proposed voluntary cooperation with the SDLP. The majority of Vanguard stayed with the UUUC and helped to form the United Ulster Unionist Movement (UUUM) under Ernest Baird. But the difficulties of keeping this coalition together grew as 'the enemy' weakened. Official Unionists could not accept the inclusion of paramilitary groups in order to stage the attempted 'loyalist strike' in May 1977. This heralded the end of the UUUC, both in Belfast as well as in London, since two Westminster MPs supported the strike. One of the more important aspects of this coalition was probably that it marked the final break between the British Conservative Party and Ulster Unionists in Parliament.[26]

After the collapse of the UUUC, the various unionist parties went their separate ways, the Official Unionists (OUP) hoping to regain some of Paisley's support and Paisley banking on some of Vanguard's votes. The political stalemate in Northern Ireland continued, and while there was negative unity on the maintenance of the border with all its constitutional and political implications, this unity could not be turned into positive proposals. The acceptance of, and some cooperation with, the SDLP which the British government demanded, none but the UPNI was willing to give. The fragmentation of unionism could thus not be overcome and the division of its supporters along class lines continued. One casualty of this division was the importance of the Orange Order which maintained its link with the OUP but could not prevent the survival and growth of the DUP; it thus lost much of its political clout.

As the economy continued to decline and bit further into protestant working-class employment, Paisley seemed to offer a better choice than the OUP for lower-class voters.[27] Throughout the 1970s the DUP consolidated its internal and financial structure, built up electioneering techniques and, after learning from a number of mistakes, refined its appeal to the voters, to emerge in the following decade as an equal partner to Official Unionism.[28] Initially the DUP benefited from being recognised as a full unionist party through its participation in the UUUC and subsequently from the disintegration and collapse of Vanguard. Paisley gained political prestige and experience through his involvement in the 1975 Convention. Probably because his party overtly integrated political and religious views, it could be, and was, more tightly organised and run than other unionist parties and organisations. That his political style of 'demagoguery [sic] and confronta-

26. See Flackes, *Directory*, for details of unionism in the 1970s.
27. Moxon-Browne, *Nation*, p. 96.
28. Smyth, *Paisley*, 154ff.

tion'[29] paid off can be seen in the results of the local government elections which followed the unsuccessful strike of 1977: the DUP established itself as the fourth major party (after the OUP with 29.6 per cent, the SDLP with 20.6 per cent and Alliance with 14.4 per cent) with 12.7 per cent of the vote. The strike had been a failure, diminishing the importance of the UDA, but the election results indicated that a large section of the protestant population, while not approving all of Paisley's methods, supported a hardline stand. With that success, attempts at reuniting unionism had failed for the time being, and the DUP could now challenge Official Unionism directly. This general picture was confirmed in the Westminster and European elections of 1979. In the latter Paisley was the single most successful candidate, polling 29.8 per cent of all first-preference votes.

By the end of the seventies unionism was thus divided not by its ultimate political aim of a revived Stormont similar to the old kind and the maintenance of the union with Great Britain, but by its rhetoric and appeal to different groups of voters within the protestant community. It was politically paralysed, since its political objective could not be achieved and it was therefore unable to initiate any kind of new policy.

In conclusion: the seventies saw the firm establishment of Direct Rule as a means to control the paramilitaries as well as the different political aspirations in the divided province. The first half of this policy proved to be largely successful, as in the second half of the decade the British government felt it could return this control increasingly to the RUC and 'criminalise' the military aspect of the political struggle.[30] The 'Ulsterisation' and criminalisation of security went hand in hand and exerted, it was hoped, ever greater pressure on moderate politicians to come to terms with a democratic compromise.

This did not, however, have the desired effect on politics in the province. The underlying reasons for the failure of all political initiatives are to a large extent the economic developments which reinforced the political perceptions of the early seventies. As the middle classes continued to do better, the consequences of the oil crisis and world over-capacity began to de-industrialise Northern Ireland. As a consequence the gap between the middle and working classes grew ever wider and any attempt at political modernisation of these low-income groups was forestalled by social and economic fears. It was therefore the respective working classes which continued to force

29. *Ibid.*, p. 114.

30. Boyle, Kevin, Hadden, Tom and Hillyard, Paddy, *Ten Years on in Northern Ireland. The legal control of political violence,* Nottingham 1980, 29ff.

moderate political leaders on both sides into retrenchment and made moderate political progress impossible. The centuries-old tribal certainties of the extremist groups appeared to be safer for the majority of the population than the vagueness of middle-class politicians who seemed to add political insecurities to the existing economic ones. Even the government's active attempts at ending economic discrimination with the Fair Employment Act of 1976 and its implementation through the Fair Employment Agency could thus often be seen to be counter-productive, because every job given to a catholic could not be given to a protestant. Since there were not enough jobs for both, each side soon felt discriminated against.

In June 1980 the two thousandth person died as a result of the political violence in the province, but the violence of the previous decade had by then been brought under control. It had become clear that it could not be eradicated and would cease only with a political 'solution'. But any such solution would depend on vast economic improvements and a long and gradual process of modernisation, conditions which were not only unlikely to materialise but were also actively resisted by those groups in the province whose interests were best served by the continuation of the status quo.

CHAPTER EIGHT

The Eighties: Political Stalemate and Vested Interests

The *modus vivendi* established in the later seventies held throughout the eighties despite various attempts by both the British government and the paramilitaries to take the initiative and change the political fortunes of the province. Economic difficulties, with a steady rise in unemployment, continued to uphold the status quo, as did the increasing involvement of paramilitary vested interests of both sides in the 'grey' as well as the ordinary economy.

The protestant working classes were now particularly affected by the stagnating economy, since the legal end of discrimination against catholics in employment effectively worked against the employment of protestants, which made it all the more difficult for them to accept the British and Irish proposals that power would be returned to them only if they were willing to share it with catholics.

The power vacuum in the province, created by the semi-colonial administration of Direct Rule, continued, too. With regional politics in limbo, its essential nineteenth-century character was once more highlighted, even though it used twentieth-century means to make its points. Mobs, demonstrations and paramilitaries can be seen as not so much extra-parliamentary but as functioning in place of proper democratic representation and access to power. At the same time, and ironically, the shake-up of the seventies had introduced the kind of class division between the parties of the sectarian blocs which marked early twentieth-century British politics: OUP and SDLP generally representing the middle classes and DUP and PSF standing generally for working-class support. With proportional representation as the electoral system the electorate had also begun to grow more sophisticated by giving, for instance, the DUP the vote in local and European elections, but sending the OUP to represent them in Westminster.

While the experience of the 1970s – that political violence can be effective – remained alive and the various groups had learnt to exploit the international publicity provided by the world's mass media, international tribunals and the American dimension, there was a drop in violence throughout the decade. Annual killings did not rise above 100 after 1981, and while the increased handover of security from the army to the UDR and the RUC meant that the relative number of deaths in these groups rose, the largest casualty numbers, as before, were to be found among civilians. There was a general decrease in street violence, and attendance at most traditional commemoration demonstrations remained low, even when boosted by the attendance of the international media. The professionalisation and modernisation of the police (which led to difficulties and incompatibilities when they had to cooperate with the much less well-trained Garda in the second half of the decade) allowed the army to take a secondary role, with now much-improved relations between the two forces, and kept the violence at an acceptable level.

Yet despite this improved picture, there was no promise of political progress. The economic, social and political circumstances of the region had not changed and tribal fears and apprehensions could still be aroused easily, as is most evident in the events surrounding the Hunger Strike or the Anglo-Irish Agreement. Before considering the attempts by the paramilitaries and governments to break out of the political stalemate, it is necessary to look again at the economic and social background of Northern Ireland, since it appears that the deprived nature of much of the province's social and economic life was one of the greatest obstacles to a political breakthrough.

ECONOMIC AND SOCIAL CONDITIONS

There can be little doubt that the continuing decline of the Northern Ireland economy underpinned the political stalemate and prevented a 'modernisation' of the working classes. Throughout the eighties the province remained the least affluent region in the UK and one of the most disadvantaged in the EC. Unemployment, averaging around 20 per cent for the decade, remained about twice the UK average. The staples continued to decline: the workforce in Harland and Wolff was down to less than 4000 in the mid eighties (from the steady 20,000 in the sixties), manufacturing industry had lost almost half its employees since the previous decade, and the construction industry declined at a similar rate.[1]

For most of the eighties (only during the last years of the decade were the policies of privatisation also applied in the province) governments continued the economic strategy employed in the 1970s, that is to provide subsidies, interest-free loans and purpose-built factories. Economic assistance was on offer through the Industrial Development Board (IDB) and the Local Enterprise Development Unit (LEDU). Harland and Wolff as well as Shorts survived only through substantial government aid. But the Conservative government of Margaret Thatcher stopped the large-scale expansion of the public services and it was largely as a result of this stagnation in the service sector that unemployment increased sharply. Added to this were the often successful attempts at greater productivity which allowed many firms to survive in an increasingly competitive national and international market.[2] But while productivity overall improved impressively, manufacturing output fell even lower than in Great Britain. This was to a large extent caused by the lack of outside investment in growth sectors of the manufacturing industry. Despite low wages and good employment records, the province's image abroad was not an attractive one, and became less so in the face of reduced government subsidies, which had attracted outside investment in the sixties and seventies, and contracting world trade.

Job promotion in the province since 1945, however, had largely depended on outside investment; only 8.5 per cent of this came out of the indigenous industries.[3] Furthermore, manufacturing industry was, and remained, export-orientated, so that slumps and slow growth in the world economy, and in particular in Great Britain, its main trading partner, affected it accordingly. As branches of international firms began to close after the end of the world economic boom in the mid seventies, there was little real incentive to open new ones in the slow-growth period of the eighties. Those which did come were smaller in scale and more often than not acquired existing firms rather than opened new ones; a substantial number of these were Eire based. The trend was not only towards acquisition investment, but also towards

1. Arthur and Jeffery, *Northern Ireland*, 27ff.
2. Rowthorn, in Teague, *Rhetoric*, 111ff.
3. *Ibid.*, p. 116.

low technology (as opposed to the high-tech multinational investment that other regions of the UK and Eire succeeded in attracting) which required a semi-skilled workforce.[4] Despite 'probably the best package of industrial incentives in Europe'[5] the image of the province abroad and the real political instability were as much as the slackening world economy ultimately responsible for the lack of new outside investment during the decade. The implications were that Northern Ireland had become both a 'satellite' and a 'workforce' economy,[6] dependent on public services and subvention from London to maintain its rising living standard and increased expenditure. In international comparison, it has been suggested, it had fallen to the bottom of the EEC in terms of transportable goods per head of population and was, 'in effect, an underdeveloped country kept afloat by subsidies from the UK'.[7] This argument is, however, somewhat misleading in so far as it treats the province as a country rather than a region, but it does emphasise the dependence of the region's economy on central government subventions.

By the middle of the decade public expenditure accounted for 70 per cent of GDP; 45 per cent of the workforce was directly employed in public services (44 per cent and 32 per cent in Great Britain respectively), and 21 per cent of it received unemployment benefit.[8] If one takes private services into account, about 70 per cent of the whole workforce was employed in the service industries. The main areas in which employment had expanded hugely in the late seventies were health, education, public administration and defence. The latter had increased particularly fast as part of the Ulsterisation policy of the government and benefited mostly male protestants. Increased state and private service employment also led to more part-time employment of women, which was still increasing at an annual rate of 2332 into the early 1980s.[9] After the failure of a number of industrial development schemes in the late seventies, industrial promotion through government agencies declined in relation to other areas, as did education, while the share taken up by health and housing rose, as did social security payments, emphasising the increase in unemployment.

4. Teague, Paul, 'Multinational Companies in the Northern Ireland Economy: An Outmoded Model of Industrial Development?', in Teague, *Rhetoric*, 166ff.

5. *Ibid.*, p. 172.

6. Rowthorn, in Teague, *Rhetoric*, 117f.

7. *Ibid.*, p. 122.

8. O'Dowd, Liam, 'Trends and Potential of the Service Sector in Northern Ireland', in Teague, *Rhetoric*, p. 183.

9. *Ibid.*, p. 194.

Despite the activities of the Fair Employment Agency (FEA) the eighties did not see a substantial decline in the sectarian inequality of employment. Lack of governmental urgency was only part of the reason for this. The west–east division of the province into catholics and protestants, and agriculture and industry respectively, had remained the same. It was Belfast, as the only conurbation, that attracted new industries and increased services. De-industrialisation and unemployment were most advanced in west Belfast where it was most difficult to invest because of the strength of PIRA in the area. Furthermore, insistence on fair employment may have operated against the profit principle, as it may have led (and occasionally did) to trouble on the shop floor; nor would workers be very enthusiastic to join a workforce which was traditionally dominated by the other side. This was probably the single most important obstacle, apart from the legal problem of positive discrimination not being permitted under British law, to the implementation of the MacBride principles. These were named after the late Sean MacBride, a former Irish Foreign Minister and recipient of both the Nobel Peace and the Lenin Peace Prize, and proposed tighter rules against discrimination in jobs against catholics; some US investors adopted the MacBride code as conditional for investment in Northern Ireland. Failure to implement MacBride therefore operated against the province's interest because it prevented some US investment which may have come, if the principle had been adopted there.

There had been an increase in catholic employment in the civil service and in the housing executive throughout the eighties. While this had not yet reached the decision-making grades in the civil service, it did help to continue the expansion and establishment of a larger catholic middle class, although this was still largely serving its own community.[10] The protestant monopoly on state power clearly no longer existed in the Northern Ireland of the 1980s which arguably weakened protestant trust in the state, while the increased participation of catholics did not increase their commitment to the state.

By the late eighties it was too early to assess the impact of the privatisation of Harland and Shorts which further decimated the workforce in these firms. It was equally difficult to estimate the importance of the 'grey' economy including the increased amount of racketeering by the paramilitaries. Annual income from the two main groups, PIRA and UDA, has been estimated at £10 million, but this might well have been exceeded.[11] It appears to be certain that, as legislation

10. *Ibid.*, p. 207.
11. White, Barry, *Belfast Telegraph*, 1 Sept. 1988, p. 9.

and the police caught up with some of the racketeering, the PIRA, at any rate, moved into legitimate business areas, thereby increasing its social and economic control.

It has been argued that sustained economic recovery in the province could happen only after a political settlement.[12] That may well be so, even though the structural and geographical problems would be very difficult to overcome and would probably remain. At the same time the economy would suffer from job losses in the security areas. But more importantly, the argument can easily be reversed: without the economic difficulties a political settlement might well have arrived at some stage. In other words, economics and politics, as so often in history, are interdependent. On the available evidence it looks as if on balance in the seventies and eighties the 'troubles' benefited the economy of Northern Ireland through greater government involvement in the public and private sectors.

Government, on the other hand, did not succeed in preventing the growth of unemployment and poverty and the arguably widening sectarian gulf in this area. The distribution of poverty within the province remained uneven, and the degree of deprivation in the province is concealed, if one looks at it only in regional comparative terms within the UK.[13] Differences in household structure – that is, generally larger families and fewer single parent and retired households – are as noticeable as the exceptionally low average income levels of the region. This suggests, given the growing income of the middle classes, that working-class families and in particular the unemployed had to cater for greater needs in larger households with a substantially lower income than in other poor regions of the UK. While there had been a greater improvement in housing since the early 1970s than in the UK as a whole, Northern Ireland had previously been a particularly backward area in this respect, and throughout the eighties there was still a correspondence between poor housing and unemployment and poverty.[14] As in the past, catholics remained over-represented among the low paid and unemployed (this is, however, based on the 1981 census figures; there is as yet little else to go on for the eighties), but there was a suggestion that the protestant advantage had begun to disappear among the sixteen to twenty-five age group. This may well have continued with the further decline of traditionally protestant-dominated industries. There is a clear link between areas of high unemployment

12. Rowthorn, in Teague, *Rhetoric*, 132ff.

13. Rowthorn, Bob, 'Unemployment: The Widening Sectarian Gap', *Fortnight*, 16 Dec. 1985; Gafikin and Morrissey, in Teague, *Rhetoric*, pp. 136–59.

14. *Ibid.*, p. 149.

and social deprivation and communal violence or clashes with the state forces, west Belfast having the worst concentration of unemployment, low pay and juvenile offences. With the fragmentation of traditional political forms under Direct Rule, localised poverty often gave rise to the emergence of community groups whose range of success and effect, however, remained rather limited.

Research on people's attitudes and the impact of violence on their mental well-being, in particular that of children, has continued and largely confirms the picture given for the seventies.[15] It has been stressed that distorted perceptions can arise out of factors such as high unemployment, potential violence and the overcrowding which the poor housing stock (which remained the worst in the UK) enforced. All of these apparently often lead to psychological disorder. The evidence suggests, however, that this has little to do with the 'troubles'. A household survey in 1983 revealed that 80 per cent of correspondents considered unemployment a greater problem than the 'troubles'. A Gallup Poll value survey of the mid eighties found that the population of the province defined itself as 'happier' than in any other area in Europe (39 per cent said they were 'very happy'). This appeared to confirm research done earlier in the decade in which the people of Northern Ireland said they were exceptionally satisfied with their present lives and were generally optimistic about the future.[16] In explanation it has been convincingly suggested that communal unrest allows people to play a role in society, even when they are unemployed. As outlined in the previous chapter, the conservative nature of society provided a social network of relatives and friends which provided stability. One might go further and argue that the ODC rate (Ordinary Decent Crime, now the official description used by the police) remained comparatively low precisely because people distinguished clearly between ordinary and political crime. This would imply, however, that the criminalisation policy of the British government had not worked, that is to say, most people in the province appeared to consider politically motivated crime as at least partly legitimate.[17] This in turn allowed paramilitary activities to continue. The late seventies and early eighties, indeed, saw one of the largest PIRA initiatives to revive its flagging fortunes through the Dirty Protest and the Hunger Strike.

15. Trew, Karen, 'Psychological Well-Being in Northern Ireland', in Ward, Alan J.(ed.), *Northern Ireland. Living with the Crisis*, London 1987, pp. 16–45.

16. Belfrage, Sally, *The Crack. A Belfast Year*, London 1988, p. 407; Trew, in Ward, pp. 23, 29.

17. Belfrage, *Crack*, *passim*.

PARAMILITARY INITIATIVES: THE H-BLOCK PROTEST AND THE HUNGER STRIKE

In the late seventies the successes of the RUC and the army had forced PIRA into a substantial reorganisation. Small active service units, often only two or three people, replaced the larger companies. This increased internal security by keeping information on plans and targets to very small numbers involved in any particular action, and thereby tightened control of the active membership. A further back-up for this policy was the 'policing' of republican areas, and the exercise of punishment, mostly in the form of 'knee-capping', for social crimes. Official policy of Provisional Sinn Fein (PSF) was at this stage still dictated largely by the Southern leaders who dominated the annual Ard Fheis (congress), and consisted primarily of the demand for British withdrawal which was to be followed by the establishment of a Four-Province Federal Ireland. How the first step would lead to the second was never made quite clear. Up to 1980 the official policy, proposed and introduced by the president, Ruairi O'Bradaigh, had been the achievement of a phased withdrawal of Britain from Northern Ireland. Then it was changed to immediate withdrawal, and a year later the whole previous federal policy was abandoned. The idea of a federal solution had been meant as a concession to the protestants in the North who were thus to have a greater say in their province. But the rising Northern leaders (Gerry Adams became Sinn Fein president in 1982) were no longer willing to compromise. By 1981 the Ard Fheis decided on the policy that Danny Morrison, PSF's director of publicity, described as 'a ballot paper in this hand and an Armalite in this'.[18] The only real policy, however, remained the taking of power in Northern Ireland, and little thought went into the question of how this power was going to be exercised once it had been acquired. While this may appear a strange programme for a political party, it does display a considerable amount of pragmatic realism. Even if PSF and PIRA had succeeded in their policy of 'Brits out', that could not have won them majority support in the province, not to mention the rest of the island. But the official arrival of this policy signified the arrival of Northern leaders and policies and the abdication of Southern attempts to control the North.

The reason for this change in direction and personnel must be

18. See Flackes, W.D. and Elliott, Sydney, *Northern Ireland. A Political Directory, 1968–88*, Belfast 1989, p. 239; Bishop and Mallie, *IRA*, 300ff.

sought to a great extent in the success of the Hunger Strike of republican prisoners in the previous years. This originated in the IRA's response to the British policy of criminalisation, which included a phased withdrawal of special category status for political prisoners who considered themselves prisoners of war. It manifested itself in the new, purpose-built H-blocks (so called because of the physical shape of the blocks) at the Maze Prison, near Belfast, formerly Long Kesh, which were ready by the mid seventies. Previously prisoners had been allowed their own organisation and discipline, indeed much like prisoners of war. Long Kesh had served as a training school for many former inmates where they learned military discipline and gained political insights. Most prisoners had been politicised through this. The British government's decision to deny them their own evaluation, and the likely result of a general lowering of morale within the prisons as well as in the movement outside, demanded some form of resistance. Decisions on how to fight against this policy were left to the prisoners themselves. Their refusal to wear prison uniforms led to the 'blanket' protest – by the end of 1976 200 men and women were 'on the blanket'.[19] All this naturally led to tension with the wardens, and prison officers became official targets for the IRA (eighteeen were killed between 1976 and 1980). The prisoners' refusal to leave their cells for fear of being beaten up by the wardens when using the washrooms escalated the protest into the 'Dirty Protest'. As wardens refused to clean the cells unless prisoners left them, the cells soon resembled cloacae. By 1978 up to 300 prisoners were on the Dirty Protest.

All this made excellent news copy, and soon the world's eyes were on the H-block prisoners: the Catholic Church, the USA, and the European Court of Human Rights took notice. The Dirty Protest, while popular with the prisoners themselves because it generated optimism through its publicity success, did not succeed in changing the government's policy, however. By 1979 a consensus emerged within the prison that the fight should be escalated into a hunger strike. Bobby Sands, the republican public relations officer within the Maze, enlisted the help of the movement outside, and in particular of the H-Block Committee and Danny Morrison. By the autumn the strike was organised and its publicity impact was kept very much in mind; in order to gain support as widely as possible six of the first seven hunger strikers who were selected came from each of the six Northern counties, and one was an INLA man. While London remained adamantly opposed to the prisoners' demands to wear their own clothes, the right

19. Bishop and Mallie, *IRA*, 278ff.

to refuse prison work, to receive one parcel from outside per week, to be granted free association with one another and to have the remission lost through the protest returned to them, the offer of talks from the Northern Ireland Office (NIO) sounded promising enough to have the strike stopped. But negotiations failed and the strike was resumed in March, prisoners now going on strike in stages to keep the momentum going and to increase the dramatic effect.

Perhaps the most important event during the whole Hunger Strike, which eventually lost the lives of ten of its participants, was the death of the MP for Fermanagh and South Tyrone. It allowed Bobby Sands, the leader of the strikers, to stand as an Anti-H-Block candidate in the by-election. It was his success in this election which made Sinn Fein consider the use of the ballot box in addition to the armed struggle. Each death in the Maze helped to retain international attention and led to rioting in the streets of Belfast and Derry on a scale not seen since the early seventies. The well-staged funerals seemed to help to consolidate the nationalist community in their support for PIRA and PSF. While the strike was watched by PSF with ambivalent feelings (its main momentum came from within the prison, and it did fall apart in the end without achieving very much), it did appear to boost republican fortunes. Now the IRA could once again be portrayed abroad as consisting of freedom fighters, while at home PSF for the first time felt some confidence in offering itself as an alternative to the SDLP as representatives of the nationalist community.

This completed the split in the catholic community into more moderate and more extremist groupings, thereby mirroring earlier developments in the protestant population. The 1982 Assembly election gave PSF over 10 per cent of the vote and five of the seventy-eight seats, all at the expense of the SDLP, thus confirming the success of its new policy. The implications of this change in policy meant that PSF had to become more attractive, better organised, and absorb more of the resources of the republican movement. Adams often had to perform a balancing act in order not to alienate PIRA, since the rationale of the movement, without which neither of its parts could continue to exist, remained violence. The greater visibility of PSF led to an influx of young people and ex-prisoners, and by the mid eighties its organisation had expanded downward to local party level. Even though there was a considerable overlap with membership of its senior partner PIRA, PSF had become a distinct organisation. It was rewarded by the electorate in the general election of 1983 with 13.4 per cent of the vote, making it the fourth strongest party in the province.

The initial impact of this success on PIRA was a drop in membership and activity. It was much more expensive to run a party and pay for electioneering than to run the IRA. In order to make the party more attractive robberies had to be cut down and the movement had to rely less on protection rackets and more on its increasing legitimate businesses and on tax fraud.[20] Money from the US had increased manyfold as a result of the Hunger Strike but was still not enough, and could not be counted on in the long run. Through the combined efforts of John Hume and the British and Irish governments the American political establishment had turned against the IRA from the mid seventies and subsequently the FBI had infiltrated Noraid (also NAC, Irish Northern Aid Committee) and prevented a number of arms deals. Furthermore, the willingness of the Americans to contribute to 'the cause' depended very much on the promotion of 'the struggle' as being successful at home. Successful RUC infiltrations as well as a number of 'super-grass' trials often made this difficult.[21]

PSF's vote in the European election of 1984 held, however, and the party began to build up a network of advice centres which were offering community services and help in getting redress from the state. This policy paid off in the 1985 district council elections when they secured 11.8 per cent of the vote and fifty-nine council seats. As security in the cities had grown more sophisticated, PIRA had been forced into the countryside. There had been a decline in the number of security forces killed and the campaign in England was renewed, culminating in the bombing of the Conservative Party Conference in Brighton in 1984.

But the SDLP, worried about the inroads into their electorate, fought back. Not only did they succed in making gun-running from the USA ever more difficult, but they also persuaded the Southern government to take the initiative in the form of the New Ireland Forum (NIF, see below) which was intended to rally all Irish political opinion against the IRA. Its efforts, together with the negative impression made by PIRA's new means of raising funds – the kidnapping of prominent businessmen – succeeded in rousing public sympathy in the Republic. While the NIF had worried PSF and PIRA, the Hillsborough or Anglo-Irish Agreement (AIA, see below) did not. But the voters, initially at any rate, were impressed by the SDLP's success, and PSF's vote dropped considerably (down to 6.6 per cent) in the following by-elections of 1986.

20. *Ibid.*, 232ff; Adams, James, *Secret Armies*, London 1987, pp. 34–40; see also Holland, Jack, *The American Çonnection*, Dublin 1989.

21. White, Barry, *John Hume. Statesman of the Troubles*, Belfast 1984, 183ff.

This put increased pressure on Adams to concentrate on the armed section of the movement and divert funds back to them. He translated the SDLP's successes into the need for creating a larger and younger following in the South. Abstentionism was therefore abandoned in the Republic, too. In the 1987 Westminster elections PSF's vote dropped by 2 per cent compared with 1983, again benefiting the SDLP. Talks between Adams and the SDLP in the following year were, not surprisingly, without success; if PSF dropped its support for violence, it could easily have been absorbed into the moderate constitutional party. The broadcasting ban of late 1988 deprived the party of much-needed public promotion and further limited its political appeal. Nationalist pressure from the South mounted and called for a reduction in accidental civilian deaths. The security services' successes, however, had deprived PIRA of much expert personnel which made the avoidance of violent accidental death more difficult.

By the end of the decade PIRA and PSF were thus caught in their own existential trap: violence was the 'cutting edge. Without it the issue of Ireland would not be an issue.'[22] A PSF in pursuit merely of the ballot box would have been a contradiction in terms and would soon have led to its demise. Therefore both violence and electioneering had to be continued against all odds. Furthermore, the continuation of violence had been made much easier by the renewal of large supplies of weaponry and semtex explosives from Libya. This guaranteed an almost unlimited supply for the foreseeable future and ensured the survival of the movement with it.[23]

The protestant paramilitaries during the eighties mostly responded to IRA and government initiatives. The UDA and its illegal arm, now naming itself Ulster Freedom Fighters (UFF), consolidated its financial base, largely through protection rackets – an estimated £3 million per year by 1988 – and underlined the unionist politicians' opposition to the NIF and the AIA.[24] The UFF committed a number of sectarian murders in response to perceived catholic and IRA successes, in particular during the Hunger Strike. The UDA continued its attempt at political participation through a new party, the Ulster Loyalist Democratic Party (ULDP). While it never attracted many votes, it appeared to represent a grass-roots desire for some form of accommodation with catholics. In 1987 the UDA itself published a programme underlining this approach, 'Common Sense', which suggested an all-party coali-

22. Gerry Adams, quoted in Bishop and Mallie, *IRA*, p. 358.
23. McKittrick, David, *Despatches from Belfast*, Belfast 1989, 83ff.
24. Flackes and Elliott, *Directory*, 275ff.

tion, a Bill of Rights and a written constitution for the province. While this was widely welcomed, nothing came of it since the UDA supported the unionists' demand for an abandonment of the AIA before any negotiations could commence. Thus by the late eighties the military within the UDA had gained the upper hand again: Andy Tyrie was ousted from the leadership and replaced by an inner council of six members exercising collective control and promising a military campaign against PIRA. In practice protestant paramilitaries were thus in the same dilemma that had developed in the seventies for all protestants: unless they were willing to accept power sharing, they could not hope to regain any power. Meanwhile they could only respond to either catholic or government initiatives.

BRITISH INITIATIVES: FROM THE NORTHERN IRELAND ASSEMBLY TO THE ANGLO-IRISH AGREEMENT

By the mid seventies (see above, p. 160) British governments had accepted that a 'solution' to the province's problems could not be imposed from Westminster and that any 'Irish Dimension' could compel unionists to rebel against London. This bipartisan policy began to be challenged from the turn of the decade by the effects of the Hunger Strike on the position of the SDLP within Northern Ireland politics as well as on international, and in particular US opinion. For a time the bipartisanship of the approach also suffered as Labour, under pressure because of the lost election of 1979, allowed its left wing to introduce a PSF-friendly policy which equated the end of partition with the arrival of socialism.[25] While this was not a very consistent policy since it contradicted Labour's official stand of 'unity by consent', it did appease its left and appeared to promise a domestic lever against the Conservative government.

By November 1978, worried by the IRA's success in attracting publicity through their protests at the Maze, the SDLP had called for a conference involving the British and Irish governments as well as the two communities in Northern Ireland. When Mrs Thatcher came to

25. Boyce, D.G., *The Irish Question and British Politics, 1868–1986*, London 1988, p. 117.

power half a year later, pressure for this increased with the United States adding their weight.[26] Governments in Dublin had come to realise over the years the threat to the stability of the Republic from the continuation of the Northern conflict. While Anglo-Irish relations had remained uneasy about the issue, both governments successfully lobbied in the USA to control fund-raising for the IRA. In May 1980 the British and Irish Prime Ministers met for the first time to explore possible cooperation over Northern Ireland. The most urgent problem for both was cross-border security, and meetings between the RUC and the Irish police, the Garda Siochana, ensued. Thatcher and Haughey, who had also become Taoiseach in the previous year, met again in December and decided to continue twice-yearly meetings into the future. As a follow-up an inter-governmental council was established to provide a forum for future discussion.[27]

These developments were much to the liking of Charles Haughey who came from a Northern family with strong republican traditions. After the allegations of gun-running against him in 1970 (see above, p. 121) he had been sacked from the Lynch government, but returned to office in charge of the Health Ministry in the new Lynch government of 1977 and succeeded him as Taoiseach and leader of Fianna Fail (FF) in 1979. He changed FF's old Sinn Fein policies on Northern Ireland from outright opposition to the British presence on the island to one of cooperation, albeit to the same end: Britain's ultimate withdrawal. After the initial rapprochement with Margaret Thatcher relations with FF deteriorated because of Britain's handling of the Hunger Strike and subsequent British policy initiatives in the North, initially including the AIA. But when Haughey's FF returned to office in 1987 relations and cooperation improved again.

Parallel with Britain's creation of institutionalised links of communication with the Southern government came a new initiative by James Prior, Secretary of State for Northern Ireland from September 1981 – 'rolling devolution', which was eventually enshrined in the Northern Ireland Act, 1982.[28] It envisaged the election of an assembly with initially only consultative functions, but eventually devolving a number of government departments to its control. Recognising the non-democratic nature of Direct Rule, this was hoped to add to and increase regional political participation in it. It would, furthermore, allow the minority population an increased say without alienating the majority and would provide the stability in the province that would attract

26. Bew and Patterson, *British State*, p. 112.
27. Arthur and Jeffery, *Northern Ireland*, p. 15.
28. Flackes and Elliott, *Directory*, p. 367.

outside investment. It would in the first instance have powers of scrutiny, to allow local politicians to question and get information from the governmental departments in the province.

The only party which whole-heartedly welcomed this development was the Alliance. Both unionist parties had reservations about the cross-community nature of the assembly and the implication of ultimate 'power sharing' which it seemed to embody. The SDLP and the Haughey government in Dublin considered it unworkable, while PSF was planning to use the elections for it to oust the constitutional nationalists from their prominent position. As a result the nationalist parties fought the elections for the assembly on 20 October 1982 on an abstentionist platform and only the Unionists and the Alliance took their seats, with the consequence that the main purpose of the assembly was defeated. Its continued existence (until June 1986, when it was dissolved), while not leading to any real power, at least gave all parties access to government departments and enabled them to offer advice on draft legislation.[29]

The SDLP had meanwhile realised that the British government was not going to force the unionists into cooperation, and it therefore hoped to salvage its fortunes against the rising PSF by enlisting the help of the South. Out of this initiative the New Ireland Forum was born, a conference of four nationalist parties: Fianna Fail, Fine Gael, the Irish Labour Party and the SDLP. They reported in May 1984 and offered three options for solving the Northern problem: a united thirty-two-county state, a federal arrangement, or joint authority within Northern Ireland by Dublin and London.[30]

Thatcher's response of 'out, out, out' to the three options was pragmatic enough. Neither the one-sided nationalist historical analysis offered in the report nor the unrealistic demands it made were acceptable to Britain, and in the province itself were approved only by the SDLP. Yet Britain recognised in the third option a substantial change in Dublin's attitude, namely the acceptance and indeed insistence that Britain should be 'in' rather than 'out' as PSF would have it. If joint responsibility was an option, then Britain could safely pursue an 'Irish Dimension' and thereby reduce American pressure for further initiatives. The British Labour Party welcomed the Forum report as a step towards a united Ireland while remaining unclear about how this could be reconciled with their 'unity by consent'.[31]

29. For a detailed account of the working of the assembly see: O'Leary, Cornelius, Elliott, Sydney and Wilford, R.A., *The Northern Ireland Assembly, 1982–1986. A Constitutional Experiment*, Belfast 1988.

30. Flackes and Elliott, *Directory*, p. 200.

31. Boyce, *Irish Question*, 121ff.

In response to the Forum report there had been a number of publications in Britain proposing more positive constitutional options most of which appeared to support an 'Irish Dimension'.[32] Meanwhile the inter-governmental meetings between London and Dublin continued and in the wake of the Forum report civil servants began discussions which culminated in the Anglo-Irish Agreement (AIA) which was signed at the former seat of the province's Governor, Hillsborough, on 15 November 1985. In constitutional terms the AIA succeeded in squaring the circle: Dublin did not concede its claim to the six counties and unionists were guaranteed a veto against unification as long as they remained in the majority in the province. It did not include any of the demands made in the Forum report but talked, in suitably vague terms throughout, about 'achieving lasting peace and stability . . . by peaceful means and through agreement'. It stressed cooperation and the joint fight against terrorism.[33] By setting up an Intergovernmental Council both governments conceded each other's interest and responsibility in the province, but stressed that neither's sovereignty was impinged on. The Irish government was encouraged to 'put forward views on proposals' for major legislation concerning Northern Ireland, while Britain did not promise that they would necessarily be taken into account (Article 5). The Council would consider security (Art. 7), legal matters (Art. 8) and in particular would further 'Cross-Border Cooperation on Security, Economic, Social and Cultural Matters'. While it had no 'operational responsibilities', the Chief Constable of the RUC and the Commissioner of the Garda Siochana would cooperate closely. Further developments in the direction of the establishment of an Anglo-Irish parliament were left to the future and the parliaments in London and Dublin.

In political terms the AIA was an extraordinary achievement for Britain. Without conceding anything except the obvious, namely that the Republic's government had an interest in the North, the British government had enrolled Dublin's support for its policy in the province, that is to encourage constitutional, moderate groups, to further the aim of devolution on the basis of 'power sharing' or at least some political cross-community cooperation, and to hasten the defeat of, or at least fight against, terrorism. Playing on the Republic's fear that terrorism might easily spill over the border, it had regained the initiative in the province, appeased the United States, and showed that it would and could stand up to unionists. It thus helped to undermine

32. O'Leary, *Assembly*, 187ff; Boyce, *ibid.*

33. The text of the Agreement can be found in Arthur and Jeffery, *Northern Ireland*, pp. 99–108.

PSF to the benefit of the SDLP, and while seriously offending unionists, had kept the terms of the Agreement sufficiently vague to prevent a serious protestant rebellion.

The AIA was in no sense a new policy for Northern Ireland; it simply proposed to continue Direct Rule until 'power sharing' was forthcoming. But it now enlisted Dublin's active support for this policy. This made it much more difficult for Fitzgerald or Haughey, who became Taoiseach again in 1987, to criticise any of Britain's policies in the province. The Agreement was welcomed in the Republic and did not threaten either its system or the constitution, as a civil war in the North or pressure for actual unification might have done. It thus largely neutralised Southern criticism of British policies in Northern Ireland and had a similar effect on US pressure.

It was Garret Fitzgerald, the leader of the Fine Gael party in the Republic since 1977, who had been the driving force behind a more conciliatory policy towards the North. His mother was an Ulster presbyterian and he therefore had close family links in the province and a better understanding of unionists than Haughey and Fianna Fail. He had launched the NIF in April 1983 and had been very disappointed by its reception in London. But it was at least in part due to his continuing pressure on both Washington and Westminster that the AIA was finally signed by Thatcher and himself, even though it would be Haughey, who was initially opposed to any cooperation with Britain on Northern Ireland, who collected any eventual benefits.

In British domestic terms the Agreement re-established the bipartisan approach to Northern Ireland; only the extreme right of the Conservative Party and the far left of Labour rejected it.[34] Mainstream politics, and indeed the general public, embraced the AIA as a reasonable and a new and successful initiative which would eventually succeed in forcing protestants to be 'rational' and 'tolerant'. Furthermore, it would help to undermine the support for PSF and PIRA, thus furthering the anti-terrorist fight. In so far as the British public had any views about the divided communities of Northern Ireland, the AIA appeared to them the recipe which 'Ulster' should adopt, freeing them of the need to pay any further attention to the problems of the province.[35]

In the Republic, too, the Agreement was generally welcomed. It preserved the aspiration of the constitution for Irish unity, allowing the anti-partitionist rhetoric to continue while also giving some guarantee

34. Boyce, *Irish Question*, p. 123.
35. *Ibid.*, p. 124 and footnote 37.

that the North's problems would not seep South.[36] It thus helped to maintain the ambivalence of Irish politics towards the province (see above, pp. 151ff). The only group which rejected it was, of course, Sinn Fein. But the Irish election results of 1987, in which it polled only 1.9 per cent of the vote despite a large electoral presence (twenty-one of twenty-four constituencies were contested) and its new non-abstentionist strategy, made it negligible even as a pressure group for the main parties.

For Britain the achievements of the AIA lay primarily in the international field: it reduced pressure from the USA by getting active cooperation from the Republic of Ireland without having had to concede any sovereignty. In the province the AIA was aimed at gaining greater support for the constitutional nationalism of the SDLP and to undermine the bullet and ballot policy of PSF. This was, by and large, successful. It was further substantiated by the gradually improving cooperation between the RUC and the Garda, the increasingly successful army intelligence and surveillance, and finally by serious investigations of the 'legitimate' PSF businesses.[37]

The cooperation between Northern and Southern police forces did not, however, progress as fast and as successfully as the British government had hoped. By 1988 the RUC comprised 8250 men and women with a 3000-strong full-time Reserve. It was a very well-trained force with its own anti-terrorist units which included covert operations and full computer-based intelligence. Peace-keeping was entirely in the hands of the police; the UDR and the army provided back-up when and where necessary. There was full cooperation between all security forces by then. Faster progress in cross-border security simply could not be achieved, because the Garda Siochana was neither as well equipped nor as well trained as the RUC, nor did it have the institutional independence from political interference.[38]

PIRA's backlash against the success of the AIA meant that greater army numbers (10,000 by the end of 1988) had to be employed in particularly vulnerable areas, that is the border, mostly to interrupt cross-border armaments movements and, often with help from the SAS, to prevent PIRA operations. Despite RUC successes in the urban centres, and particularly in Belfast, PIRA's destructive potential remained high as it succeeded in remaining well supplied with explo-

36. Mair, Peter, 'Breaking the Nationalist Mould: The Irish Republic and the Anglo-Irish Agreement', in Teague, *Rhetoric*, pp. 81–110.

37. Adams, *Secret*, *passim*.

38. Flackes and Elliott, *Directory*, 386f; Ryder, Chris, *The RUC: A Force under Fire*, London 1989, *passim*.

sives, arms and ammunition, largely from Libyan sources. The British government further tried to control republican activities in 1988 by its ban on broadcasting for members of proscribed organisations and supporters of violence, and by requiring a declaration of the renunciation of violence from candidates in local elections.[39]

By the end of the decade the British government had thus still not succeeded in establishing consensus government. Direct Rule was firmly, and largely successfully, in place. It was now actively supported by the Dublin government. The governing of the province remained semi-colonial, despite the fact that the Conservative Party began to organise there in 1989. Direct Rule would cease only once political cooperation between catholics and protestants was achieved. But neither PSF nor any of the unionist parties was willing to share power and the AIA thus served only the interests and purposes of the SDLP in the region itself.

LIVING WITH THE ANGLO-IRISH AGREEMENT: REGIONAL POLITICS

While attempting to make it clear to unionists that their former privileged political position in the province had ended, the AIA was, of course, not guaranteeing the SDLP more than a guard against the encroachment of PSF. Only if the unionists were actively to accept power sharing could John Hume and his party hope ever to have a real say in Northern Ireland's politics again. Hume has often been considered the main architect of the Agreement and he certainly seems to have had a considerable say in its origins.[40] The SDLP's response to both the signing of the Agreement at Hillsborough and to the protestant protest against it, however, highlights both the dilemma the party found itself in and Hume's shortcomings as a politician.

Hume had succeeded Gerry Fitt as party leader in 1979, when the latter felt his party was moving towards nationalism and losing its social democratic and labour credentials in the process. Despite Hume's denials there can be little doubt that he felt forced by the consolida-

39. Adams, *Secret, passim*; Ryder, *RUC, passim*; Flackes and Elliott, pp. 416, 396.

40. For example White, *Hume*; McKittrick, *Despatches*, p. 9; O'Dowd, in Teague, p. 27.

tion of PIRA to move in that direction. This view was soon reinforced by the success of the Hunger Strike and the emergence of PSF as a serious election contender for the SDLP's vote. Ever since, Hume had cleverly performed a balancing act between the rejection from unionists and the pressure from the nationalist extremists. By refusing to cooperate with any British initiative that would not guarantee power sharing as of right, he eventually had his principle accepted and guaranteed, but at the price of having real political participation postponed for a lengthy time. He left socialism to the small Workers Party, the former Official IRA, and incorporated constitutional nationalism, represented in the party by Seamus Mallon, his deputy leader.

The signing of the Agreement at Hillsborough was a triumph for the SDLP, and it was only after the much stronger than expected negative response from unionists that Hume felt compelled to placate protestants by stressing the potential for reconciliation in the accord. But even though protestant politicians would not listen to him, the SDLP gained two marginal seats from them in the next Westminster elections, both of which also showed a clear decline in the PSF vote. Hume tried to follow this up with talks with its president, Gerry Adams, and attempted to persuade him that the implication of the AIA was that the attitude of the British government had changed with regard to Northern Ireland, and that violence was no longer necessary. Not surprisingly nothing came of these talks except the confirmation to unionists that PSF and the SDLP were merely different sides of the same coin, both trying to deprive them of their perceived democratic right to rule the province. By the late eighties catholic public opinion did not appear to have been very impressed by the results of the Agreement, nor did they expect to gain very much from it.[41]

Hume's conviction that the two cultural traditions needed to be recognised and reconciled, which differed markedly from the republican extremists who held unionism to be artificial and a concept which would disappear with the British presence on the island, did not permit any doubt as to the rationality or desirability of this view. This was its limitation and ultimate political short-sightedness, since the unionist community not only did not want his kind of reconciliation but feared it as its final defeat. Hume's international success in portraying the 'Ulster Problem' as solvable, if only the protestants would be reasonable and rational, was thus based on a false assumption. Historical experience and its specific interpretation in the light of more recent events did not allow unionists to trust nationalists. The SDLP's

41. Flackes and Elliott, *Directory*, p. 257.

dilemma arose out of this: it depended on the Anglo-Irish Agreement to fend off PSF on the one hand and to achieve power sharing on the other. For their part, unionists were compelled to bracket both nationalist groupings together as one and to see the AIA as the achievement of both, adding to their inability to accept it. It can therefore also be argued, as it has been,[42] that the AIA was less a success for the SDLP than testimony of its failure in the province's politics.

It was thus Hume's apparent inability to understand the nature of the protestant cultural tradition, while recognising its existence, that made him underestimate the negative unifying effect of the Agreement on the protestant community. The British government had been better prepared, having at long last begun to understand unionists a little better. It appeared to have expected more of a backlash than protestants could in the end muster.[43] But for the first time since 1974 the AIA provided unionists with an anti-nationalist issue on which the vast majority of protestants could agree.

Not surprisingly, unionists had not been consulted in the run-up to the signing of the Agreement. After Thatcher's rejection of the New Forum report and the continuing existence of the assembly, unionists had probably considered themselves safe from another attempt at forcing them into power sharing. The AIA put an end to this relative security. Unionists were shocked and outraged. Only a fortnight before the signing of the accord, Molyneaux and Paisley, the respective leaders of the OUP and the DUP, had warned the Prime Minister against any consultative role for the Republic in the affairs of Northern Ireland. Soon afterwards a campaign was launched to set up 'Ulster Clubs' across the province in readiness for any such development. After the Agreement was signed all Unionist Westminster MPs resigned their seats in protest, and a massive demonstration in Belfast was attended by an estimated 100,000 people.

James Henry Molyneaux had become leader of the OUP in 1979, soon after Paisley's triumph in the first European election. Under his leadership the party had to fend off the challenge from the DUP in the face of what looked like ever closer cooperation between London and Dublin. As a result Official Unionism moved away from Westminster and became more than ever before centred in the province. Molyneaux adopted a much more conscious public profile than any of his predecessors. He was generally successful in holding the corrosion

42. Aughey, Arthur, *Under Siege: Ulster Unionism and the Anglo-Irish Agreement*, Belfast 1989, p. viii.

43. McKittrick, *Despatches*, p. 22.

of the party's grass-roots support by the DUP, and in several instances even succeeded in reversing the trend back in favour of the OUP.

In the by-elections of January 1986, following the AIA, the Unionists increased their vote, gaining protestant votes from the Alliance Party, even though they lost one seat to the SDLP. Molyneaux's personal majority in Lagan Valley almost doubled from over 17,000 to almost 30,000. On 3 March a 'Day of Action' was organised, leading to strikes, disruptions in commerce and communication, barricades manned by masked loyalists and some rioting at night in Belfast. The OUP and DUP, united in their desire to destroy the Agreement, condemned the resulting violence and intimidation but demanded the abolition of the Agreement and refused any further cooperation with the government. Even the RUC, which had tried to maintain law and order, were branded as representatives of Westminster, and several policemen and their families were driven out of their homes by loyalists.[44] The unionist protest, under the slogan of 'Ulster Says No', gradually modified its demands from scrapping the Agreement to suspending it, after which, they said, they would be willing to talk to the SDLP about devolution and power sharing. When the Secretary of State, Tom King, refused this, the ways of the OUP and the DUP parted over the form they wanted the protest to take. Molyneaux and the OUP wanted to mobilise passive resistance and lawful demonstrations, while the DUP, with Peter Robinson, its hard line deputy leader, initially more prominent than Paisley himself, wanted to make the province ungovernable. But despite a great deal of rioting, sectarian clashes, fights with the RUC, and the dissolution of the assembly in June 1986, active support for the campaign began to decline after the marching season of the summer, while the rhetoric of it remained unchanged to the end of the eighties.

Since no unionist could agree to the AIA, there were only two options for opposition to it: the lawful and democratic one through elections and demonstrations which was followed by the OUP, and the revival of the 1912 inheritance which appeared to have worked in 1974 and which was taken up by the DUP. Neither of these succeeded. By 1987 the DUP had given up any notion of rebellion and physical resistance, and when the 1980s closed, the AIA was still in existence.

The division of unionism on how to resist the Agreement can to a large extent be explained in terms of the final political aim of the two unionist parties. Since the early eighties Paisley had supported devol-

44. Ryder, *RUC*, 317ff.

ution as the only chance protestants would ever have of holding power again in the province and as a bulwark against a united Ireland.[45] It thus made sense to fight the state by any means available if it defied the wishes of the majority in the region. But Molyneaux, to some extent under the influence of Enoch Powell, Unionist MP for South Down between 1974 and 1987, had opted for integration, which made an argument for violent resistance to the state into which he wanted fully to be integrated that much more difficult. Ironically, the OUP was itself divided on the issue and the majority within the party was probably devolutionist which made it easier for them to support, at least rhetorically, the DUP's more violent stand.[46]

The difficulty about 'bringing the Agreement down' was that there was very little specific to bring down. As opposed to 1974 the form of government had not changed and the Northern Ireland Office could not be defeated short of defeating Westminster. There was a limited physical manifestation of the AIA, and the little that existed was duly attacked: the Secretary of State, the police, the administrative Secretariat at Maryfield in Belfast. Furthermore, there was no obvious and manifest increase in catholic power. In other words, in practice the AIA changed very little in the life of the province, which may have disillusioned catholics if they had ever hoped for much from the Agreement, but by the same token allowed protestants to relax a little. It is this which largely accounts for the rapid decline of much active hostility to the Agreement in the late eighties.

While the AIA united all unionists in opposition to it, it was also vague enough to frustrate their attempts to resist it, since it was not meant to introduce a new policy for the province. The power vacuum thus continued and in one respect at least regional politics in Northern Ireland had come full circle: as catholics had said no to unionist rule in the twenties, so unionists now said no to Direct Rule from London with an 'Irish Dimension'. Unionists now were as united against the AIA as catholics then had been against partition and unionist rule, and they had equally good reasons for their behaviour: in each instance a substantial group was excluded from full participation in the state. Both acted on principle and out of fear, expecting the worst from the respective rulers and fearing that any compromise, in the form of active participation in whatever diminished role in order to increase and improve that role, would indeed compromise not only their respective principles but also their ultimate chance of power.

45. Aughey, *Siege*, p. 116; O'Malley, *Uncivil Wars*, pp. 169–203.
46. McKittrick, *Despatches*, pp. 58–65.

The impact of the AIA on the province's politics did not therefore result in a substantial change. While stabilising the political fortunes of the SDLP without necessarily improving them, it had no real impact on either the substance of the PSF electorate or on the violence of the PIRA. It increased the uncertainties of unionists whose desire to remain full members of the United Kingdom was officially made conditional on a majority in Northern Ireland continuing to support that wish (ironically, in view of their insistence on majority rule). There could therefore be little expectation that unionists were likely in the foreseeable future to give way to the pressures for power sharing with the SDLP. Direct Rule was thus likely to continue in largely unchanged form with hardly any devolved powers even at local level.

The eighties re-established Northern Ireland as a constitutionally specific region within the UK whose citizens were not considered to have equal political rights with those in the rest of the state. The uncertainty of its status within the UK was confirmed by the AIA with at least the underlying idea of getting rid of the territory altogether. Britain had found that she had to accept the methods and arguments of her opponents: violence and the ballot box on the one hand and nationalism on the other. Her own outdated democratic system had proved no help in establishing democracy in the province, even though she introduced proportional representation there. The economic, social and political problems of the region probably gave the British government little choice. As PIRA and PSF had succeeded in getting support and supplies from the USA, and as the SDLP tried to counterbalance that and had succeeded in persuading Dublin to act on its behalf, Britain could reduce the pressure only by something like the AIA, even if that implied a rebuke to unionists and made their cooperation even more uncertain. The eighties thus finished as they had begun; the twin policies of encouraging moderation through support of the constitutional sections of each community and the fight against the extremists of both sides had only confirmed the political stalemate. In the political turmoil of the previous two decades the extremists, however, can arguably be seen as the winners, since they succeeded in establishing themselves firmly in the economic, social and political fabric of the province's society, and it remained in their interest to maintain the status quo.

The twenty years of the most recent 'troubles' in Northern Ireland have allowed all political groups within it to make their aspirations publicly known. The complexities of the province's history lie in the more often than not mutually contradictory and exclusive nature of these aspirations which could have been accommodated rationally only if everyone concerned had been willing to subscribe to democratic and constitutional modes of politics. Since this was never the case, and since some groups were also willing to take up non-constitutional means if they thought their perceived constitutional rights under threat, the problems of the province could only be contained, not solved. The British government, after a considerable time of apprenticeship, appeared to have learnt that lesson by the late eighties. If ignorance of Irish history and politics by British politicians had led to the form the partition of Ireland took, then twenty years of 'troubles' had forced Whitehall and Westminster to catch up with a considerable amount of homework and to recognise that the constitutional compromise of 1920 could not be easily undone.

CHAPTER NINE

The Nineties: From the Anglo-Irish Agreement to the 'Peace Process' – The Problem Accommodated?

The momentous changes which took place in Eastern Europe and South Africa during the early nineties, while not on the scale of those commented on by Churchill after the First World War, made at least one journalist conclude that 'Ulster's crisis seems quite petty'.[1] Yet while the general pattern of development in Northern Ireland saw only little change, there was a sudden upsurge in political activity in the middle of the decade which led to what might become a new chapter in the history of the province. From the perspective of the later nineties and in the light of intense journalistic research,[2] which revealed the previous ten years' secret diplomacy between Dublin, Belfast and London, political developments since the mid-eighties need to be re-examined, even though their full story can only be told once all the archives have been opened.

The years following the Anglo-Irish Agreement saw a continuation of the search for consensus, but now British governments put mounting pressure on unionists. The consultative involvement of Dublin in any initiatives taken in the province and the inclusion of even the American President made unionists feel that they were confronted by an ever-growing 'pan-nationalist front'. The seeming, if tentative, vic-

1. Quoted in Bardon, Jonathan, *A History of Ulster*, Belfast 1992, p. 826.
2. In particular Mallie, Eamonn and McKittrick, David, *The Fight for Peace. The Secret Story Behind the Irish Peace Process*, London 1997.

tory of the ballot box over the bullet within the republican camp increased this pressure. In particular the first of the two ceasefires called by the IRA to facilitate Sinn Fein's participation in political talks drew worldwide media attention, encouraged by outbreaks of peace and reconciliation elsewhere.

As republicans appeared to put greater emphasis on politics, so the loyalist paramilitaries began to change. They formed political parties in order to carry their demands into politics: the Ulster Democratic Party (UDP) representing the UDA and UFF, and the revived Progressive Unionist Party (PUP, in existence since 1979) now representing the UVF. This more pragmatic approach was finally also adopted by the Unionist Party, which showed an increasing, if cautious, willingness to enter into dialogue with nationalism. John Taylor, the new deputy leader of the UUP,[3] admitted the 'effectiveness and ingenuity of Sinn Fein'.[4] This in turn alienated the DUP and its supporters, while by and large the Orange Order, even though now at a greater distance from the UUP than in the past and increasingly taking the DUP's side in internal unionist debates, seems to have been willing to compromise on some of the crucial issues concerning the routes of their marches. By 1997 David Trimble, leader of the party since 1995 and with the reputation of a hard-liner, was willing to enter talks which included Sinn Fein.

The Conservative government under John Major had depended on the unionist vote in the House of Commons, but the new Labour government, which had been returned with the largest majority this century, could theoretically disregard the unionists completely although Tony Blair, while still in opposition, had toned down its previous anti-partitionist stand on Northern Ireland. Nationalists' hopes were thus high, but by the same token the new Secretary of State, Mo Mowlam, could and did act more even-handedly than her predecessors. Thus Britain could pursue its aims of pushing the province towards some form of self-government with a much strengthened domestic hand.

The governments of the Republic, with a hugely improving economy behind them,[5] and with guidance from John Hume, embraced

3. In 1989 the OUP, under Molyneaux's guidance, reverted to its original title, the Ulster Unionist Party (UUP). See Purdy, Ann, *Molyneaux: The Long View*, Antrim 1989, p. 92.

4. Quoted in Bew, Paul, Gibbon, Peter and Patterson, Henry, *Northern Ireland 1921–1996. Political Forces and Social Classes*, London 1996, p. 236.

5. See for instance O'Toole, Fintan, 'In the Land of the Emerald Tiger', in a supplement with the *Irish Times*, 28 Dec. 1996.

the opportunity to become peace-makers. This was particularly welcome to Hume, who could hope to diminish support in the USA for the violent tradition of republicanism and to replace it, with the active help of the President of the United States himself, with support for the united nationalist front of the Irish government and the SDLP. By allowing Sinn Fein leaders openly to travel to the States and meet the American President, it was hoped to put further pressure on SF to abandon terror and enter constitutional politics.

The drawback in these developments was the electoral improvement that SF reaped as a result of its willingness to follow the political path in a more serious fashion. As Adams began to overshadow Hume as peace-maker, so some non-voters and some of those who had previously stuck with the SDLP turned to SF. As politics advanced from the first to the second ceasefire, the losers appeared to be the DUP and the SDLP. But after the latter ceasefire the UUP under Trimble at long last seemed to be willing to engage directly with Hume and his party in the hope of prising it away from SF.

Out of these developments, and with a great deal of pressure now on SF from both the White House and Dublin to continue on the path of the ballot rather than the bullet, finally came the Good Friday Agreement, which brought the paramilitaries into politics and offered a compromise between unionist and nationalist politics, and the elections for the first self-governing Northern Ireland Assembly in June 1998.

POLITICAL DEVELOPMENTS: THE TALKS PROCESS

A good deal has now been revealed about the secret diplomacy that took place from the late eighties between SF, the SDLP and the British and Dublin governments, and about the growing politicisation of loyalist paramilitary groups.[6] Even before the signing of the Anglo-Irish Agreement there had been some contact between John Hume and Gerry Adams in which the former tried to persuade the latter to give up the armed struggle in favour of full involvement in politics. Little came of this, but by 1987, the same year in which it became known that the IRA had amassed a huge arsenal of Libyan armoury,

6. See Mallie and McKittrick, *The Fight for Peace*; Cusack, Jim and McDonald, Henry, *UVF*, Dublin 1997.

SF seemed to realise that its military campaign had to be underpinned and accompanied by more realistic politics.[7] The talks between Adams and Hume, beginning seriously the following year, were attempts to develop a more pragmatic approach and to explore what might be achieved for the republican movement by political means.

A change in British attitudes emerged with the arrival of the new Secretary of State, Peter Brooke, who suggested that the government might talk to SF, if the IRA renounced violence. In a response to questions from journalists in November 1989 to mark his 100th day in office, he conceded that a military defeat of the IRA was impossible, but that it could be contained, which in turn might make the terrorists consider whether 'the game had ceased to be worth the candle'[8] and think of abandoning their campaign of violence in favour of politics. This was against the background of a year in which the IRA had carried its bombings and killings to England and Germany; their violence being matched by tit-for-tat responses from loyalists.

The violence continued throughout the following year, with loyalist paramilitaries in particular targeting catholic taxi drivers and the IRA murdering army personnel in Germany, as well as continuing its campaign in England. But Brooke continued his cautious moves to get talks going on several levels. While public opinion on both sides began to accept the AIA – a *Belfast Telegraph* poll showed that neither side thought it made much difference – and at first district councils and then the UUP ended their boycott of the Northern Ireland Office, official relations worsened. Relations between Dublin and London grew troubled over several Irish Supreme Court decisions which went against Northern Ireland, the unionists refused to agree to any talks, and the SDLP appeared to turn ever greener, when both Hume and Mallon suggested that no 'internal affairs of Northern Ireland' existed and that devolution had proved in the past to be unworkable – in other words, only an All-Ireland solution could be contemplated.

The month of November 1990, when John Major became Conservative leader and Prime Minister of the UK, also saw an interesting development in the Republic of Ireland where Mary Robinson was elected President and John Bruton became Fine Gael leader. Both had

7. The information in this section is largely based on the following: Mallie and McKittrick, *The Fight for Peace*; Flackes, W.D. and Elliott, Sydney, *Northern Ireland. A Political Directory, 1968–1993*, Belfast 1994; Bew, Paul and Gillespie, Gordon, *Northern Ireland. A Chronology of the Troubles, 1968–1993*, Dublin 1993; Bew and Gillespie, *The Northern Ireland Peace Process 1993–1996. A Chronology*, London 1996; *Belfast Telegraph*; *Fortnight*.

8. Mallie and McKittrick, *The Fight for Peace*, p. 99.

a record of wanting unionist interests treated fairly – Robinson had resigned from the Labour Party in protest against the AIA, and Bruton proposed amendments to Articles 2 and 3 of the Irish Constitution (see above, pp. 151) to the effect that Irish unity could be achieved by consent. These were rejected by the Dail in December.

Meanwhile Peter Brooke stayed on as Secretary of State. He had made a significant speech to his constituency during the election campaign in which he had said, 'The British government has no selfish strategic or economic interests in Northern Ireland: our role is to help, enable and encourage. Britain's purpose, as I have sought to describe it, is not to occupy, oppress or exploit, but to ensure democratic debate and free democratic choice.'[9] This has to be understood against a background of the opening of secret contacts between his officials and the leadership of the republican movement which he had authorised earlier in the year.[10] This 'back-channel' of communication was kept open during the coming years, although not made public until much later. That Christmas the IRA had its first official ceasefire for fifteen years.

In the new year, however, the violence continued and increased. 1991 saw loyalists kill more people than the IRA, while the latter's military strength and sophistication continued to improve. There were more, and more efficient, bombs than there had been since 1978. The nationalist paramilitaries began to use 'human bombs' (that is, forcing the driver of a hijacked vehicle to drive the bomb to its destination) in a number of openly sectarian attacks on protestant housing estates. The choice of 'soft targets', – commercial as well as government and service providers to the security forces – meant that more civilians were killed, and the loyalist paramilitaries, under a new hard-line leadership, retaliated by killing those catholics who they thought were IRA or SF activists. As a result more civilians were killed by both sides. There was also what was later to become known as a 'spectacular', namely a mortar bomb attack on Downing Street.

Brooke started a new talks initiative in which the notion of the three strands of relationships was first introduced: first, relations within Northern Ireland; secondly, North–South relations; and thirdly, the relationship between the UK and the Republic of Ireland. While initially supported by the constitutional parties, not much came of this, as violence escalated during the summer. At the same time, though, the 'back-channel' communications continued, and in the autumn the

9. *Ibid.*, p. 107.
10. *Ibid.*, pp. 104ff.

first results of Hume's discussions with Adams emerged secretly in the form of a draft for a joint declaration by the British and Irish Prime Ministers. This had been worked out in consultation with Adams and Haughey and contained most of the concepts that later went into the Downing Street Declaration, with its emphasis on self-determination, and the need for agreement between the two sides and for Britain to play the role of facilitator for democratic debate and compromise.

1992 saw very little change in the general pattern, although with hindsight one can see significant movement under the surface. The violence from both sides continued along familiar lines, peaking in the run-up to the April elections, but continuing thereafter. Again loyalists 'outkilled' republicans and there were some particularly outrageous and gruesome tit-for-tat mass-killings. Libya severed its links with the IRA in March, but by then its stockpile of weapons was sufficient for many years to come. In November the IPLO (Irish People's Liberation Organisation), a particularly militant and violent splinter-group of the INLA, disbanded itself after a series of attacks by the IRA in which one of its members was killed and others seriously wounded.[11] In July the Royal Irish Regiment, an amalgamation of the UDR and the Royal Irish Rangers, came into existence.

Brooke's talks could not be revived before April, but during the election campaign there were some indications that the Labour leader Neil Kinnock by and large supported the government line. In the province the elections brought a slight move to the centre, with SF and DUP votes declining by about 1.5 per cent. Gerry Adams was replaced as an MP by the SDLP's Joe Hendron with the help of some protestant voters. Sir Patrick Mayhew replaced Brooke as Secretary of State. While perceived as more patrician and less open-minded than Brooke, he none the less revived the talks and proceeded with the three-strand initiative, to which the constitutional parties initially responded quite positively, with the unionists in particular showing willingness to talk even to the Dublin government – indicating that government policies, as implied in the AIA, appeared to be making some progress. But by September the DUP had walked out of Strand Two, complaining that Articles 2 and 3 of the Republic's constitution were not to be debated, only returning when these reappeared on the agenda as part of the overall programme for discussion. But with the continuation of the vicious violence, and the collapse of the coalition government in Dublin in November, the talks broke down when the unionists walked out shortly thereafter.

11. Holland, Jack and McDonald, Henry, *INLA. Deadly Divisions*, Dublin 1996.

Behind the scenes Mayhew continued with the 'back-channel' talks, although with less confidence in their success than Brooke. In February Albert Reynolds had succeeded Haughey as FF leader and Taoiseach and had immediately suggested that Articles 2 and 3 could be discussed as part of 'global talks', i.e. including the Government of Ireland Act of 1920. In contrast, the opposition leader, and leader of Fine Gael, John Bruton, proposed in May that Articles 2 and 3 should be changed unilaterally and not used as a bargain in negotiations with the unionists. In the November elections in the Republic the Labour Party doubled its vote, at the expense of FF and FG which each lost about 5 per cent, to become the third largest party. In January 1993 this resulted in the first FF–Labour government, with a large majority in the Dail strengthening its domestic hand in the pursuit of peace in Northern Ireland.

Reynolds was more active than any Taoiseach before him with regard to the North and in support of the Hume–Adams initiative. Sinn Fein's 'Towards a Lasting Peace', published in February 1992, showed a much more political approach and a willingness to pursue non-violent avenues. On the basis of this draft suggestions for a British–Irish joint government declaration continued to be passed between and argued over by SF, John Hume and the Irish government. Mayhew meanwhile offered SF admittance to talks provided the IRA would abandon violence.

This theme continued to be followed by both British and Irish governments during the following year. The violence persisted throughout the year, and in particular the summer's marching season showed increased loyalist hostility towards the RUC. In October the IRA's bombing of protestants in the Shankill Road resulted in ten people dead and 57 injured, and the retaliatory shooting by the UFF in Greysteel killed seven people and wounded 13, but there was also an upsurge of political activity in public and even more so behind the scenes.

Throughout 1993 there were public offers from both governments to SF to enter talks on condition that the IRA cease its violence. There were suggestions of US involvement[12] – an American fact-finding delegation, accompanied by an unofficial ceasefire, visited the province in September – and the hitherto secret meetings between Hume and Adams became public knowledge in April, continuing in more public fashion thereafter. The existence of the 'back-channel' was leaked in November, as were the Irish draft proposals for a joint

12. O'Clery, Conor, *The Greening of the White House. The Inside Story of how America Tried to Bring Peace to Ireland*, Dublin 1996.

declaration by the two governments. The 'back-channel' was suspended, but the hectic activity between Hume, the leadership of SF, Reynolds and Dick Spring, the Labour leader who had become Reynolds's Foreign Minister, together with the involvement of both catholic and protestant clergy as well as the White House, finally produced the Downing Street Declaration (DSD) on 15 December 1993.

The DSD was a masterpiece of diplomatic ambiguity in appearing to offer all sides some of the things they wanted without rejecting any of their aspirations. It was based on the many drafts that had come out of the Hume–Adams discussions, with additions from Reynolds and his advisers. Mainstream unionist support was achieved by allowing Molyneaux and Archbishop Eames to participate in the final drafting.[13] While granting the right of self-determination to the Irish people, it guaranteed unionists the right to remain within the UK as long as the majority in Northern Ireland so wished. The Provisional movement was offered participation in the democratic talks process provided it renounced violence. This showed two important shifts from previously held positions. The British government moved away from trying to find a consensus in the centre of politics and towards trying to bring the men of violence into politics, and the Irish government moved away from the notion of a united Ireland towards one of an agreed Ireland which by necessity accepted that a unionist majority in the North implied the continuation of partition. Both Spring and Mayhew insisted that any ceasefire would have to be given credentials by the handing over of some weapons.

Responses to and discussions about the DSD continued throughout 1994, while republican and loyalist violence continued, and SF asked for a long series of clarifications on the Declaration. There was a good deal of encouragement and even pressure from Dublin and the USA to move further along the road of politics and away from violence. In January the Irish broadcasting ban against SF was lifted and its leaders were granted visas to visit the States. Adams's subsequent visit there put further pressure on the SF leader, while Mayhew agreed that there now was a 'broad shape of a possible agreement'[14] emerging. Even though it was difficult to see how the DSD, or its eventual clarification by the NIO and Reynolds, could meet any of the demands that SF/IRA were making, from July speculations about an IRA ceasefire intensified. On 31 August the IRA announced that 'there will be a complete cessation of military operations'.[15]

13. Bew and Gillispie, *The NI Peace Process 1993–1996*, p. 37.
14. *Ibid.*, p. 52.
15. *Ibid.*, p. 63.

The immediate response from the international media and from Dublin were enthusiastic, while Britain and the unionists wondered how permanent the ceasefire might be. The general public in the province were generally more muted in their response: only 30 per cent believed that the ceasefire would be permanent.[16] But now Britain, too, ended the broadcasting ban on SF, and Adams was allowed back into the USA to stress the benefits peaceful policies might bring. In mid-October the loyalists declared their own ceasefire, which was to be conditional on the permanence of that of the IRA. It also offered 'to all the loved ones of all innocent victims over the past 25 years, abject and true remorse'.[17] Loyalist representatives were promptly received in Dublin and the USA. The presence of the British army on Northern Ireland's streets was gradually reduced and the police began to patrol without flak-jackets.

The British Labour Party meanwhile replaced its openly pro-nationalist spokesperson on Northern Ireland, Kevin MacNamara, with Dr Marjorie Mowlam. In Dublin Reynolds opened a Forum for Peace and Reconciliation shortly before he had to resign as leader of the party and was replaced by Bertie Ahern. After the subsequent elections Fine Gael formed a coalition with Labour and the Democratic Left and John Bruton became Taoiseach while Spring remained Deputy and Foreign Minister.

Northern Ireland was offered increased aid from the USA and the EU, and the doors of Stormont finally opened for exploratory talks with SF. But the real difficulty was the lack of any shadow of political agreement. SF expected the government to accept the IRA's ceasefire at its face value and to be treated as an equal partner in peace negotiations, while unionists did not trust the political transformation of the paramilitaries' party. As a result 1995 was dominated by discussions on the ambiguity of the ceasefire and requests for decommissioning of weapons in advance of any admittance of SF to serious talks.

There was, however, a general easing of tension, foremost on the streets of the province, where bombs and killings ceased. But, as is now known,[18] the IRA only ceased its direct military activity, while continuing its recruiting, policing, fund-raising, intelligence gathering and military contingency planning; there was also an increase in the number of punishment beatings which occurred. A similar trend could be observed on the loyalist side of the divide. However, the security

16. *Belfast Telegraph*, 2 Sept. 1994.
17. Bew and Gillespie, *The NI Peace Process, 1993–1996*. p. 72.
18. Mallie and McKittrick, *The Fight for Peace*, p. 319.

presence was reduced, some troops withdrawn, more prisoners released, most towns opened their security gates, and some of the security budget was transferred to other areas of spending.

But for most of the year there was no political progress, since unionists refused to join any talks with SF as long as decommissioning was not agreed on first. Even though both loyalist paramilitary parties and the RUC made it clear that decommissioning was impractical, not likely to be forthcoming, and perhaps unnecessary, the British government could not persuade the unionists to accept this. The Framework Documents which both governments had offered in February promised compromise to appease both sides of the community without giving either enough, while annoying the unionists in particular with a strong emphasis on North–South cooperation. July saw some ugly confrontations between police and loyalist mobs after a stand-off in Drumcree, near Portadown, over an Orange march, highlighting the frustration protestants felt about the peace process, which appeared to them to be going forward entirely at their expense. In the subsequent years Drumcree became the symbol of sectarian hatred on both sides.[19] The new unionist leader, David Trimble, who succeeded Molyneaux in September, certainly gave the impression of representing the hardliners of unionism. By the autumn stalemate had been reached.

It was only towards the end of the year and under pressure from President Clinton's late-November visit to Northern Ireland that a new approach, the Twin-Track Strategy, was agreed between Dublin and London. This proposed all-party talks by February 1996 and an international body, under the former US Senator George Mitchell, to look into and advise on the decommissioning issue. Clinton's visit elicited a huge emotional response in Belfast and Derry, and was clearly an attempt to carry further what the White House had been trying to do throughout the year, namely encourage and promise support for the ceasefire.

The emotional shot in the arm which Clinton's visit appeared to have given the peace process barely outlived the year. By January the military faction within the republican movement appeared to assert itself, while the unionists pressed for an elected body to be instituted before any talks commenced. On 24 January 1996 the Mitchell Commission reported. It circumvented the decommissioning issue by proposing decommissioning in parallel to talks, while its only preconditions for participation in talks were commitments to democracy and

19. Ryder, Chris, *The RUC 1922–1997. A Force under Fire*, London 1997, pp. 461–6, 476.

exclusively peaceful methods. An elected body was declared a possible addition. Major went along with these proposals and also offered unionists elections to a Northern Ireland Forum in the spring.

While an opinion poll in late January suggested that 83 per cent of people in the province supported decommissioning before talks, the government clearly felt it needed to offer a compromise to SF on the issue, while also appeasing unionist demands for an elected Forum. In February the Dublin Forum for Peace and Reconciliation submitted its Report, which included a stress on the need for unionist consent in any future arrangements for Northern Ireland. Thus SF could not subscribe to the Report. Shortly thereafter the IRA's ceasefire ended and the IRA blamed British intransigence for its demise. Most of the resulting bombing occurred in England, and Northern Ireland did not return to full-scale violence. The loyalist ceasefire held, if sometimes only precariously.

Nonetheless security was gradually increased on the streets. While Gerry Adams declared 'the peace process is over',[20] strenuous attempts were made by the Irish, British and American governments to move towards a return of the ceasefire. Perhaps partly as a result of this, and in spite of SF's obvious continuing policy of not ruling out violence, in May Adams announced SF's acceptance of Mitchell's preconditions. This appears to have helped his party's results in the subsequent Forum elections, in which it polled 15.5 per cent, its best result ever. The elections of 30 May, which also determined which ten parties were to participate in the multi-party peace talks from June, returned a predictable Forum, with a weakened middle ground and an increase for SF.

The renewed stand-off over Drumcree around 12 July had been preceded by a wave of IRA violence, and was accompanied by such widespread loyalist rioting that the RUC felt it had to change its policy and allow the march to proceed against catholic residents' wishes. In the wake of this sectarian hatred flared up everywhere and violence increased with it. The IRA suffered some setbacks, with arms-finds and arrests in both Britain and Ireland. After the particularly shocking attacks on Thiepval army barracks in Lisburn, a second Hume–Adams document, coincidental to these events, offered a new ceasefire, but was rejected, possibly because of the events in Lisburn. When both Blair and Major, independently of each other, paid visits to Belfast in December, the peace process was still very much in abeyance.

The beginning of 1997 was dominated by pre-election wrangles during which both Hume and Bruton attacked SF and suggested a

20. Bew and Gillespie, *The NI Peace Process 1993–1996*, p. 173.

vote for it was a vote for murder, while the political talks were adjourned until after the election. Pressure on Adams and the IRA to renew the ceasefire continued from Dublin, London and Washington, while the uncertainty of the loyalist ceasefire became clear when a new anti-ceasefire group emerged, the Loyalist Volunteer Force (LVF). Throughout the year sectarian hatred, often taking the form of church arson, was much in evidence.

In the national elections of 1 May the UUP with 32.7 per cent of the vote, the SDLP (24.1 per cent), the DUP (13.6 per cent) and the Alliance Party (6 per cent) roughly maintained their position, while SF increased its vote to 16.1 per cent, sending two MPs to Westminster – Adams retook West Belfast, and Martin McGuinness won the seat for Mid-Ulster, even though both refused to take their seats. The new Labour administration with Dr Mo Mowlam as Secretary of State for NI was generally welcomed by nationalists, and SF signalled that it was 'ready to do business with the government'. It improved its electoral standing even more in the local elections, where it polled 16.9 per cent of the first-preference votes. Tony Blair, the new Prime Minister, with a huge majority in the Commons, permitted contacts with the party provided conditions on the ground allowed it, and he and Mowlam promised participation in talks after a credible ceasefire. The decommissioning precondition was removed.

In the run-up to that year's Drumcree, Hume and Trimble met to try to find a solution to the annual marching difficulties but failed to reach a workable compromise, while in June Britain and Ireland gave the IRA a five-week deadline for a ceasefire which was duly delivered in July. But almost immediately it became clear that there were sections within the military side of the movement who were not happy about the implications of the Mitchell principles. Not only Republican SF and the IRSP were against a renewed ceasefire, but a new splinter group, the Continuity Army Council (CAC), emerged which continued the campaign, despite being hampered by limited supplies. Adams's difficulties in holding the movement together re-emerged later in the year when there were some serious defections from the IRA and speculations on a split in the movement were rife,[21] but by the end of the year the worst of the storm appeared to have been weathered, or at least it was no longer blowing in public.

In mid-September the talks had resumed, while police on both sides of the border reported less paramilitary activity than during the previous ceasefire.[22] Hume and Adams had been in consultation again

21. Mullin, John, *Guardian*, 9 Dec. 1997.
22. Cusack, Jim, *Irish Times*, 13 Sept. 1997.

soon after the elections, and, with unionists having lost their balancing power in Westminster, a new FF government in Dublin, and the success of FF's Northern candidate, Mary McAleese, in the presidential elections, the nationalists' fortunes seemed to be rising. By December Adams had met Blair in Downing Street, much to the unionists' distaste, and throughout the last months of the year there was frequent serious rioting in protestant areas of working-class Belfast and some catholic rioting against loyalist marches in Derry. In December the leader of the LVF, Billy Wright, was killed within the Maze prison by a member of the INLA. This was followed by revenge killings of catholics. Much would depend on whether the new government could maintain the balanced approach that Mowlam had shown on the marching issue in the summer, as 1998 started with increased tension on the ground and with accusations from republicans that Britain did not move fast enough and from loyalists that all concessions had so far gone to republicans. The loyalist ceasefire at least seemed to hang by a thread, and the continuation of the talks was only achieved when Mowlam went to talk to convicted prisoners in the Maze to get their support. However, discussions in the Forum and the peace talks continued under increasing pressure from government to meet the Easter deadline.

The Forum, which had had no real power and suffered from the non-participation of the nationalist parties, none the less provided the first political debates by an elected body in the province for decades, and produced some useful social and economic reports. It was abolished on 24 April after the acceptance of the Agreement by the parliaments in London and Dublin. The multi-party talks continued until Good Friday, 10 April 1998, when an agreement was finally reached. With a deliberate policy of reaching no preliminary conclusions, the talks operated on two levels: the 'private' political one where, away from public scrutiny, the minimal and maximal positions were threshed out and some compromise arrived at, and the public one, fought out in front of the media, which often suggested that very little progress was being made. But by Easter a result had been achieved.

The Agreement provided in Strand One for a 108-member assembly with full legislative and executive powers and with safeguards 'to ensure all sections of the community can participate'.[23] On the most controversial Strand Two a North–South ministerial council was

23. *The Agreement.* n.d., no place [government publication, distributed to all households in NI in April 1998], p. 5.

agreed 'to develop consultation, co-operation and action within the island of Ireland . . . on matters of mutual interest'.[24] On Strand Three there would be a British–Irish council and a British–Irish intergovernmental conference. There were also provisions for constitutional change, i.e. the repeal of the Government of Ireland Act 1920, and changes to Articles 2 and 3 of the Irish constitution, once the electorate, North and South, had accepted the Agreement. The losers appear to have been SF, who got neither 'free-standing' cross-border bodies nor the retention of the Irish territorial claim, which Adams had declared to be 'minimum requirements' right up to the final days before the Agreement was signed. Trimble, on the other hand, had achieved a change in Articles 2 and 3, North–South bodies were to be responsible to the Assembly, and Northern Ireland remained firmly within the UK.

In the subsequent referendum campaign a vast majority of nationalists, led by SF and the SDLP, supported the Agreement, but unionism remained split, with the DUP and the UKUP arguing for a no vote and the UUP in great difficulties with its own dissenters. Opinion polls suggested that only half of all unionists were in favour of the Agreement. The main issues of their concern were decommissioning of paramilitaries' weapons, the early release of prisoners and the future of policing. The referendum returned an overall (i.e. North and South counted together) yes vote of 85.46 per cent. But in the North this was only 71.12 per cent, on a turnout of 81 per cent, compared to the massive 94.39 per cent in the South. A detailed analysis of this vote is nearly impossible, since the whole province was treated as one constituency, and counted and returned as one. The implication is, however, that a majority, if not a very large one, of unionists voted in favour The assembly elections on 25 June were conducted through the single-transferable-vote system from the 18 parliamentary constituencies in the province, and, after a transitional period of seven months, the assembly was to take over the legislative and executive authority from the NIO for Finance and Personnel, Agriculture, Economic Development, Education, Environment and Health, and Social Services, while Security and Prisons remained with the NIO. The election results confirmed the referendum: unionist votes were split in half between those who supported the Agreement and wanted the Assembly to work and those who resented the presence of SF and the Irish dimension. Much would depend on Trimble's ability to keep his own dissenters in line. He was elected First Minister on 1 July with Hume's second-in-command, Seamus Mallon, as his Deputy.

24. *Ibid.*, p. 11.

ECONOMY AND SOCIETY

The general trends in the economy, as outlined above (p. 180ff.), continued into the early nineties as a reflection of local conditions as much as of developments in Great Britain and the world economy beyond. By the late nineties the decade was judged to have been economically successful, with Northern Ireland by then being one of the fastest-growing regions within the UK.[25] Because of the political restraints on Thatcherism in the region its impact on Northern Ireland is disputed.[26] It was certainly unevenly applied, and there was a time-lag, brought about by the necessity to produce special legislation through Orders in Council. Because of the political imperative which demanded the inclusion of economic and social policies in solving the political crisis, British governments could not avoid spending relatively more in the province than on any other region, even if the cost of security is not taken into account. In 1993, for instance, the fiscal transfer from Britain amounted to £3.4 billion,[27] accounting for 28 per cent of GDP.

In part as a result of this Northern Ireland was less severely affected by the recession than other regions. But the structural changes the economy had undergone during the previous decade also played a role: the private sector, and in particular the small business sector, had expanded, as had the service sector. Small firms often performed better than the multinationals and a good deal of diversification had occurred. While economists do not yet agree on an overall interpretation of the province's economic performance, there is some consensus on the role of public spending, the lack of the eighties' boom helping to prevent a recession, and improvements in productivity.[28] Northern Ireland's industrial output continued to grow faster than the UK average from the late eighties to the mid-nineties (see Table I.5, p. 252). By then unemployment also began to fall, while turnover and profits increased. A third of all employment, however, was still provided by

25. Simpson, John, *Belfast Telegraph*, 25 Mar. 1998.

26. Gaffikin, Frank and Morrissey, Mike, *Northern Ireland: The Thatcher Years*, London and New Jersey 1990.

27. Roche, Patrick J. and Birnie, J. Esmond, *An Economic Lesson for Irish Nationalists and Republicans*, Belfast 1995, p. 16.

28. Gillespie, Norman, 'Employment, Unemployment and Equality of Opportunity: An Introduction', in McLaughlin, Eithne and Quirk, Padraic (eds), *Policy Aspects of Employment Equality in Northern Ireland*, Belfast n.d. [1996], p. 9. Volume II of *Employment Equality in Northern Ireland*, published by Standing Advisory Commission on Human Rights (SACHR II).

the public sector, rising as high as 42 per cent by the early nineties.[29] Gross average weekly earnings had reached 90 per cent of the UK average by 1997 (up from 84 per cent in 1992), yet social security benefit remained the second most important source of income, and 60 per cent of GDP was due to public expenditure.

These statistics thus say little about the underlying real picture, which seems to show a more unequal distribution of income than elsewhere.[30] While it remained about 15 per cent cheaper to live in the province than elsewhere in the UK, largely due to cheaper housing in the owner-occupier sector, and the effective average expenditure per household was higher than in the rest of the UK, spending per person was lower (see Table I.6, p. 253). This indicates not only larger households, but also a higher proportion of low-income households than elsewhere. Moreover, while there was increased employment, there were few long-term economic prospects, and by the later nineties the relative growth-rate began to slow down, only to pick up again after the second ceasefire had begun. By the summer of 1997 unemployment had reached its lowest level since 1980 and manufacturing output was rising faster than UK averages again.[31] By the autumn the province was expected to move up from its position as the poorest region in the UK. Falls in unemployment, by then at a fairly steady rate of 7 per cent, and increases in employment were expected to continue offsetting the expected drop in public expenditure.[32]

It is well to be reminded (see above, p. 184) that the political unrest in the province has arguably been on balance economically beneficial, in particular through the expenditure on security and its knock-on effect on the economy overall. After the first ceasefire, tourism increased by 56 per cent, leading to a regional growth of 3.6 per cent against a national rate of 2.6 per cent. The £286 million saved on the security budget was reallocated to social services and education, but clawed back when the ceasefire ended.[33] The ceasefire thus had an initially positive impact on the service sector and on trade generally, but whether this will be so in the long term, if a permanent ceasefire can be maintained, remains an open question. Economic benefits could also be seen in the continuation of partition, since the EU

29. Gaffikin, Frank and Morrissey, Mike, *The New Unemployed. Joblessness and Poverty in the Market Economy*, London and New Jersey 1992, p. 162.

30. Simpson, John, *Belfast Telegraph*, 9 Jan. 1995.

31. Simpson, John, *Belfast Telegraph*, 17 July 1997.

32. Gudgin, Graham, *The Economic Outlook and Medium Term Forecasts 1997–2000*, Northern Ireland Economic Research Centre, Sept. 1997; John Simpson, 'Are We No Longer the Weakest Region in the UK?', *Belfast Telegraph*, 28 Oct. 1997.

33. Ryle, Sarah and Sharrock, David, *Guardian*, 20 Feb. 1996.

favoured marginalised border areas, from which both governments, and thus the North and the South of Ireland, gained advantages.[34]

The Republic had certainly improved its economic performance greatly. From the mid-nineties its economy had the fastest national growth within the EU. It had been exceptionally successful in attracting inward investment and EU Structural Funds and Cohesion Fund projects. This puts in perspective the relative success of the Northern economy, where productivity in particular still lagged behind the UK at between 8 per cent and 13 per cent, especially when one considers that industry in the Republic was at a serious cost disadvantage compared to Northern wages, rates and non-trade service costs.[35]

The rise of unemployment in the first half of the nineties and its fall in the second half was accompanied by a very gradual but steady change in the employment ratio of protestants and catholics, from 64.1 per cent and 35.9 per cent respectively in 1990 to 61.9 per cent and 38.1 per cent in 1997, which was beginning to approximate the division in the population.[36] The fair employment legislation, strengthened in 1989, when the FEA became the Fair Employment Commission (FEC) with stronger legal teeth than its predecessor, had begun to make real progress (see Table I.7, p. 253). There was evidence of a decline in the numbers of catholics feeling discriminated against in employment. The legislation had been accepted, 'albeit grudgingly in some quarters'.[37] Parties, organisations and public opinion agreed on the need for legislation and affirmative action, while rejecting positive discrimination. After some initial doubts employers were satisfied with the results, since they too could now call upon the law to resolve any difficulties. Both communities benefited from the legislation, although many protestants continued to feel that it worked against their interests by giving catholics preferential treatment.

34. On the economic advantages of NI remaining part of the UK see also: Gudgin, Graham, 'The Economics of the Union: Romance and Reality', in Foster, John Wilson (ed.), *The Idea of the Union. Statements and Critiques in Support of the Union of Great Britain and Northern Ireland*, Vancouver 1995, pp. 75–88.

35. Simpson, John, *Belfast Telegraph*, 4 Feb. 1997.

36. For this section in general see: Bardon, *A History of Ulster; Belfast Telegraph*; SACHR II; SACHR III: McVey, John and Hutson, Nigel (eds), *Public Views and Experiences of Fair Employment and Equality Issues in Northern Ireland,* Belfast n.d. [1996]; Stringer, Peter and Robinson, Gillian (eds), *Social Attitudes in Northern Ireland. The Second Report. 1991–1992*, Belfast 1992 (NISA 91/92); Breen, Richard, Devine, Paula and Robinson, Gillian (eds), *Social Attitudes in Northern Ireland. The Fourth Report. 1994–1995*, Belfast 1995 (NISA 94/95); Dowds, Lizanne, Devine, Paula and Breen, Richard (eds), *Social Attitudes in Northern Ireland. The Sixth Report. 1996–1997*, Belfast 1997 (NISA 96/97).

37. SACHR III, p. 11.

Despite the greater equality in employment, inequality remained in unemployment: catholics were still twice as likely to be without jobs as protestants (see Table I.1, p. 250; Table I.3, p. 251; and Map 4, p. 262). The reasons for this are disputed,[38] but geographical distribution, with more protestants living in economically more active areas, rather than the discrimination of the past appears to have been the main cause. Not the political unrest but their communally differential distribution affected the availability of jobs to each community. The catholic share in employment had increased particularly in the public sector, with the exception of jobs in the construction industry. Their overall share was 37 per cent by 1996, and in health and education they held 43 per cent of posts (see Table I.7, p. 253).

Non-political crime remained among the lowest nationally and internationally.[39] The public was also less worried about being the victim of crime than elsewhere; and as far as these crimes were concerned both protestants and catholics felt that the RUC dealt well with them. Attitudes in the more political areas of life, however, showed only very limited change.[40] While protestants felt the RUC dealt fairly with everyone, catholics continued to feel that they were not receiving equal treatment from the security forces; only among the younger generation was there a change, in that young protestants conceded that the security forces did not treat catholics equally (although in other respects Northern Ireland is still unusual in its lack of a marked generation gap).[41] Generally, though, catholics remained suspicious of the state, while protestants supported it. Both were united in their high level of intolerance towards religious membership, but also in their support for the welfare system. Despite the inroads of Thatcherism, Keynes's and Beveridge's were the value systems subscribed to by almost everyone across class, religion or gender divides. Gender remained secondary to religious identification, although there was a considerable increase in female economic and the beginning of more female political activity.[42] Statistically there appears

38. Simpson, John, *Belfast Telegraph*, 24 Mar. 1997; SACHR II.

39. Bennetto, Jason, *Independent*, 30 July 1997.

40. Brewer, John D., 'The Public and the Police', in NISA 91/92, pp. 52–66.

41. Cairns, Ed and Tara, 'Children and Conflict: A Psychological Perspective', in Dunn, Seamus (ed.), *Facets of the Conflict in Northern Ireland*, London 1995, p. 98.

42. Sales, Rosemary, *Women Divided: Gender, Religion and Politics in Northern Ireland*, London 1997; Walker, Lynda, 'Godmothers and Mentors. Women, Politics and Education in Northern Ireland', M.Ed. thesis, QUB 1996; Morgan, Valerie and Fraser, Grace, 'Women in the Northern Ireland Conflict: Experiences and Responses', in Dunn, Seamus (ed.), *Facets of the Conflict in Northern Ireland*, pp. 81–96; on gender imbalance within unionist politics see: Cochrane, Feargal, *Unionist Politics and the Politics of Unionism since the Anglo-Irish Agreement*, Cork 1997, pp. 47–52.

to have been a very gradual move towards slightly more liberal attitudes.[43]

Some of these may have been caused by changes in the field of education. Northern Ireland continued to achieve higher academic standards than elsewhere in the UK at the top end of the quality scale, but it also had an exceptional number of young people without any educational qualifications.[44] By 1997 25 per cent of the economically active population had no formal qualifications, compared to an average of 18 per cent for the UK. Integrated education, that is schools which deliberately recruited from both sides of the religious divide, made great strides in the nineties, and new schools were being built or founded at a steady rate. Public opinion was generally content with the quality of education available and fully in favour of its state funding, including higher education. The majority, however, was against the selection procedure of the 11-plus exam, which was still in force in the province, and most catholics were in favour of comprehensive schools.[45] There were government directed and aided EMU (education for mutual understanding) schemes which tried to teach subjects in a cross-communities and cross-curriculum manner, although it is difficult to assess the effect of these.[46] It was part of the wider attempt by government to encourage mutual cultural understanding with which the Northern Ireland Community Relations Council was entrusted. But the stress on the 'two traditions' may indeed have been counter-productive in that it encouraged exclusive cultural identification. The initiative, together with the ever-increasing number of inter-community groups in the voluntary sector, has remained marginal in successfully addressing 'the deep-seated nature of the conflict and the intractability of deeply held values and the difficulty of securing a meeting of minds where a fundamental change in attitudes is required, and where positions are historically determined and reinforced and fortified by a race memory that recalls only the hurts received and not the wounds inflicted'.[47] It was these problems which politics had to address, if there was ever going to be political change in the province.

43. NISA 94/95; NISA 96/97.

44. Walker, Gail, *Belfast Telegraph*, 8 Oct. 1997.

45. Osborne, Richard D., 'Social Attitudes in Northern Ireland: Education', in NISA 94/95, pp. 33–48.

46. Smith, Alan, 'Education and the Conflict in Northern Ireland', in Dunn, Seamus (ed.), *Facets of the Conflict in Northern Ireland*, pp. 168–86.

47. Hayes, Maurice, *Minority Verdict. Experiences of a Catholic Public Servant*, Belfast 1995, pp. 316f.

THE NATIONALIST CAMP

The initiative for the political developments of the mid-nineties clearly goes back to John Hume's attempts at weaning Gerry Adams and the republican movement off violence and into politics, which he had pursued ever since the AIA. As outlined above (p. 198f.), the major difficulty lay in the different perception each had of the role and position of unionism in the province. While Hume lacked a real grasp of the unionists' apprehensions, he did talk, if often from a protestant perspective in rather patronising terms, a great deal about the need to reconcile them, while Adams barely recognised their existence in any future political developments. There was throughout the period great pressure on the latter to take them seriously into account, not only from Hume and Britain, but also from Dublin and to some extent even from Washington. The other big and almost insurmountable problem was the question of the political unity of the island. This was not only relevant to whether or not a united Ireland could be achieved in the foreseeable future, but also to a number of issues in republican perception. The most important of these, that of self-determination, for instance, involved for them the population of the whole island and excluded a separate right of the province's population to determine its own future. How Hume, with help from Dublin, London and Washington, succeeded in persuading the representatives of the violent tradition at least to try to address these issues is still not quite clear, and possibly never will be, since none of the issues appears to have been completely resolved.

Hume's dilemma had grown worse ever since the emergence of PSF. Not only did the continuing existence of a strengthened IRA make another Sunningdale (see above, p. 162ff.) with a promise of some cross-border institutions impossible, but the arrival of republican political representation began to eat into the votes of the SDLP. If nationalism was to make any political progress, it had to be united. Hence Hume's serious and intense pursuit of Adams and his movement and his often astonishing insistence on the importance of peace even over and above his own party's interests.

The AIA had been the first successful step in that direction. It allowed Hume to argue that Britain's position and intentions had changed and that a gradual move towards unity was possible. The fact that SF abolished its abstentionist policy in the South, accompanied by a split in which Republican Sinn Fein (RSF) maintained the puritan line that active involvement in politics would weaken the revolutionary intent of the movement, seemed to suggest for the first time that its conversion to constitutional politics was a real possibility. In military terms the republican movement was very successful in the second half of the eighties, but its political fortunes appeared to decline: voters in the South only gave it 2 per cent of the vote, while the Southern political establishment was clearly anti-republican and the AIA only confirmed this. The propaganda war was going badly, with the disaster of the Enniskillen bombing and the interception and discovery of armament supplies in boats off the Irish coast in November 1987.

Thus Hume's argument that Britain was now neutral on partition and the IRA campaign therefore unnecessary, if not even counterproductive, made some sense to the Provisional leadership. In the subsequent meetings the crucial issues were kept ambiguous: self-determination was never clearly defined, while the existence of unionist disagreements, independent of Britain, was stressed.

Sinn Fein, under the more flexible leadership of Adams and McGuinness, realised that the military campaign was insufficient and a much clearer emphasis needed to be put on political developments, or, as SF's press officer, Richard McAuley, put it, in an interview with a US journal in 1992, 'We're not going to realise our full potential as long as the war is going on in the north and as long as Sinn Fein is presented the way it is with regard to armed struggle and violence.'[48] During the eighties Sinn Fein developed a very efficient party machinery which operated as successfully on constituency as on national and international levels; while their relations with the media clearly outshone any other party in Northern Ireland. Since 1985 they had participated in district council elections and by May 1993 held ten seats on Belfast City Council; 'They were joining the system, not tearing it down',[49] as one commentator put it. The policy that followed was in essence a continuation of the Armalite and ballot box, but now with much greater emphasis on politics, and the Armalite often in partial hiding. In order to keep its support for both these policies SF had to maintain its anti-partitionist and anti-British tradition and keep the Armalite ready to avoid any splits in the movement. This made for continued tension not only within the movement, but also with the SDLP, and for continuing suspicion from unionists who, however hard they were pushed, found it difficult to trust the republican politicians and by extension anyone who cooperated with them.

48. Quoted in *Fortnight* 309, Sept. 1992, p. 5.

49. O'Brien, Brendan, *The Long War. The IRA and Sinn Fein from Armed Struggle to Peace Talks*, Dublin 1993/95, p. 50.

Brooke's active support of SF's exploration of non-violent means finally resulted in their discussion document 'Towards a Lasting Peace' of 1992, which for the first time seriously examined the viability of using unarmed means to achieve their goal, and in the process to modernise the movement.[50] The one principle, though, which was maintained throughout was that an internal settlement was out of the question: in other words, there had to be official involvement by Dublin in the province's affairs. This remained the stumbling-block, since ultimately neither the unionists nor Dublin found this acceptable.

But from then onwards SF sought talks that might lead to peace, even though they maintained throughout that an internal settlement was unacceptable and that unionists would somehow have to be forced to accept a settlement. This did, however, also imply that Britain should stay in the province until it had succeeded in persuading the unionists into a united Ireland.[51] The SDLP leadership appears to have hoped that this was sufficient, provided SF could be made to accept a semi-internal agreement with strong input from Dublin, and at various stages Adams did indeed talk about his willingness to accept some such 'transitory' arrangement. Once put to the vote, North and South, and accepted by the electorate throughout the island, it was hoped that any further violence would have lost its historical legitimacy, since all the people would have expressed their will to end it. The difficulty was to keep the republican movement united and to give SF sufficient leeway to appease its supporters. The danger – and perhaps the SDLP occasionally overlooked the seriousness of this – was that the required speed was bound to offend unionists unless they too could be appeased, which in turn was likely to weaken the nationalist case. With the unexpected help from David Trimble, however, these difficulties were overcome and, once the Agreement was delivered and accepted by the public, the SDLP could afford to turn towards the UUP, while rejecting an electoral pact with SF in the campaign for the June 1998 elections for the new NI Assembly.

There can be little doubt about the leadership quality, the political acumen and the astute grasp of political manoeuvring of Gerry Adams, who, while remaining ignorant about unionists as well as the substantial changes which had taken place in the Republic during his lifetime,[52]

50. Mallie and McKittrick, *The Fight for Peace*, pp. 138ff. and *passim*; O'Brien, *The Long War*, p. 224.

51. Cf. Cox, W. Harvey, 'From Hillsborough to Downing Street – and After', in Catterall, Peter and McDougall, Sean (eds), *The Northern Ireland Question in British Politics*, London 1996, p. 196.

52. Foster, Roy, *Irish Times*, 4 Jan. 1998.

succeeded in carrying both side of the movement and retaining their support. To this end his international successes in the USA were put to as much use as his continuing support for the military tradition which was kept alert throughout the first ceasefire, and the channelling of supporters' frustrations and expectations into citizens' action groups which were particularly prominent during the marching season of the summers.[53] As long as supporters could see that some progress had been made and the ultimate aim of a united Ireland was not lost, Adams's status and trust within the movement kept it united. Another good example of this was the TUAS option which was debated within the movement from 1994. The meaning of this changed from the 'Totally Unarmed Struggle', which suggested a ceasefire was possible because 'all the major Irish nationalist parties [were] rowing in roughly the same direction', to, after the end of the first ceasefire, the 'Tactical Use of Armed Struggle'.[54] One commentator has seen a 'fusion of the IRA and Sinn Fein'[55] in these developments, which might, alternatively, suggest a victory of the political over the military faction within the republican movement.

Adams's strategy was remarkably successful. It achieved concessions from Britain and from the unionists which in turn increased SF's popularity and hence its vote. SF had moved from the 'mindless' use of violence to its use in a politically meaningful sense, but its overall political framework remained contradictory and vague, perhaps as a necessary part of this strategy. There appear to be two possible interpretations of this. It can either be seen as a genuine attempt to demilitarise the IRA very gradually and slowly, showing its members in the process that politics could achieve what they ultimately had not and possibly never could, namely the unity of Ireland. Alternatively these policies can be seen as a straightforward continuation of the bullet and ballot method without any real intention to demilitarise until Britain had finally withdrawn from the North. Either of these interpretations fits the available evidence, and it might even be possible to see them as one and the same, a pragmatic and flexible approach using whichever promises better results under any given circumstances. The real difficulties began with SF's participation in the official political talks, where eventually they would have to agree to a settlement which could only meet the most limited of their objectives, while hoping that any splits in the movement could be kept to a minimum.

53. O'Doherty, Malachi, *Belfast Telegraph*, 10 Mar. 1997.
54. Mallie and McKittrick, *The Fight for Peace*, pp. 401ff.
55. O'Brien, *The Long War*, p. 328.

Adams's policies had gained support within the movement, when after the first ceasefire the IRA succeeded militarily only in England, while it experienced heavy losses through arrests of leading figures in the Republic and the RUC continuously intercepted operations in the North. As the talks proceeded, the INLA and CAC, as well as on at least one occasion the IRA itself, interrupted progress through bombs in the province. This, however, does not appear to have led to a split within the movement overall.

Until the final signing of the Agreement the paramilitary threat was maintained. But after Good Friday 1998 there was no further talk of reviewing the ceasefire in July. The message, accepted by both sides of the movement, was that the armed struggle was over and that the Agreement's 'transitional arrangement' would carry them into a finally united Ireland within a generation. This appears to have been widely accepted by the Northern IRA membership. Dissent came mainly from members in the Republic and the border areas 'who had escaped the brunt of the loyalist and security force actions'.[56]

Dublin governments played a crucial role in supporting the Hume–Adams initiative, but also in stressing the pragmatic necessity of taking account of the unionists' existence and expectations. They had finally decided that keeping the North at arm's length would not solve the long-term potential of the conflict spilling over the border, a frequent worry and fear ever since 1969. With the exception of much of Charles Haughey's policies, Dublin governments had been anti-'republican' since Garret Fitzgerald's premiership for that very reason,[57] while public opinion in the Republic did not always follow suit, even though it was unwilling to vote for SF to any extent. Even FF[58] began to push SF to give up their absolute anti-partitionist stand and to seek unionist consent. Albert Reynolds, in particular, went out of his way to mediate between Dublin, London and Washington in order to accommodate and further the Hume–Adams initiative, even after the first ceasefire broke down. All this clearly implied that SF was being asked to join the constitutional nationalist camp, to abandon any legitimacy of holding arms against the North, and to reconcile itself to the Northern union with Britain. To some extent SF had accepted such a possible outcome by accepting the 'principle of consent of a majority of the people of NI', as embodied in the AIA and the Framework

56. Jim Cusack, *Irish Times*, 25 April 1998.

57. See Fitzgerald, Garret, *All in a Life. An Autobiography*, Dublin 1991.

58. On traditional FF attitudes towards the North see, for instance, Horgan, John, *Sean Lemass. The Enigmatic Patriot*, Dublin 1997, pp. 252–88 and *passim*.

Documents of 1995 and by signing up to the Mitchell principles thereafter, which ultimately took away the *raison d'être* of the republican movement.[59]

US governments had promised economic aid, if significant progress towards peace was made, ever since 1977,[60] but active support for the new peace policy in the USA goes back to the Clinton campaign of 1992, which wooed the Irish-American vote by promising an envoy for Northern Ireland and a visa for Adams, if the Democrats won.[61] The British Conservative anti-Clinton stance during the campaign may have increased the candidate's pro-Ireland line. Not all the election promises, however, became policies, when he was elected. The envoy idea was abandoned, but the pro-nationalist Jean Kennedy Smith was made ambassador to the Republic and contacts with Dublin and Sinn Fein were kept active at various levels of government involvement. While the American understanding of the problems in NI rarely reached very sophisticated levels, their involvement, with some guidance from Dublin, certainly helped to push Hume's and the Irish government's argument by diminishing support for the IRA in the States and encouraging Adams on the path of politics rather than violence. It also helped to further the Sinn Fein leader's policy within his movement. The carrot and stick method of visits to the USA, which included permission for political fund-raising once the ceasefire was in place, certainly gained Adams support and prestige, but also tied him more firmly to the peace policy, as can be seen in the icy response in Washington to the end of the first ceasefire, which had been planned and prepared at the time Clinton visited Ireland. But Adams's new image as peace-maker survived and was easily resurrected with the new ceasefire. With ex-senator Mitchell chairing the peace talks, the US administration was committed to supporting the constitutional nationalist policy.

With the signing of the Agreement and its subsequent confirmation by the parliaments in London and Dublin as well as by the electorate in the North and South of Ireland, constitutional policies within the nationalist camp had won over the violent tradition. Sinn Fein had conceded the legitimate presence of Britain in Northern Ireland, even though it perceived it to be a 'transitional phase'.[62] As emerged soon

59. See McCann, Eamonn, *Belfast Telegraph*, 26 Feb. 1997 and 5 Nov. 1997.

60. Fitzgerald, *All in a Life*, p. 576.

61. O'Clery, *The Greening of the White House*, pp. 7ff.; Mallie and McKittrick, *The Fight for Peace*, p. 280.

62. Mitchel McLaughlin, *Belfast Telegraph*, 15 May 1998.

after the referendum on the Agreement, John Hume was now in a position to cooperate with unionism, provided the UUP was in a position to return the favour, without having to look constantly over his shoulder at SF. This appeared to be a 'Sunningdale' which could work. The nationalist electorate confirmed its support for these developments in the elections for the Assembly by giving the SDLP the highest share of all parties in first-preference votes (22 per cent), and SF's proportion rose to its highest yet at 17.6 per cent.

BRITISH POLICIES

As shown in previous chapters, the purpose of British Direct Rule was to allow a consensus in the political middle ground to emerge which would enable catholic and protestant parties to share power and make devolution possible. Up to and including the AIA (see above, p. 194ff.), all initiatives to break the log-jam of sectarian intransigence had focused on the moderate centre where liberal unionism and liberal nationalism could meet, in the hope that once an agreement in the centre was reached, a ripple effect would gradually draw the rest of society in, until the extremes were isolated. The existence of such a centre, however, turned out to be illusory, like Alice's Cheshire Cat: in relatively quiet times the moderate ground seemed to be large and sound, but as soon as sectarian tension grew, it paled into insignificance or disappeared altogether – not entirely unlike the opinion polls, which invariably showed a huge majority of the population in favour of peace without necessarily investigating what kind of peace the individuals polled had in mind. It thus became clear that Direct Rule could and would have to continue into perpetuity, unless a different method of tackling the problem could be found.

Peter Brooke appears to have been the first Secretary of State who tried to approach the province's political difficulties from the opposite end, namely by trying to persuade the extreme and violent ends of the political spectrum to move towards the middle. The end of this policy, pursued by all subsequent NI Secretaries, was the same as the previous one, a devolved power-sharing government in Northern Ireland, but the means of arriving there had radically changed. If polarisation could be reduced from the outside in, and an agreement reached on that basis, then a stable settlement might be achieved and Direct Rule could be phased out. In two respects the AIA had prepared the ground for such a development: it had produced full cooperation from

Dublin governments with British policies in the North, and it had put unionists under pressure to accept a compromise.

The initial success of this approach was greatly facilitated by tentative feelers from nationalist and loyalist paramilitaries for a more certain way into politics. Hume's talks with Adams on the one hand, and the conviction of loyalist ex-prisoners that the working classes could only lose by continued violence, had initiated this process. British governments had been in contact with the IRA leadership on and off since 1972, much to the annoyance of Irish governments, who felt that any contact with 'terrorists' undermined the democratic process and their own stand against them.[63] But until 1989 this had been part of a general intelligence-gathering exercise with little hope that more could come out of these contacts. The AIA had strengthened the SDLP's electoral hand against SF, and the republican movement's leadership began to consider ways out of their own impasse, namely that violence in conjunction with the ballot box seemed to have reached the limit of what it could achieve. This held promise not only for Hume's approach, but also for British initiatives. If, as appeared to be the case, loyalist violence was reactive, that is conditional on nationalist activities, then priority had to be given to finding ways of bringing SF into the political process. This line was thus followed by Thatcher, Major and Blair.

The dangers and risks of such a policy were in principle no greater than before: a false move or wrong timing could incite one of the opposing sides to renewed or increased violence, but that had always been the case. Whether the focus was on the political middle ground or its extremes, any attempt to resolve the province's entangled problems meant walking a tightrope. As in the past, as Labour became more electable it softened its pro-nationalist stand and bipartisanship was re-established. A new learning process had, however, to be set in motion, with the need for closer collaboration with Dublin, which initially resulted in many misunderstandings and mutual accusations. This was not surprising, given that there had been very little direct cooperation before and that the Irish governments were not handed any real power but were asked to help persuade radical nationalists to take the constitutional path. The Irish government had, however, changed its own attitude considerably since the AIA and was now willing to accept unionism's claims as legitimate.[64]

63. Fitzgerald, *All in a Life*, p. 104 and *passim*.

64. Cf. Catterall, Peter and McDougall, Sean, 'Introduction: Northern Ireland in British Politics', in Catterall and McDougall (eds), *The NI Question*, p. 8.

Since unionists were increasingly isolated politically as a result of this approach, a prime task of all British governments – eventually with help from Dublin, once unionist leaders were willing to listen to it – was to reassure them of the consent principle, which now no longer meant an absolute guarantee of the constitutional status quo but still offered a guarantee that a united Ireland would not be forthcoming without their consent, provided they retained a majority in the North. At the same time pressure was relentlessly exerted upon unionists to accept the notion of power-sharing as a *sine qua non* of devolution.

One way of assuring the unionists that no deals were made with the republican movement behind their backs was an emphasis on an ever more sophisticated security policy against the IRA. This also served the purpose of reinforcing the arguments about the unarmed struggle within SF. Since the AIA there had been more, and more effective, cooperation in this from the South, although on a political level Dublin was only willing to go so far, unless the judicial system in the North was reformed. John Hermon, who had considered the policing of the protestant AIA day of action the RUC's breakthrough to impartiality, was replaced by Hugh Annesley in May 1989. With a Northern father, but raised in Dublin, the hopes were that it would be easier for him to cooperate with the Gardai and to increase recruitment from the catholic section of the population, thus not only pleasing the unionists but making security more acceptable to nationalists. Catholic membership remained at 8 per cent overall throughout the nineties, but was higher in senior posts. Annesley made inroads into paramilitary racketeering and continued with the professionalisation of the RUC, but, as previous Chief Constables, he could only go as far as politics allowed him to, and catholics' reluctance to join the police continued. While he showed a generally more democratic style than his predecessor and improved the managerial and command structure of the force, his reluctance to tackle the male-dominated protestant ethos of the police meant that the RUC was particularly ill suited to confront the increased protestant violence of those years.[65] The RUC was given a clean bill of health by the Stevens inquiry which reported on links between loyalist paramilitaries and the police. The UDR, however, was shown to have an exceptionally large number of members with criminal records, poor internal security and clear links to loyalist paramilitaries. Out of this came its reorganisation under Brooke, in July 1992, when the Royal Irish Regiment was set up, thus showing the government's clear intent of providing impartiality in

65. Ryder, *The RUC 1922–1997*, pp. 401–7, 416, 464–71.

its security organisations as well as improving their efficiency. In November 1996 Annesley was succeeded by Ronnie Flanagan, whose North Belfast working-class background and reputation for openness and accountability promised well for the necessary reforms in the RUC.[66]

As governments hardened their official attitude towards SF and the IRA through broadcasting bans, tighter security, and the banning of SF from all political talks, while trying to convince them in private that they were now neutral facilitators in an all-Irish dispute, unionists remained suspicious of any secret dealings with republicans. The increasingly frustrated mood of much loyalist public opinion flared up regularly during the marching season and found its focus in the Drumcree issue, which showed London how bitter the communal hatred remained. It clearly indicated that much headway still needed to be made, even if republicans could be persuaded to accept a largely internal settlement. While SF had initially insisted that Britain should impose a settlement on the protestants of the North, it gradually began to accept that neither Britain nor the government of the Republic had any intention of doing this.

The main difficulty for Brooke and his successors thus remained to mediate and find a balance between unionists' fears of a blueprint pointing towards a united Ireland and the nationalists' insistence that an internal settlement was insufficient. The three-stranded approach was an imaginative one, and, after some initial resistance, unionists accepted the principle of power-sharing in Strand One and some North–South cooperation. But it was the North–South relations of Strand Two which remained the major stumbling-block. As Trimble seemed to accept the principle, the SDLP raised its aims, and it was the question of how much power any joint body should be given which remained the greatest problem throughout the negotiations.

With each step Britain took forward it tried to balance what it offered each side: the Select Committee in the House of Commons was finally granted to unionists, followed by the DSD, which showed the complete agreement of the two governments on the way forward for the province. It was also the furthest Britain had moved from active involvement in the province: as one commentator put it, '[the DSD] is in fact a shedding of the British population of Ulster'.[67] Unionist unease was lessened by the loyalist ceasefire, which was as much a response to the DSD as it was to the republicans' previous

66. *Ibid.*, pp. 474f.
67. Foster, John Wilson, *Fortnight*, May 1994, pp. 35–6.

ceasefire. Loyalist paramilitaries felt that the union was safe, which enabled Trimble to move away from the DUP, which felt that Britain was increasingly paving the way towards a united Ireland, and towards a cautious compromise. The Framework Documents of 1995, which put a greater, and more uncertain, emphasis on North–South cooperation than the unionists liked and failed to propose a substantial enough change to Articles 2 and 3 of the Irish constitution, were balanced by the Heads of Agreement paper which was tabled on behalf of the two governments at the beginning of the final talks in January 1998, which promised an inter-governmental committee alongside cross-border bodies. This in turn displeased SF, but it had become difficult for them to withdraw from the talks at this stage. In many respects the DSD and the Framework Documents were Britain's final triumph in its policy: both governments ceased to be protectors of the separate parts of the population of Northern Ireland and became neutral observers willing to help both sides as best they could to come to an agreement which they would then be willing to underwrite and guarantee. As the AIA had brought the support of the SDLP, so the DSD dropped Britain's commitment to the majority in the province, thus opening the door for SF. It has been suggested that this was the final recognition that not SF but unionists were the problem for the British government because of their insistence on Britain's obligation to stay in the province.[68]

By the spring of 1998, with SF and the UDP back at the talks and the degree of actual progress difficult to assess, as the participating parties continued to attack each other in front of the media, the British government appeared confident that an agreement could be reached before the next summer's marching season. Confirmation of this might have been found in the increased violence from the paramilitary breakaway groups on both sides: the LVF's and CAC's bombings and killings continued and seemed to intensify. Whether or not, in view of this, SF and the unionists could stay on the road of compromise remained to be seen. The talks, or indeed any agreement which could be concluded by May/June, might yet be pulled asunder by the violence of those who rejected it.

During the referendum campaign there was a last-minute scare, when opinion polls suggested a sudden plunge in support for the Agreement among unionists which was at least in part brought on by the NIO, Dublin and London bending over to help Sinn Fein to secure IRA support by temporarily releasing some of the worst con-

68. Cox, W. Harvey, 'From Hillsborough to Downing Street', p. 209.

victed bombers. Only several visits by Tony Blair to the province secured a final unionist majority vote. From then onwards British policy looked promising again: the centre ground expanded and was now represented by the parties which had campaigned for a yes vote. British policy at last appeared to have put Northern Ireland on the rails, even though the final outcome could yet be wrecked.

UNIONIST RESPONSES

After the initial frustration with the AIA (see above, p. 199ff.), which shook even the unionist middle classes out of a decade of political apathy,[69] unionists had learned to live with it.[70] It appeared after all to be helping to keep violence at an acceptable level, even though it deprived them of any political initiative. In essence and at least until the ceasefires, however, unionists were still trying to defend what they had lost in 1972, even though the unity that this common aim provided was as fragile as ever. Not surprisingly perhaps, the move towards compromise and peaceful negotiations with nationalists did not come from the centre of traditional unionism, which had too much to lose, but from the paramilitary fringes, even though this could only come to fruition if it was taken up by the UUP – without such an initiative, however, it is doubtful whether Trimble could have followed that direction.

As early as 1987 the UDA had published a document, entitled 'Common Sense', which proposed a written constitution, a bill of rights, a Supreme Court, and power-sharing in the form of proportionality within a devolved government, to which the UVF responded that it had proposed similar ideas in 1977,[71] even though very little attention was given to them at the time.[72] The increased politicisation of the loyalist paramilitaries can be traced back, albeit in an interrupted

69. Coulter, Colin, 'Direct Rule and the Unionist Middle Classes', in English, Richard and Walker, Graham (eds), *Unionism in Modern Ireland: New Perspectives on Politics and Culture*, London 1996, p. 178.

70. Cochrane, *Unionist Politics*, pp. 88f.

71. Cusack, *op. cit.*, p. 253.

72. Bruce, Steve, *The Red Hand: Protestant Paramilitaries in Northern Ireland*, Oxford 1992, p. 239.

line, to the traditional unionist parties' response to the AIA, which was perhaps perceived as more of a threat to the union by the former groups than by the latter's politicians. As a result, rather than saying simply no, to which official unionism and the DUP confined themselves, they began to develop constructive policies which were more moderate than either of the conventional parties'. By the late eighties there was considerable mistrust of Paisley and his party in particular. In the nineties the focus of violence became deliberately more political, and, if not always successfully, switched from targeting catholics in general to aiming at SF members. But there was also the realisation – as previously in security circles and then in the IRA – that the war could not be won militarily.

The Stevens inquiry relieved the UDA of most of its leadership and a 'more determined, ruthless and dedicated organisation'[73] emerged thereafter. By spring 1991 the two groups had moved closer together and the Combined Loyalist Military Command (CLMC) was formed, claiming to work towards peace in the form of ceasefires and a political settlement. Cooperation in practice, however, often proved difficult because of internal power struggles and rivalries[74] between the groups and their members, and was not helped by the fact that the UDA was reluctant to abandon its largely sectarian nature, or many of its leaders their income from non-political paramilitary activities. As individual political leaders emerged in the UDP and PUP, prominent among them David Ervine of the PUP and Gary McMichael of the UDP, the image of the loyalist paramilitaries changed – they became more adept in dealing with the media, and, even though they distrusted the Hume–Adams alliance and opposed any North–South joint authority, their conviction grew that only a political settlement involving compromise could end the conflict in Northern Ireland. To that end they were willing to and did make contact with the Dublin government. To what extent they succeeded in carrying their still largely sectarian grass-roots with them remains difficult to assess, although by and large their ceasefire held. But as with the republican end of the spectrum those disagreeing openly found refuge in the new splinter-group of the LVF, and what Steve Bruce suggested for an earlier period might still hold true: 'If you want defence or attack, you support your local UVF and UDA. When you want political representation, you can choose from a variety of unionist parties.'[75]

73. Cusack, *op. cit.*, p. 263. See also Bruce, Steve, *The Edge of the Union: The Ulster Loyalist Political Vision*, Oxford 1994.

74. Cf. Bruce, *Red Hand*, pp. 124ff., and *passim*.

75. *Ibid.*, p. 242.

The limited initial impact of the new parties on the electorate can be seen in the Forum elections of 1996 in which the PUP polled 3.5 per cent and the UDP 2.2 per cent of the vote, while the DUP, which considered the union unsafe since the DSD, held to 17.8 per cent. The DUP was effectively driven into ever greater inflexibility, and its electorate appears to represent the hard core of those groups within unionism who perceive any compromise with nationalism as the beginning of the end of their cultural and political identity and thus as a threat to their very existence. They continued to view any Southern Irish involvement in Northern affairs as evidence of the Republic's encroachment on Northern territory. An unlikely ally for Paisley turned out to be the leader of the UK-Unionists (UKUP), Robert McCartney, a QC and former UUP member, who had called the DUP leader a fascist in 1981,[76] but now stood with him against the DSD and any weakening of the union. Both parties campaigned for a no vote in the referendum, hoping for a revival of their political fortunes through a combined effort with the Orange Order and UUP dissenters to rout Trimble.

The greatest danger for mainstream unionism was thus a return to the seventies, and Sunningdale parallels were often quoted:[77] Trimble might end up as another Faulkner, isolated within the party; traditionally unionist leaders fell because they appeared to grow 'soft' on the union: 'signs of compromise were equated with weakness and treachery rather than statecraft'.[78] However, when David Trimble was elected over John Taylor to succeed Molyneaux as leader of the UUP in September 1995, he was perceived to be a hard-liner who would, even more than his predecessor, reject any overtures by the British government to press unionism into power-sharing with nationalists. This was not dissimilar to Faulkner's image in the O'Neill administration (see above, p. 92f.). Taylor was considered to be 'a tough old campaigner', but with 'the clout and vision to take his people . . . into the peace process'.[79] Trimble had been a law lecturer in Queen's University, Belfast, had entered politics in the early seventies, was involved with the UUUP and Vanguard (see above, pp. 125, 140f., 169), and in the late seventies had finally rejoined the OUP, where he represented the most radical anti-AIA wing within the party. He was elected as MP for Upper Bann in 1990.

76. Flackes and Elliott, *Northern Ireland*, p. 217.
77. e.g. David McKittrick, *The Nervous Peace*, Belfast 1996, p. 79.
78. Cochrane, *Unionist Politics*, p. 387.
79. McKittrick, *The Nervous Peace*, p. 147.

From the moment of his election as leader Trimble turned out to be much more visible than Molyneaux, initially promoting the hard-line image, when he openly posed in support of loyalism in Drumcree, and much more aggressive in promoting unionism in front of the television cameras. The opportunity, or possibly necessity, to change course came with the DSD, which from a unionist perspective was a much more serious step by Britain away from its commitment to the union that the AIA had been.[80] Staying with the DUP and rejecting it was a much less attractive option, given that both British and Irish governments supported it and that the loyalist paramilitaries' representatives considered the union sufficiently guaranteed by it. With some courage Trimble went for the option of putting unionism back into a negotiating position rather than one of simple opposition. After that decision his problems were, if anything, worse than Gerry Adams's: he had to carry the greatest possible majority of his notoriously fractured party with him into any agreement and could only hope that the supporters of the LVF and other defected paramilitaries would not give their vote to the DUP, which was in some respects the superficially more attractive party for unionist voters since it did not try to break with tradition or try to 'modernise'.[81]

This explains the rather confusing picture that emerged subsequently: the UUP appeared to be talking with one hard-line voice and all 'soft' dissent seemed to have disappeared, while in fact Trimble sat down with nationalists to negotiate the future of Northern Ireland. Initial attempts to prise the SDLP from its 'pact' with SF continued to be pursued even after it became clear that this approach could not succeed, but relations with constitutional nationalism improved considerably. Yet Trimble could not afford to acknowledge any of SF's political demands in public, in view of his larger constituency. The resulting good relations with the SDLP, however, opened the door for compromise.

Apart from taking the toughest possible stand in public, Trimble, in order to keep the party together and not have too much of his electorate defect to the DUP, had to get concessions for unionism which, if not on the scale of those made to nationalists, would at least guarantee the continuation of Northern Ireland's constitutional position as part of the UK and a say by unionists in any future form of government that was at least in proportion to their strength. By and large he

80. See, for instance, Foster, John Wilson, 'The Declaration and the Union', in Foster (ed.), *The Idea of the Union*, pp. 100–3.

81. Cf. Cochrane, *Unionist Politics*.

succeeded in this. From the time he met Taoiseach Bertie Ahern in November 1997 the unionist leader succeeded in getting assurances that the envisaged cross-border bodies would have executive functions but not executive power and that the Republic was indeed willing to modify its constitutional claim to the territory of the North. With this achieved his party executive gave Trimble a free hand to negotiate the best he could for unionism in the talks. In many respects Trimble picked up where the modernisation of unionism had faltered under O'Neill and Faulkner. While keeping the tough stance to appease the right wing of his party and to avoid his predecessors' mistakes, he was equally willing to compromise and allow unionism to enter a new democratic alliance with all forces in Northern Ireland who were willing to do the same.

After the signing of the Agreement a rather complicated picture emerged. Unionism appeared to be split down the middle: eight unionist MPs (UUP, DUP and UKUP) opposed the Agreement in the debate in the House of Commons and only three supported it. As the campaigns for the referendum on 22 May started, the supporters of a no vote stressed the issues of the future of the RUC, prisoner releases, decommissioning of weapons, and the prospect of former IRA men sitting in a government of Northern Ireland. Against the background of unionist tradition to resist any change, since it was considered to benefit only nationalists, the anti-Agreement campaign had a psychological advantage and certainly appeared to be more articulate and vociferous in its negativity than any pro-Agreement voices. The DUP, UKUP and the Orange Order all weighed in against the Agreement, utilising the ancient fears of the unionist community. For a time their cause was helped by the insensitive release of convicted terrorists to attend respective republican and loyalist meetings.

During the campaign there were attempts to split the UUP as the basis for a majority unionist no vote. Given the weak position of Trimble's stance among the parliamentary party this looked promising and Jeffrey Donaldson made a bid for the future leadership. But he had to retreat before the referendum when the British government's and Trimble's efforts appeared to increase the yes vote among unionists beyond the dissenters' expectations. The thin majority of the unionist yes vote in the referendum encouraged renewed cooperation with the SDLP, which refused an offered pact with SF and urged its voters to give their transfer votes to other 'yes-parties', explicitly including the UUP, in the elections to the assembly. Because of the proportionate nature of decision-making in that body (any major legislation needed majority support from parties of both communities) the

Trimble-faction of unionism needed a clear majority in the first election to it or else the new parliament could be wrecked from within and effectively made inoperable. If one counted the two elected PUP candidates they just about managed that, even though some of their own elected members had been no-campaigners and much would depend on how well Trimble could keep the party together. Whether or not his position as First Minister would help him in this remained to be seem.

As the century draws to a close the constitutional and political framework of Northern Ireland appears to have changed considerably. The constitutional compromise of 1920 has made room for the *de jure* recognition by the Republic and the province will be able to exercise, initially limited, but eventually full, self-government within the UK. This by itself and in the short term of course does nothing to diminish perceived prejudices and sectarian expectations on both sides of the divided community. Only if self-government can be made to succeed in the long run, and in economic as much as in political terms, can the divisions eventually be accommodated and a modernised and more democratic society emerge.

The constitutional compromise of 1920, however, was changed for good. While the province might yet prove itself to be not quite ready for self-government – and the omens, with the next Drumcree as controversially as ever on the early summer horizon, were not good – the changes to the Irish constitution made it unlikely that either side in the conflict could continue to articulate itself in quite the same traditional forms. The 'armed propaganda'[82] which the IRA provided for Sinn Fein looked likely to become rhetoric rather than a real threat for the time being, while unionism still had to come to terms with its new position, which in terms of the Agreement negotiations was a victory but was seen by very many unionists as a Pyrrhic one at best in which a Trojan horse in the form of Sinn Fein had been forced into their midst.

82. Gerry Adams's phrase, quoted by Malachi O'Doherty, *Belfast Telegraph*, 25 May 1998.

Bibliography

Adams, James, *Secret Armies*, London 1987.

Adams, James, Morgan, Robin and Bambridge, Anthony, *Ambush. The War between the SAS and the IRA*, London, Sydney and Auckland 1988.

The *Annual Register*, a Record of World Events, Vols 187–229, 1945–1987, London, New York and Toronto 1946–88.

Arthur, Max, *Northern Ireland Soldiers Talking*, London 1987.

Arthur, Paul, *The People's Democracy 1968–1973*, Belfast 1974.

Arthur, Paul, *Government and Politics of Northern Ireland*, London and New York 1984 (2nd edn).

Arthur, Paul and Jeffery, Keith, *Northern Ireland Since 1968*, Oxford 1988.

Aughey, Arthur, *Under Siege. Ulster Unionism and the Anglo-Irish Agreement*, Belfast 1989.

Aunger, Edmund A., 'Religion and Occupational Class in Northern Ireland', in *Economic and Social Studies*, Vol. 7, No. 1, 1975, pp. 1–18.

Bardon, Jonathan, *A History of Ulster*, Belfast 1992.

Barritt, Denis P. and Carter, Charles F., *The Northern Ireland Problem. A Study in Group Relations*, London 1962.

Barritt, Denis, *Northern Ireland – a Problem to every Solution*, London 1982.

Barton, Brian, *Brookeborough. The Making of a Prime Minister*, Belfast 1988.

Beckett, J.C., 'Ulster Protestantism', in Moody, T.W. and Beckett, J.C. (eds), *Ulster Since 1800*, second series, *A Social Survey*, London 1958 (2nd edn).

Beckett, J.C., *The Making of Modern Ireland 1603–1923*, London 1966.

Beckett, J.C., 'Northern Ireland', in *Journal of Contemporary History*, Vol. 6, No. 1, 1971, 121ff.

Belfrage, Sally, *The Crack. A Belfast Year*, London 1988.

Bell, Geoffrey, *The Protestants of Ulster*, London 1976.

Bell, J. Bowyer, *The Secret Army. The IRA 1916–1979*, Dublin 1979 (3rd edn).

Bell, J. Bowyer, *Back to the Future. The Protestants and a United Ireland*, Dublin 1996.

Beresford, David, *Ten Men Dead. The Story of the 1981 Irish Hunger Strike*, London 1987.

Bew, Paul, Gibbon, Peter and Patterson, Henry, *Northern Ireland 1921–1996. Political Forces and Social Classes.* London 1996.

Bew, Paul and Gillespie, Gordon, *Northern Ireland. A Chronology of the Troubles, 1968–1993*, Dublin 1993.

Bew, Paul and Gillespie, Gordon, *The Northern Ireland Peace Process 1993–1996. A Chronology*, London 1996.

Bew, Paul and Patterson, Henry, *The British State and the Ulster Crisis. From Wilson to Thatcher*, London 1985.

Birrell, Derek and Murrie, Alan, *Policy and Government in Northern Ireland. Lessons of Devolution*, Dublin 1980.

Bishop, Patrick and Mallie, Eamonn, *The Provisional IRA*, London 1987.

Bleakley, David, *Faulkner. Conflict and Consent in Irish Politics*, London and Oxford 1974.

Bloomfield, Ken, *Stormont in Crisis. A Memoir*, Belfast 1994.

Boulton, David, *The UVF 1966–73. An Anatomy of Loyalist Rebellion*, Dublin 1973.

Boyce, D.G., *The Irish Question and British Politics, 1868–1996*, London 1996 (2nd edn).

Boyd, Andrew, *Holy War in Belfast*, London 1969.

Boyle, Kevin, Hadden, Tom and Hillyard, Paddy, *Ten Years on in Northern Ireland. The Legal Control of Political Violence*, Nottingham 1980.

Breen, Richard, Devine, Paula and Robinson, Gillian (eds), *Social Attitudes in Northern Ireland. The Fourth Report. 1994–1995*, Belfast 1995.

Bruce, Steve, *God Save Ulster! The Religion and Politics of Paisleyism*, Oxford and New York 1986.

Bruce, Steve, *The Red Hand: Protestant Paramilitaries in Northern Ireland*, Oxford 1992.

Bruce, Steve, *The Edge of the Union: The Ulster Loyalist Political Vision*, Oxford 1994.

Buckland, Patrick, *Ulster Unionism and the Origins of Northern Ireland 1886–1922*, 2 vols, Dublin and New York 1973.

Buckland, Patrick, *The Factory of Grievances*, Dublin and New York 1979.

Buckland, Patrick, *James Craig Lord Craigavon*, Dublin 1980.

Buckland, Patrick, *A History of Northern Ireland*, Dublin 1981.

Cairns, Ed, *Caught in Crossfire: Children and the Northern Ireland Conflict*, Belfast and New York 1987.

Callaghan, James, *A House Divided. The Dilemma of Northern Ireland*, London 1973.

Catterall, Peter and McDougall, Sean (eds), *The Northern Ireland Question in British Politics*, London 1996.

Clarke, Liam, *Broadening the Battlefield: The H-Blocks and the Rise of Sinn Fein*, Dublin 1987.

Cochrane, Feargal, *Unionist Politics and the Politics of Unionism since the Anglo-Irish Agreement*, Cork 1997.

Cole, John, *As it Seemed to Me. Political Memoirs*, London 1996.

Committee on the Administration of Justice, 'Police Accountability in Northern Ireland', CAJ Pamphlet No. 11, Belfast 1988.

Coogan, Tim Pat, *The IRA*, London 1970.

The Crossman Diaries. *Selections from the Diaries of a Cabinet Minister 1964–1970,* London 1979.

Cusack, Jim and McDonald, Henry, *UVF*, Dublin 1997.

Darby, John, *Conflict in Northern Ireland: The Development of a Polarised Community*, Dublin and New York 1976.

Darby, John (ed.), *Northern Ireland: The Background to the Conflict*, Belfast 1983.

Darby, John, *Intimidation and the Control of Conflict in Northern Ireland*, Dublin 1986.

Devlin, Bernadette, *The Price of My Soul*, London 1969.

Devlin, Paddy, *Straight Left. An Autobiography*, Belfast 1993.

Dowds, Lizanne, Devine, Paula and Breen, Richard (eds), *Social Attitudes in Northern Ireland. The Sixth Report. 1996–1997*, Belfast 1997.

Downey, James, *Them and Us: Britain, Ireland and the Northern Question 1969–82*, Dublin 1983.

Duignan, Sean, *One Spin on the Merry-go-round*, Dublin, n.d. [1995]

Dunn, Seamus (ed.), *Facets of the Conflict in Northern Ireland*, London 1995.

Edwards, Owen Dudley, *The Sins of our Fathers. Roots of Conflict in Northern Ireland*, Dublin 1970.

Elliott, Sydney (comp. and ed.), *Northern Ireland Parliamentary Results 1921–1972*, Chichester 1973.

English, Richard and Walker, Graham (eds), *Unionism in Modern Ireland: New Perspectives on Politics and Culture*, London 1996.

Faligot, Roger, *Britain's Military Strategy in Ireland. The Kitson Experiment*, London 1983.

Falls, Cyril, 'Northern Ireland and the Defence of the British Isles', in Wilson, T. (ed.), *Ulster under Home Rule*, Oxford 1955.

Farrell, Michael, *Northern Ireland: The Orange State*, London 1980 (2nd edn).

Faulkner, Brian, *Memoirs of a Statesman* (ed. John Houston), London 1978.

Fitzgerald, Garret, *All in a Life. An Autobiography*, Dublin 1991.

Flackes, W.D., *Northern Ireland: A Political Directory, 1968–83*, London 1983.

Flackes, W.D. and Elliott, Sydney, *Northern Ireland. A Political Directory, 1968–1993*. Belfast 1994.

Foster, John Wilson (ed.), *The Idea of the Union. Statements and Critiques in Support of the Union of Great Britain and Northern Ireland*, Vancouver 1995.

Foster, R.F., *Modern Ireland 1600–1972*, London 1988.

Gaffikin, Frank and Morrissey, Mike, *Northern Ireland: The Thatcher Years*, London and New Jersey 1990.

Gaffikin, Frank and Morrissey, Mike, *The New Unemployed. Joblessness and Poverty in the Market Economy*, London and New Jersey 1992.

Gordon, David, *The O'Neill Years. Unionist Politics 1963–1969*, Belfast 1989.

Gray, Tony, *The Orange Order*, London 1972.

Green, Arthur J., *Devolution and Public Finance. Stormont from 1921 to 1972*, Glasgow 1979.

Gudgin, Graham, *The Economic Outlook and Medium Term Forecasts 1997–2001*, Northern Ireland Economic Research Centre. September 1997.

Guelke, Adrian, *Northern Ireland: The International Perspective*, Dublin 1988.

Hadden, Tom and Boyle, Kevin, *The Anglo-Irish Agreement: Commentary, Text and Official Review*, London and Dublin 1989.

Hamill, Desmond, *Pig in the Middle: The Army in Northern Ireland, 1969–1984*. London 1985.

Hanna, Eamon (ed.), *Poverty in Ireland*, Lurgan 1988.

Harbinson, Jeremy and Joan (eds), *A Society under Stress. Children and Young People in Northern Ireland*, West Compton House, Somerset 1980.

Harbinson, John F., *The Ulster Unionist Party, 1882–1973. Its Development and Organisation*, Belfast 1973.

Harkness, David, *Northern Ireland Since 1920*, Dublin 1983.

Harris, Rosemary, *Prejudice and Tolerance in Ulster: A Study of Neighbours and 'Strangers' in a Border Community*. Manchester 1972.

Hayes, Maurice, *Minority Verdict. Experiences of a Catholic Public Servant*, Belfast 1995.

Hennessey, Thomas, *A History of Northern Ireland 1920–1996*, Dublin 1997.

Hermon, John, *Holding the Line. An Autobiography*, Dublin 1997.

Heskin, Ken, *Northern Ireland: A Psychological Analysis*, Dublin 1980.

Holland, Jack, *The American Connection*, Dublin 1989.

Holland, Jack and McDonald, Henry, *INLA. Deadly Divisions*, Dublin 1996.

Horgan, John, *Sean Lemass. The Enigmatic Patriot*, Dublin 1997.

Isles, K.S. and Cuthbert, N., 'Economic Policy', in Wilson, T. (ed.), *Ulster under Home Rule*, Oxford 1955.

Johnson, D.S., 'The Northern Irish Economy 1914–1939', in Kennedy, Liam and Ollerenshaw, Philip (eds), *An Economic History of Ulster, 1820–1939*, Manchester 1985.

Johnson, D.S. and Kennedy, L., 'The Two Irish Economies Since 1920', in Moody, T.W., Martin, F.X., Byrne, F.J. and Vaughan, W.E (eds), *A New History of Ireland*, VII, Oxford (forthcoming).

Kennedy, David, 'The Catholic Church', in Moody, T.W. and Beckett, J.C. (eds), *Ulster Since 1800*, second series, *A Social Survey*, London 1958 (2nd edn).

Kennedy, Dennis, *The Widening Gulf. Northern Attitudes to the Independent Irish State, 1919–49*, Belfast 1988.

Kennedy, Liam and Ollerenshaw, Philip (eds), *An Economic History of Ulster, 1820–1939*, Manchester 1985.

Keogh, Dermot and Haltzel, Michael H. (eds), *Northern Ireland and the Politics of Reconciliation*, Cambridge 1993.

Lawrence, R.J., *The Government of Northern Ireland*, Oxford 1965.

Lee, J.J., *Ireland 1912–1985: Politics and Society*, Cambridge 1989.

Lyons, F.S.L., *Ireland Since the Famine*, London 1982 (revised edn).

MacManus, Francis (ed.), *The Years of the Great Test*, Dublin and Cork 1967.

Magee, Jack, 'The Teaching of Irish History in Irish Schools', in *The Northern Teacher*, Winter 1970.

Mallie, Eamonn and McKittrick, David, *The Fight for Peace. The Secret Story Behind the Irish Peace Process*, London 1997.

McAllister, Ian, 'Political Opposition in Northern Ireland: The National Democratic Party, 1965–1970', in *Economic and Social Review*, 6:3, 1975, pp. 353–66.

McAllister, Ian, *The Northern Ireland Social Democratic and Labour Party. Political Opposition in a Divided Society*, London 1977.

McCann, Eamonn, *War and an Irish Town*, Harmondsworth 1974.

McKittrick, David, *Despatches from Belfast*, Belfast 1989.

McKittrick, David, *The Nervous Peace*, Belfast 1996.

McLaughlin, Eithne and Quirk, Padraic (eds), *Policy Aspects of Employment Equality in Northern Ireland*, Belfast n.d. [1996] (Volume II of *Employment Equality in Northern Ireland*, published by Standing Advisory Commission on Human Rights).

McNamee, Peter and Lovett, Tom, *Working-Class Community in Northern Ireland*, Belfast 1987.

McVey, John and Hutson, Nigel (eds), *Public Views and Experiences of Fair Employment and Equality Issues in Northern Ireland*, Belfast n.d. [1996] (Volume III of *Employment Equality in Northern Ireland*, published by SACHR).

Miller, David, *Don't Mention the War. Northern Ireland, Propaganda and the Media*, London 1994.

Moloney, Ed and Pollak, Andy, *Paisley*, Dublin 1986.

Moody, T.W. and Beckett, J.C. (eds), *Ulster Since 1800*, second series, *A Social Survey*, London 1958 (2nd edn).

Moody, T.W., 'The Social History of Modern Ulster', in Moody, T.W. and Beckett, J.C. (eds), *Ulster Since 1800*, second series, *A Social Survey*, London 1958 (2nd edn).

Moxon-Browne, Edward, *Nation, Class and Creed in Northern Ireland*, Aldershot, Hampshire 1983.

Murphy, Dervla, *A Place Apart*, London 1979.

Murray, Dominic, *Worlds Apart: Segregated Schools in Northern Ireland*, Belfast 1985.

O'Brien, Brendan, *The Long War. The IRA and Sinn Fein from Armed Struggle to Peace Talks*, Dublin 1993/95.

O'Brien, Conor Cruise, *States of Ireland*, London 1974.

O'Clery, Conor, *The Greening of the White House. The Inside Story of how America Tried to Bring Peace to Ireland*, Dublin 1996.

O'Dowd, Liam, Rolston, Bill and Tomlinson, Mike (eds), *Northern Ireland: Between Civil Rights and Civil War*, London 1980.

O'Leary, Cornelius, Elliott, Sydney and Wilford, R.A., *The Northern Ireland Assembly, 1982–1986. A Constitutional Experiment*, Belfast 1988.

Oliver, John Andrew, *Working at Stormont*, Dublin 1978.

O'Malley, Padraig, *The Uncivil Wars. Ireland Today*, Belfast 1983.

O'Malley, Padraig, *Questions of Nuance*, Belfast 1990.

O'Neill, Terence, *Ulster at the Crossroads*, London 1969.

O'Neill, Terence, *The Autobiography of Terence O'Neill, Prime Minister of Northern Ireland 1963–1969*, London 1972.

Palley, Claire, 'The Evolution, Disintegration and Possible Reconstruction of the Northern Ireland Constitution', in *Anglo-American Law Review*, Vol. I, 1972, pp. 368–476.

Paor, Liam de, *Divided Ulster*, Harmondsworth 1971.

Parkinson, J.R., 'Shipbuilding', in Buxton, Neil K. and Aldcroft, Derek H. (eds), *British Industry between the Wars*, London 1982.

Patterson, Henry, *The Politics of Illusion. A Political History of the IRA*, London 1997.

Porter, Norman, *Rethinking Unionism. An Alternative Vision of Northern Ireland*, Belfast 1996.

Probert, Belinda, *Beyond Orange and Green. The Political Economy of the Northern Ireland Crisis*, London 1978.

Purdy, Ann, *Molyneaux: The Long View*, Antrim 1989.

Rees, Merlyn, *Northern Ireland. A Personal Perspective*, London 1985.

Roche, Patrick J. and Birnie, J. Esmond, *An Economic Lesson for Irish Nationalists and Republicans*, Belfast 1995.

Rolston, Bill and Tomlinson, Mike, *Unemployment in West Belfast. The Obair Report*, Belfast 1988.

Rose, Richard, *Governing without Consensus. An Irish Perspective*, London 1971.

Rose, Richard, *Northern Ireland. A Time of Choice*, Washington, DC 1976.

Rowthorn, Bob, 'Unemployment: The Widening Gap', in *Fortnight*, 16 Dec. 1985.

Ruane, Joseph and Todd, Jennifer, *The Dynamics of Conflict in Northern Ireland: Power, Conflict and Emancipation*, Cambridge 1996.

Ryder, Chris, *The RUC 1922–1997. A Force under Fire*, London (1989/92) 1997.

Sales, Rosemary, *Women Divided: Gender, Religion and Politics in Northern Ireland*, London 1997.

Sayers, John E., 'The Political Parties and the Social Background', in Wilson, Thomas (ed.), *Ulster under Home Rule*, Oxford 1955.

Shea, Patrick, *Voices and the Sound of Drums. An Irish Autobiography*, Belfast 1981.

Smyth, Clifford, *Ian Paisley. Voice of Protestant Ulster*, Edinburgh 1987.

Stewart, A.T.Q., *The Ulster Crisis*, London 1967.

Stewart, A.T.Q., *The Narrow Ground*, London 1977.

Stringer, Peter and Robinson, Gillian (eds), *Social Attitudes in Northern Ireland. The Second Report. 1991–1992*, Belfast 1992.

Sunday Times Insight Team, *Ulster*, Harmondsworth 1972.

Teague, Paul (ed.), *Beyond the Rhetoric. Politics, the Economy and Social Policy in Northern Ireland*, London 1987.

Toibin, Colm, *Walking along the Border*, London 1987.

'The Ulster Debate', report of a Study Group of the Institute for the Study of Conflict, London, Sydney, Toronto 1972.

Utley, T.E., *Lessons of Ulster*, London 1975.

Van Voris, W.H., *Violence in Ulster: An Oral Documentary*, Arnherst 1975.

Walker, Lynda, 'Godmothers and Mentors. Women, Politics and Education in Northern Ireland', M.Ed. thesis, QUB 1996.

Wallace, Martin, *Northern Ireland. 50 Years of Self-Government*, Newton Abbot 1971.

Walsh, Pat, *From Civil Rights to National War. Northern Ireland Catholic Politics 1964–1974*, Belfast 1989.

Ward, Alan, J. (ed.), *Northern Ireland. Living with the Crisis*, London 1987.

White, Barry, *John Hume. Statesman of the Troubles*, Belfast 1984.

White, Barry, 'Putting the Squeeze on the Terrorist Cash Flow', in *Belfast Telegraph*, 1 Sept. 1988, p. 9.

Whyte, J.H., *Church and State in Modern Ireland, 1923–1979*, Dublin 1980 (2nd edn).

Whyte, J.H., *Interpreting Northern Ireland*, Oxford 1990.

Wilson, Andrew J., *Irish America and the Ulster Conflict, 1968–1995*, Belfast 1995.

Wilson, Harold, *Final Term. The Labour Government 1974–1976*, London 1979.

Wilson, Thomas (ed.), *Ulster under Home Rule*, Oxford 1955.

Wilson, Tom, *Ulster: Conflict and Consent*, Oxford and New York 1989.

Government publications (in chronological order)

Quekett, Arthur S., *The Constitution of Northern Ireland. Part III: A Review of Operations under the Government of Ireland Act 1920*, HMSO, Belfast 1946.

Ulster Year Book 1947–1986, HMSO, Belfast 1947–1987.

Blake, John W., *Northern Ireland in the Second World War*, HMSO, Belfast 1956.

Isles, K.S. and Cuthbert, N., *An Economic Survey of Northern Ireland*, HMSO, Belfast 1957.

'Report of the Joint Working Party on the Economy in Northern Ireland' (Hall Report), HMSO, London 1962, Cmd 1835.

'Economic Development in Northern Ireland' (Wilson Report), HMSO, Belfast 1965, Cmd 479.

'Disturbances in Northern Ireland: Report of the Committee appointed by the Governor of Northern Ireland' (Cameron Report), HMSO, Belfast 1969, Cmd 532.

'A Commentary by the Government of Northern Ireland to Accompany the Cameron Report', HMSO, Belfast 1969, Cmd 534.

'Report of the Advisory Committee on the Police in Northern Ireland' (Hunt Report), HMSO, Belfast 1969, Cmd 535.

'Review of Economic and Social Development in Northern Ireland', HMSO, Belfast 1971, Cmd 564.

Shearman, Hugh, *Northern Ireland 1921–1971*, HMSO, Belfast n.d. [1971].

'Report of the enquiry into allegations against the security forces of physical brutality in Northern Ireland arising out of events on 9th August 1971' (Compton Report), HMSO, London 1971, Cmd 4823.

'Report of the Tribunal appointed to inquire into the events on Sunday, 30th January 1972, which led to loss of life in connection with the procession in Londonderry on that day by the Rt. Hon. Lord Widgery, OBE, TD' (Widgery Report), HMSO, London 1972.

'Violence and Civil Disturbances in Northern Ireland in 1969: Report of the Tribunal of Enquiry' (Scarman Report), 2 vols, HMSO, Belfast 1972, Cmd 566.

'The future of Northern Ireland', a paper for discussion, HMSO, London 1972.

'Report of a Committee to consider, in the context of civil liberties and human rights, measures to deal with terrorism in Northern Ireland' (Gardiner Report), HMSO, London 1975, Cmd 5847.

'The protection of Human Rights by Law in Northern Ireland', HMSO, London 1977, Cmd 7009.

The Chief Constable's Annual Report, RUC, Belfast 1996.

Statistics on the operation of the Northern Ireland (Emergency Provisions) Act. Annual statistics 1997, NIO 1997.

The Agreement, n.d., no place [government publication, distributed to all households in Northern Ireland in April 1998].

Geddis, Paul W. (ed.), *Northern Ireland Annual Abstract of Statistics*, Belfast 1998.

Newspapers and periodicals

The Belfast Telegraph
Fortnight
The Guardian
The Independent
The Irish Times

Tables

I. SOCIAL AND ECONOMIC

Table I.1 Percentage of unemployed in NI by region (*Source*: Wilson, *Ulster*, p. 106, and *Northern Ireland Annual Abstract of Statistics* 1998, p. 103)

		1971	*1987*	*1995*	*1997*
East:					
Ballymena	(25.9)	5.6	14.4	7.4	4.8
Belfast	(27.3)	7.4	18.2	10.0	6.5
Coleraine	(23.9)	10.6	22.9	12.7	8.8
Craigavon	(39.1)	7.4	19.1	9.2	6.0
Newry	(71.4)	16.7	29.8	16.4	10.7
West:					
Cookstown	(49.2)	10.5	14.9	31.6	8.6
Dungannon	(52.3)	21.0	13.0	26.6	8.6
Enniskillen	(52.5)	15.0	12.2	25.0	9.2
Londonderry	(64.3)	14.7	15.7	27.5	11.6
Magherafelt	(54.7)	9.2	12.1	29.3	7.5
Omagh	(62.1)	12.2	12.0	23.3	9.2
Strabane	(56.9)	19.9	17.7	34.7	12.6

Figures in brackets are the percentage of catholics in the total population in 1971; 1971 figures refer to males only, 1987, 1995 and 1997 include females.

Table I.2 Employment composition by industry (*Source*: DED, census of population, 1991, quoted in SACHR II, p. 195)

	Public sector share		*Employment change 1989–93*		*Catholic share 1991*
	1989	1993	Public sector (%)	Total	
Production	6.6	4.8	30.2	4.4	31.8
Construction	12.2	5.2	62.9	13.9	46.9
Distribution	0.9	0.8	4.5	13.3	33.8
Trans. & comms.	42.0	42.4	3.8	4.6	37.4
Fin'l & bus. services	12.3	10.7	1.2	13.9	32.5
Public admin. & defence	99.5	99.9	4.0	3.5	27.0
Sanitary services	29.5	21.3	1.6	41.1	31.5
Education	89.5	87.5	1.8	4.1	43.4
Research & development	86.0	82.3	21.7	18.2	25.0
Health services	87.4	71.6	6.7	13.8	43.0
Other public services	56.5	50.8	8.7	1.3	40.0
Recreation/ cultural services	52.8	49.3	10.2	18.0	38.8
Personal services	14.9	10.3	36.7	8.2	40.9
Total	38.5	35.8	-3.1	4.2	35.6

Table I.3 Unemployment rates for protestants and catholics in 1971, 1981 and 1991 (*Source:* SACHR II, p. 4)

	Men			*Women*		
Census	Prots.(a)	Cath.(b)	Ratio (a)to(b)	Prots.	Caths.	(a)to(b)
1971	6.5%	17.3%	2.6	3.6%	7.0%	1.9
1981	12.4%	30.2%	2.4	9.6%	17.1%	1.8
1991	12.7%	28.4%	2.2	8.0%	14.5%	1.8

Table I.4 Employment manufacturing in NI and the Republic of Ireland, 1967–94 (*Source:* SACHR II, p. 248)

	NI (thousands)	*ROI (thousands)*
1967	174.0	200.0
1970	179.7	213.0
1974	167.3	222.0
1979	142.2	226.7
1984	109.5	197.0
1989	106.3	185.6
1994	100.7	198.3
1967–94	-42%	-1%

Table I.5 Percentage change in output, employment and labour productivity, 1984–94, NI, Scotland, Wales and the Republic of Ireland (*Source:* SACHR II, p. 249)

	Northern Ireland	*Scotland*	*Wales*	*Rep. of Ireland*
1984–89				
Output	+18.8	+11.4	+14.3	+49.5
Employment	-1.2	-7.4	+11.8	-5.8
Output/head	+20.2	+20.3	+2.2	+58.7
1989–94				
Output	+11.4	+7.4	+5.2	+41.5
Employment	-5.3	-11.9	-6.3	+6.8
Output/head	+17.6	+21.9	+12.2	+32.5
1984–94				
Output	+32.4	+19.8	+20.2	+111.4
Employment	-6.2	-18.4	+4.7	+0.7
Output/head	+41.2	+46.8	+14.8	+109.9

Table I.6 Regional comparisons (*Source: Social Attitudes in Northern Ireland*, 1991–92, p. 6)

	Percentage rise in house prices, 1983–90	*Consumers' spending per capita 1990* (UK=100)	*Percentage rise in labour market* participation rate *1983–90*	*Unemployment rate*
Scotland	65.0	92.5	2.5	8.2
North	113.3	87.8	1.8	7.7
Wales	94.0	83.9	5.2	6.6
Midlands	128.9	88.1	1.8	5.6
South	138.2	116.5	6.9	3.8
N. Ireland	41.0	83.2	0.1	14.0
UK	119.2	100.0	4.2	5.8

Table I.7 Change in the catholic percentage of the NI workforce (public and private sector concerns with 26 or more employees) by SOC 1990–94 (*Source:* FEC, 1996, quoted in SACHR II, p. 7)

	1990 %	*1991* %	*1992* %	*1993* %	*1994* %	*overall change* %
SOC1 (Managers & admin.)	30.50	31.30	32.50	33.60	34.40	3.90
SOC2 (Professional occ.)	33.40	34.40	35.90	36.80	38.80	5.40
SOC3 (Ass. prof. & techn.)	40.10	40.10	40.60	41.20	41.80	1.70
SOC4 (Clerical & secretar.)	34.20	34.60	35.20	36.40	37.10	2.90
SOC5 (Craft & skilled man.)	34.30	33.20	33.40	34.10	34.50	0.20
SOC6 (Pers. & protect. serv.)	28.50	29.60	30.20	30.50	30.40	1.90
SOC7 (Sales occupations)	33.30	34.00	35.00	35.60	36.70	3.40
SOC8 (Plant & machine oper.)	38.50	39.00	39.70	40.70	41.50	3.00
SOC9 (Other occupations)	38.80	39.80	39.50	39.20	40.30	1.50
Total	34.90	35.30	35.80	36.50	37.20	2.30

Table I.8 Religious attendance 1991 (*Source:* SANI 1991–92, p. 152)

Question: Apart from special occasions such as weddings, funerals and baptisms, how often nowadays do you attend services or meetings connected with your religion?

	18–34 yrs%	*35–54 yrs%*	*55+yrs%*	*All*
Weekly	44	53	58	52
Never	22	17	16	18

		Caths.	*Prots.*	*Britain*
18–34 yrs	Weekly	77%	26%	13%
	Never	4%	22%	34%
35–54 yrs	Weekly	88%	44%	20%
	Never	2%	10%	33%
55+ yrs	Weekly	91%	49%	20%
	Never	3%	16%	33%

Table I.9 Percentage answering 'yes' to whether religion will always make a difference in NI (*Source:* SACHR III, p. 59)

1968		*1989*		*1991*		*1993*		*1994*	
Caths.	Prots.	Caths.	Prots.	Caths.	Prots.	Caths.	Prots.	Caths.	Prots.
70.3	56.3	87.3	93.5	81.9	90.2	85.3	89.6	86.6	91.3

Table I.10 National identity in NI (*Source:* SANI 1995, p. 17)

Question: Would you describe yourself as . . . (%)

	Catholic			*Protestant*		
	1986	1989	1993	1986	1989	1993
... British	9	8	12	65	68	69
... Irish	61	60	61	3	3	2
... Ulster	1	2	1	14	10	15
... Northern Irish	20	25	24	11	16	11

Table I.11 National identity, by religion, class and sex (%) (*Source:* SANI 1997, p. 125)

	Protestants		*Catholics*	
	Salariat	*Working class*	*Salariat*	*Working class*
Men				
British	56	67	15	5
Irish	8	3	49	75
Ulster	8	15	6	–
Northern Irish	23	13	30	20
Other	5	2	–	–
Women				
British	61	64	19	15
Irish	9	6	51	59
Ulster	6	15	–	4
Northern Irish	22	12	28	21
Other	2	2	2	1

Table I.12 Party identification, by religion and class (%) (*Source:* SANI 1997, p. 124)

	Protestants		*Catholics*	
	Salariat	*Working class*	*Salariat*	*Working class*
UUP	48	42	0	–
DUP	8	23	0	–
SDLP	1	1	60	48
Sinn Fein	0	0	1	8
Alliance	22	5	16	6
Other	9	4	7	4
None	8	19	14	26
Other/Don't know/NA	3	6	3	6

Table I.13 Long-term constitutional preference, by religion, class and sex (%) (*Source*: SANI 1997, p. 128)

	Protestants				*Catholics*			
	Salariat		*Working class*		*Salariat*		*Working class*	
	M	F	M	F	M	F	M	F
Part of UK	83	85	94	86	31	28	22	37
United Ireland	10	8	–	8	64	59	63	49
Other	7	3	4	2	6	4	4	2
Don't know	–	4	2	4	–	9	10	11

II. SECURITY

Table II.1 Deaths, August 1969–December 1996 (*Source*: Flackes and Elliott, *Directory*, p. 467, 1994; Chief Constable's Annual Report, 1996)

	RUC	*RUCR*	*Army*	*UDR/RIR*	*Civilians*	*Annual death toll*
1969	1	0	0	0	12	13
1970	2	0	0	0	23	25
1971	11	0	43	5	115	174
1972	14	3	103	26	321	467
1973	10	3	58	8	171	250
1974	12	3	28	7	166	216
1975	7	4	14	5	217	247
1976	13	10	14	15	245	297
1977	8	6	15	14	69	112
1978	4	6	14	7	50	81
1979	9	5	38	10	51	113
1980	3	6	8	9	50	76
1981	13	8	10	13	57	101
1982	8	4	21	7	57	97
1983	9	9	5	10	44	77
1984	7	2	9	10	36	64
1985	14	9	2	4	25	54
1986	10	2	4	8	37	61
1987	9	7	3	8	66	93
1988	4	2	21	12	54	93
1989	7	2	12	2	39	62
1990	7	5	7	8	49	76
1991	5	1	5	8	75	94
1992	2	1	4	2	76	85
1993	3	3	6	2	70	84
1994	3	–	1	2	56	62
1995	1	–	–	–	8	9
1996	–	–	1	–	14	15
Total	196	101	450	203	2262	3212

Note: Figures for civilians include terrorist suspects and prison officers

Table II.2 Violence, 1969–96 (*Source*: Flackes and Elliott, *Directory*, p. 471, 1994; Chief Constable's Annual Report, 1996; *Northern Ireland Annual Abstract of Statistics*, p. 38, and RUC Information Centre.)

	Shooting incidents	*Explosions*	*Bombs defused*	*Malicious fires*	*Armed robberies*	*Amounts stolen* £
1969	u/a	8	u/a	u/a	u/a	u/a
1970	213	153	17	u/a	u/a	u/a
1971	1,756	1,022	493	u/a	437	303,787
1972	10,628	1,382	471	u/a	1,931	790,687
1973	5,018	978	542	587	1,215	612,015
1974	3,206	685	428	636	1,231	572,951
1975	1,803	399	236	248	1,201	572,105
1976	1,908	766	426	453	813	545,340
1977	1,181	366	169	432	591	446,898
1978	755	455	178	269	439	203,750
1979	728	422	142	315	434	568,359
1980	642	280	120	275	412	496,829
1981	815	398	132	536*	587	894,929
1982	382	219	113	499	580	1,392,202
1983	290	266	101	528	622	830,258
1984	230	193	155	840	627	701,903
1985	196	148	67	740	459	655,690
1986	285	172	82	906	724	1,207,152
1987	489	236	148	506	858	1,900,098
1988	537	253	205	518	742	1,388,599
1989	566	224	196	307	604	1,079,399
1990	559	167	120	333	492	1,728,685
1991	499	230	137	333	608	1,672,884
1992	506	222	149	419	738	1,665,863
1993	476	206	83	196	643	1,514,878
1994	348	123	99	58	555	1,709,000
1995	50	1	1	129	421	838,000
1996	125	8	17	152	405	2,840,000
Total	35,233	9,983	4,927	10,215	19,798	£27,129,000

*No figures available for April–June 1981.
Amounts stolen 1994–96 and total figure rounded to nearest £000.

Table II.3 Arms finds and house searches, 1969–96 (*Source*: Flackes and Elliott, *Directory*, p. 472, 1994; Chief Constable's Annual Report, 1996; *Northern Ireland Annual Abstract of Statistics*, p. 38; Statistics on the operation of the Northern Ireland (Emergency Provisions) Act, NIO 1997, p. 11, and RUC Information Centre.)

	Firearms found	*Explosives found (kg)*	*Ammunition found (rounds)*	*Number of house searches*
1969	14	102	2,236	u/a
1970	324	305	43,095	3,107
1971	717	1,246	157,944	17,262
1972	1,264	18,819	183,410	36,617
1973	1,595	17,426	187,399	74,556
1974	1,260	11,848	147,202	74,914
1975	825	4,996	73,604	30,002
1976	837	9,849	70,306	34,919
1977	590	1,728	52,091	20,724
1978	400	956	43,512	15,462
1979	301	905	46,280	6,452
1980	203	821	28,078	4,106
1981	398	3,419	47,070	4,104
1982	321	2,298	41,453	4,045
1983	200	1,706	32,451	1,497
1984	197	3,871	27,211	1,282
1985	238	3,344	13,748	812
1986	215	2,443	29,061	1,273
1987	267	5,885	19,796	1,523
1988	489	4,728	105,052	4,136
1989	246	1,377	37,700	3,027
1990	176	1,969	22,452	3,568
1991	164	4,167	18,175	2,961
1992	194	2,167	29,131	3,415
1993	196	3,944	20,066	3,264
1994	178	1,285	13,196	2,880
1995	118	5	17,678	331
1996	98	1,677	10,049	580
Total	11,290	113,286	1,519,496	358,315

Maps

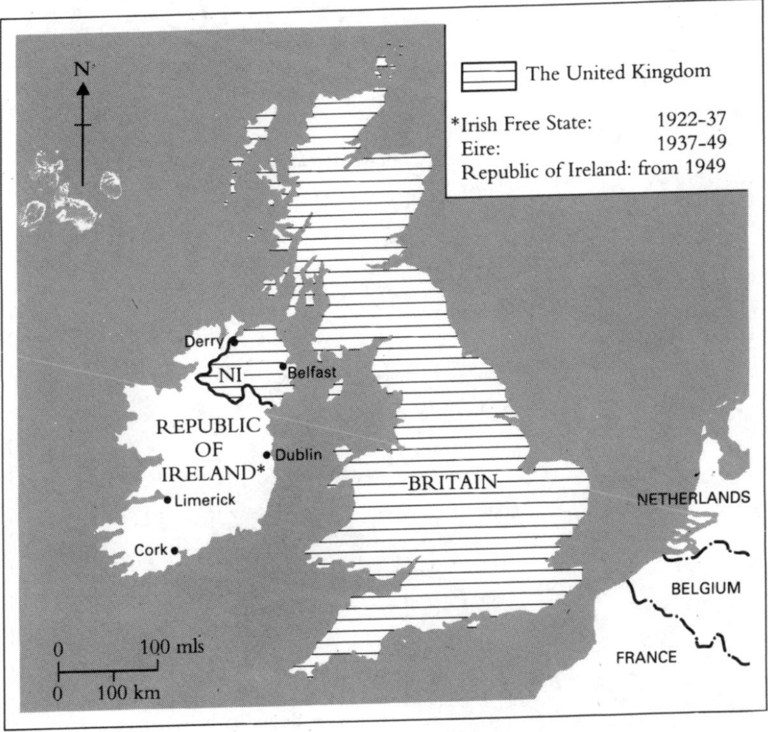

Map 1 The British Isles

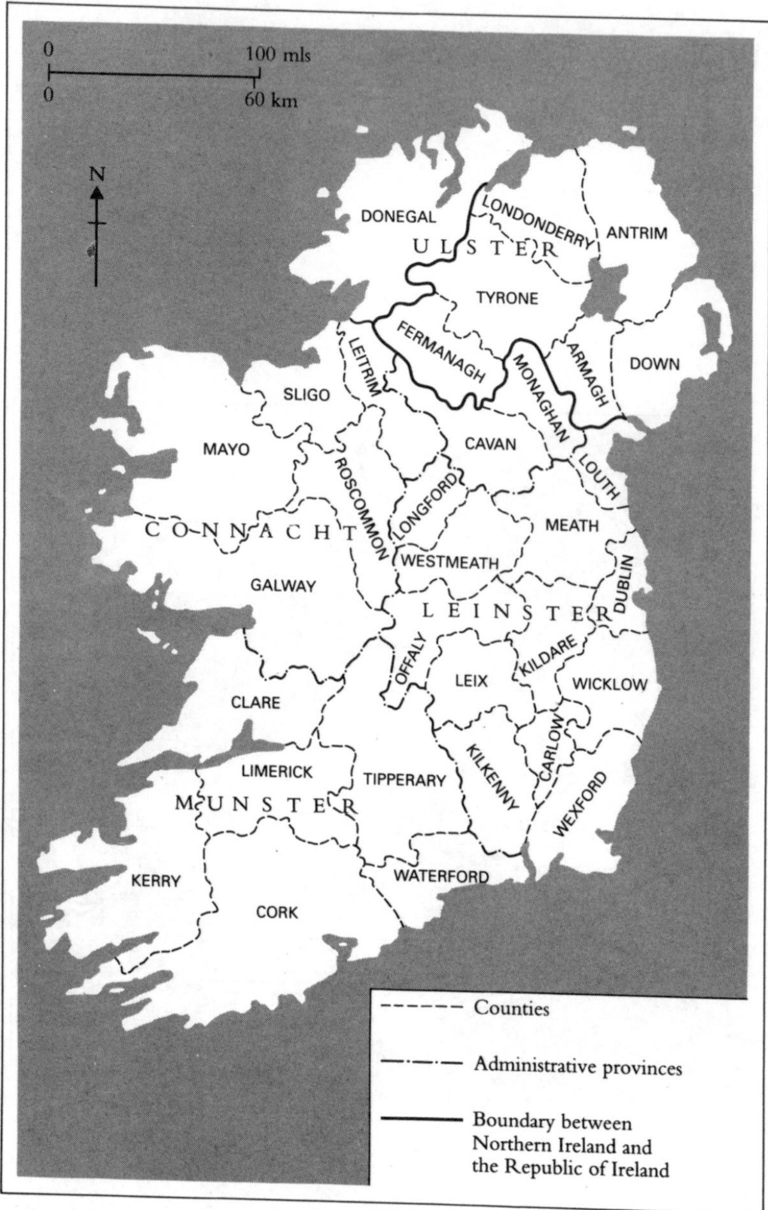

Map 2 Ireland

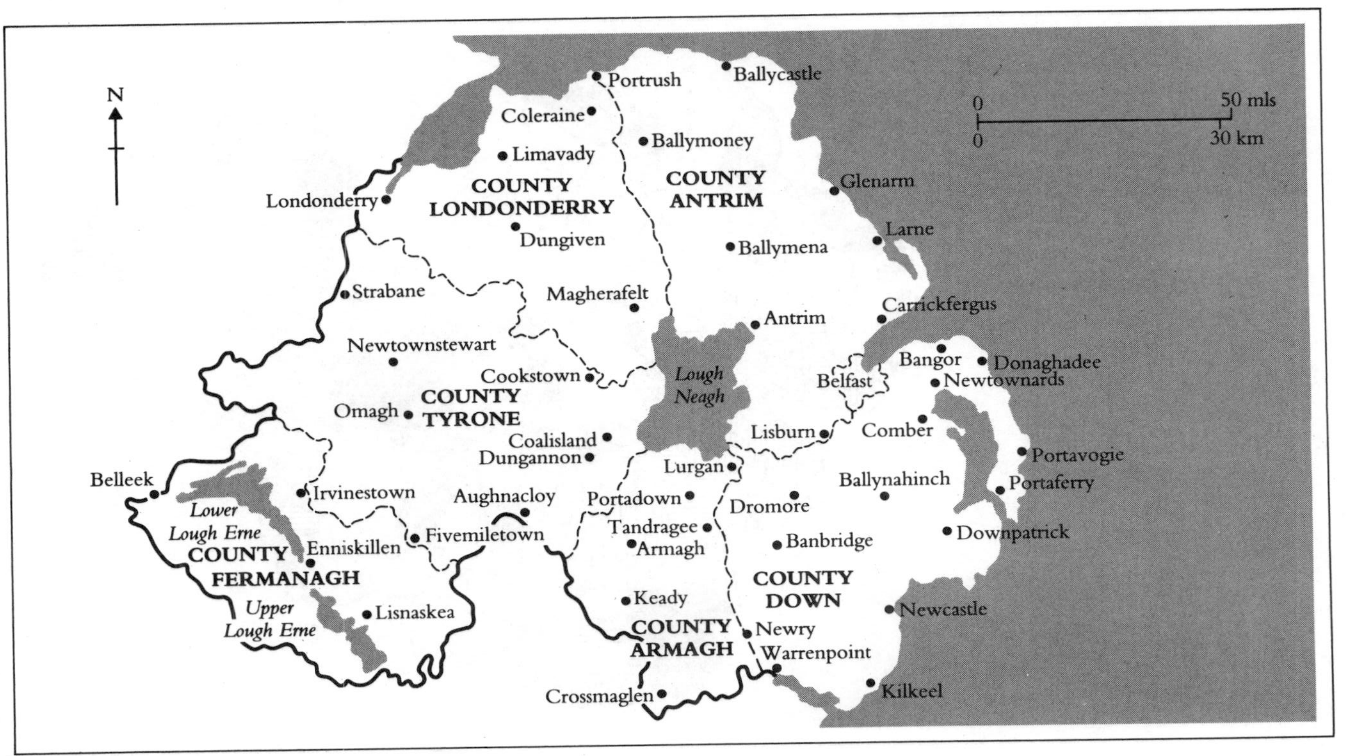

Map 3 Northern Ireland

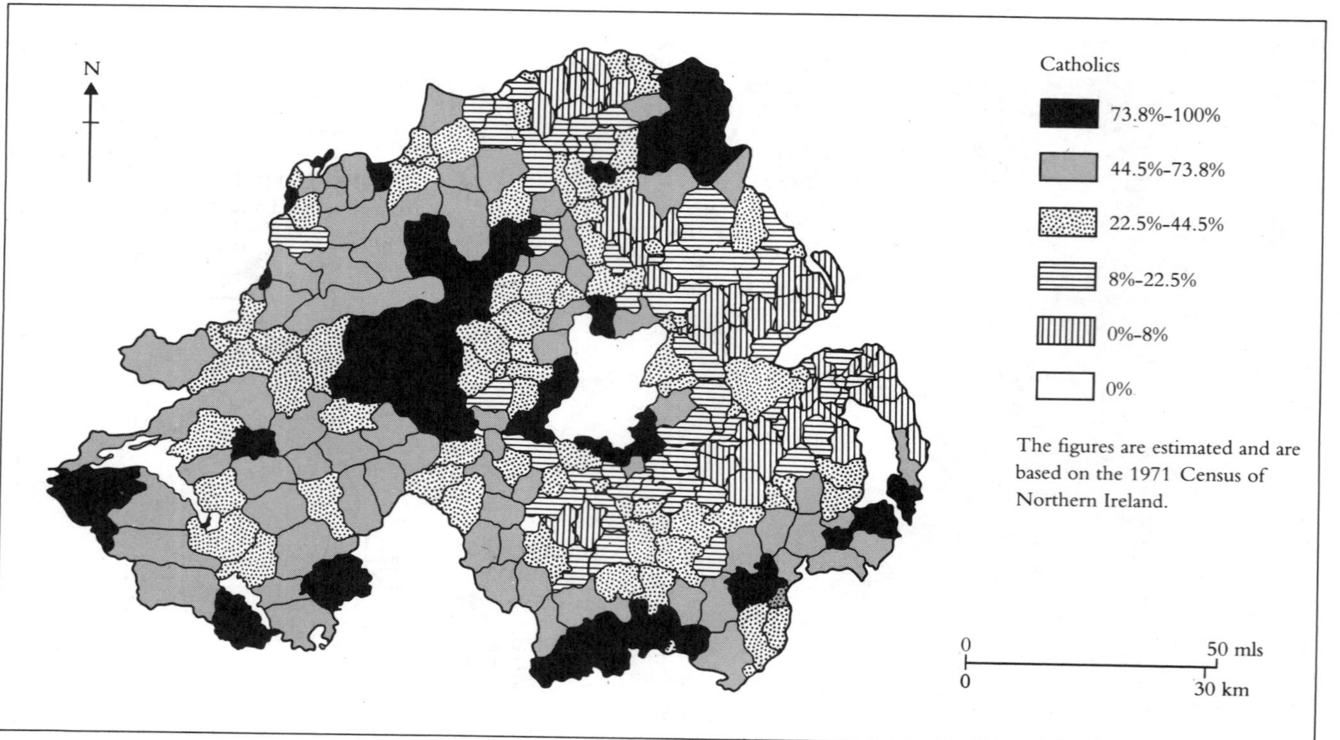

Map 4 Sectarian population distribution

Index